D1122420

JACOB

JACOB

JIMMY SWAGGART

Jimmy Swaggart Ministries
P.O. Box 262550 • Baton Rouge, Louisiana 70826-2550
Website: www.jsm.org • Email: info@jsm.org
(225) 768-7000

ISBN 978-1-941403-00-6
09-123 • COPYRIGHT © 2014 Jimmy Swaggart Ministries®
14 15 16 17 18 19 20 21 22 23 24 / RRD / 13 12 11 10 9 8 7 6 5 4 3 2 1

TABLE OF CONTENTS

INTRODUCTION

All of the Bible characters, with their own personalities and their own ways of doing things, are interesting beyond compare; however, Jacob, in one sense of the word, proves a most interesting case study.

Even though it was Old Testament times and actually at the very birth of the Nation of Israel, still, the great Doctrine of Sanctification is portrayed in the life of this man, this man called Jacob, perhaps greater than any other.

Jacob was fully human, even warts and all, but, at the same time, he proved to be one of the greatest Men of God who ever lived. The great Faith statement, *"The God of Abraham, Isaac, and Jacob,"* puts this man in a category that was only held by two others. Actually, the Nation of Israel was born out of his loins. It was a people who would be given the Word of God, and who would serve as the Womb of the Messiah. Yes, they are a distinct people totally unlike any other on the face of the Earth.

THE PROPHECY

A wayward Prophet by the name of Balaam gave some of the greatest Prophecies concerning Israel of anything found in the Word of God.

As it regards Israel, the Holy Spirit, through this wayward character, gave the following word to the world:

"And he took up his Parable, and said, Balak the king of Moab has brought me from Aram, out of the mountains of the east, saying, Come, curse me Jacob, and come, defy Israel.

"How shall I curse, whom God has not cursed? or how shall I defy, whom the LORD has not defied?

"For from the top of the rocks I see him, and from the

hills I behold him: lo, the people shall dwell alone, and shall not be reckoned among the nations" (Num. 23:7-9).

For instance, there are no people on the face of the Earth who have been scattered all over the world as Israel was for nearly 2,000 years, and then, after that length of time, come together to form a cohesive nation as did these people. Despite the fact that they rejected the Lord Jesus Christ, thereby, bringing upon themselves untold suffering, still, many Prophets proclaim the Restoration of these people, which actually began in 1948. The truth is, they will ultimately accept Jesus Christ as their Saviour, their Lord, and their Messiah. It will be at the Second Coming, but all of this, one might say, began with Jacob.

WHAT KIND OF MAN WAS HE?

We hope to address that question in this Volume. However, whatever it is we do say, still, I think one can say that Jacob is so outsized and, in a sense, so multi-faceted that I personally feel it's virtually impossible to capture this individual in totality. And yet, our modern Faith is anchored securely in the three individuals referred to as *"Abraham, Isaac, and Jacob."* It was and is because of their Faith. Despite their problems, they believed God.

A PROFILE

I feel that in some way you will see yourself in Jacob. As we follow him through his victories and defeats, to be sure, we will see ourselves. However, that's what the Holy Spirit intends.

While the story of Jacob is the story of ancient history, in a sense, it is also the story of every Believer who has ever named the Name of the Lord.

"I love to tell the story of unseen things above,
"Of Jesus and His Glory, of Jesus and His Love,
"I love to tell the story, because I know 'tis true,
"It satisfies my longings, as nothing else can do."

"I love to tell the story; more wonderful it seems,
"Than all the golden fancies of all our golden
dreams,
"I love to tell the story; it did so much for me;
"And that is just the reason I tell it now to thee."

"I love to tell the story; 'tis pleasant to repeat,
"What seems each time I tell it, more wonderfully
sweet.
"I love to tell the story, for some have never heard,
"The Message of Salvation from God's Own Holy
Word."

"I love to tell the story; for those who know it best
"Seem hungering and thirsting to hear it like the
rest.
"And when, in scenes of Glory, I sing the new,
new song,
"'Twill be the old, old story, that I have loved so
long."

JACOB

Chapter One

THE BIRTH OF JACOB

THE BIRTH OF JACOB

"And Isaac entreated the LORD for his wife, because she was barren: and the LORD was entreated of him, and Rebekah his wife conceived" (Gen. 25:21).

Now begins the story of one of the greatest Men of God who ever lived, Jacob. In this account we will find that the Lord portrayed this man in both his strengths and weaknesses.

As we said in the introduction, when we see Jacob, in a sense, we are seeing a microcosm of our personal lives.

Satan hindered the birth of this man for some 20 years. However, God overruled all things to emphasize once more the great truth that He displays the riches of His Grace and Glory where nature is dead. This is a principle in the Spiritual Life which nature is unwilling to learn.

BARREN

While Satan hindered the birth of Jacob for some 20 years, we find that the Lord allowed him to do such.

Why?

Anything and everything that Satan does, he does only by permission from the Lord. To be sure, he is subject to the Lord in every capacity (Job, Chpts. 1 and 2).

So, as it regards Believers, this means that the Lord uses Satan in order to strengthen the Faith and trust of Believers. How does He do that?

As mentioned, the Lord allows Satan a modicum of latitude. Of course, Satan means to hurt us and even destroy us, but the Lord's Reasons are altogether different, as should be overly obvious.

He wants us to do exactly what Isaac did.

ENTREATED THE LORD

Twenty years is a long time, but Isaac didn't give up. During this time, he kept entreating the Lord to heal Rebekah so that she might be able to conceive and bear children.

As well, even though he and his wife naturally wanted children, and wanted them very much, the real reason was far more important. The birth of a son to this union was just as important as Isaac's Miracle birth had been as it regarded his father and mother, Abraham and Sarah. For the Plan of God to be brought forth, which pertained to the Redemption of all of mankind, Isaac and Rebekah would have to have a son.

As far as Rebekah was concerned, nature was dead. In other words, she could not have a child. However, God is able to overrule all of these things. He wanted Isaac to continue to believe Him. In other words, this was a test of Faith, as all things, as it pertains to Believers, are tests of Faith.

The answer ultimately came because the Lord was entreated of him, and Rebekah conceived.

What was the Lord's Reasoning behind all of this, and we speak of the barrenness of both Sarah and Rebekah?

Among other things, it was to show that the children of the Promise were not to be simply the fruit of nature but the Gift of Grace.

THE STRUGGLE

"And the children struggled together within her; and she said, If it be so, why am I thus? And she went to inquire of the LORD" (Gen. 25:22).

Rebekah's language in the Verse just given in essence says, *"If in answer to prayer God is about to give me this joy of being a mother, why am I so physically oppressed that I am in danger of death?"*

Why should such an answer to prayer be accompanied by such mysterious suffering?

Rebekah took her questions to the Lord, which is exactly where we should take them, also!

The phrase, *"And the children struggled together within her,"* pertains to the fact that there were twins in her womb; however, the *"struggle"* carries with it a tremendous spiritual meaning.

Two energies, the one believing and the other unbelieving, struggled within her and were present even before they were born. It is like the two natures, sin nature and Divine Nature, within the Believer.

So, as we had in the union of Abraham and Sarah the beginning of the Divine Plan, we have with Isaac and Rebekah the opposition by Satan to that Divine Plan, which, strangely enough, centers up in the same family.

As we shall see, Jacob and Esau represent the two natures struggling within the Believer. There is only one way that victory can be achieved over the sin nature, and that is by subscribing to God's Prescribed Order, which is the Cross.

THE QUESTION

The question, *"If it be so, why am I thus?"* probably means, *"If I have thus conceived in answer to my husband's prayers, why do I suffer in this strange manner?"*

In answer to this question which plagued her heart, she took it to the Lord.

"And the LORD said unto her, Two nations are in your womb, and two manner of people shall be separated from your bowels; and the one people shall be stronger than the other people; and the elder shall serve the younger" (Gen. 25:23).

THE ANSWER TO PRAYER

The two nations God told her about are the Edomites and Israelites. From her womb, that is, from the time of their birth, Jacob and Esau would be separated, divided, and even hostile, for they would have nothing in common. Exactly as the Lord said would happen, the elder people descended from Esau, who was born first. They served the people descendent from the younger son, Jacob.

This was fulfilled when the Edomites were made subject to king David (II Sam. 8:13-14).

However, the greater fulfillment will have to do with the coming Millennial Reign. Then, Israel will be the supreme Nation on Earth, and all other nations will look to her, with Jesus Christ at her head. In essence, Israel will be the Priestly Nation of the world in that hour.

As well, the descendants of Esau would also fall in with the descendants of Ishmael, both being the Arab people, with the animosity between these and Israel continuing even unto this hour.

THE SPIRITUAL SENSE

While continuing in the material and physical sense, the phrase, *"And the one people shall be stronger than the other people; and the elder shall serve the younger,"* also carries over greatly into the spiritual.

As we have stated, the two boys may represent the two natures in the Christian. We speak of the sin nature and the Divine Nature (II Pet. 1:4). In one sense, that was the reason for the struggle between the two unborn babies while they were yet in their mother's womb.

Esau was born first and represents the sin nature, with which every person is born due to Adam's fall.

This simply means that the nature of the person is bent totally and completely toward sin, disobedience, and rebellion to God.

When the believing sinner is Born-Again, he now has the Divine Nature, which is stronger than the sin nature. So, when the human being is first born, he has the sin nature as well as a human nature. When he is Born-Again, he now has, as well, the Divine Nature.

However, the sin nature doesn't leave once the believing sinner is Born-Again. If the Believer doesn't understand God's Prescribed Order of Victory, which speaks of the sanctified life, the sin nature will once again dominate the person exactly as it did before Conversion. This is sad but true! In fact, because they do not understand God's Prescribed Order of Victory, at this very moment, untold millions of Christians are being dominated by *"Esau,"* i.e., *"the sin nature,"* even though they love the Lord very much,

THE APOSTLE PAUL

When the Apostle Paul set out to inform the Believer as to how to walk in victory in this life that we live for the Lord, he began in the Sixth Chapter of Romans to explain to us the sin nature.

Some preachers teach that once the person comes to Christ, the sin nature is forever gone. My answer to that is, that being the case, why did the Holy Spirit through Paul take up so much time explaining to Believers how to have victory over this monster when it doesn't exist? Listen to Paul:

"Neither yield you your members as instruments of unrighteousness unto (the) *sin (Paul is speaking here of the sin nature): but yield yourselves unto God, as those who are alive from the dead, and your members as instruments of Righteousness unto God"* (Rom. 6:13).

If it's not possible for the Believer to yield himself to unrighteousness, with the sin nature once again dominating him, why would Paul warn us here of these things?

The truth is, the sin nature, although continuing to abide in the heart and life of the Believer, doesn't have to be a problem at all. As we have explained in other commentary, the truth is, we are to be dead to the sin nature, in a sense, because it is unplugged, so to speak. If it is to be noticed, the Scripture doesn't tell us that the sin nature is dead, but that we are to be dead to the sin nature. Again, listen to Paul:

"Likewise reckon you also yourselves to be dead indeed unto (the) *sin, but alive unto God through Jesus Christ our Lord"* (Rom. 6:11).

THE SIN NATURE

In the original Greek Text, there is a term referred to as *"the definite article."* In fact, in the Sixth Chapter of Romans alone, this definite article is used some 15 times and is implied one other time. In other words, he said, *"How shall we, who are dead to* (the) *sin, live any longer therein?"* (Rom. 6:2).

The way the King James translators gave it to us, it makes it seem as though Paul is talking about particular sins; however, he is actually speaking of the sin nature. We know that because he included the definite article, i.e., *"the sin."*

Once again, he didn't tell us here that the sin nature was dead, but that we are dead to the sin nature.

THE CROSS

It is because of the Cross that we are dead to the sin nature. Paul explains this in Romans 6:3-5. We died with Christ, were buried with Him, and raised with Him in Newness of Life.

As far as what we once were, all of that is dead. That's why he said, *Knowing this, that our old man is crucified with Him, that the body of* (the) *sin might be destroyed (the guilt of sin removed and the power of sin broken, thereby, made ineffective), that henceforth we should not serve* (the) *sin"* (Rom. 6:6).

WHAT IS THE SIN NATURE?

It had its origin, at least as far as the human race is concerned, with Adam and Eve. When they fell, they fell from a place of total God-consciousness down to a place of total self-consciousness. When they fell, their entire nature became that of disobedience, sin, ungodliness, and rebellion against God. In other words, it governed them 24 hours a day, seven days a week, even as it governs every unsaved person in the world. That's the reason for all the wars, man's inhumanity to man, criminal activity, etc.

Inasmuch as Adam was the father of the entirety of the human race, so to speak, his failure passed on to all. That's what we meant when we said that every individual is born with a sin nature, with that sin nature dominating him until he comes to Christ, at least, if he comes to Christ.

HOW DO WE STAY DEAD TO THE SIN NATURE?

We stay dead by continuing to maintain our Faith in the Cross, understanding that it was there that all victory was won. That's why Paul also said: *"But God forbid that I should glory (boast), save in the Cross of our Lord Jesus Christ, by Whom the world is crucified unto me, and I unto the world"* (Gal. 6:14).

If the Believer constantly maintains his Faith in Christ and the Cross, understanding that it is what Jesus did at the Cross that makes everything possible, he'll have little problem with the sin nature.

FAITH

However, this is where the fight commences, even the struggle between Jacob and Esau, so to speak.

Paul also said: *"Fight the good fight of Faith, lay hold on Eternal Life, whereunto you are also Called, and have professed a good profession before many witnesses"* (I Tim. 6:12).

This *"good fight of Faith"* is the only fight in which we are called upon to engage. That's where the struggle is. Satan tries to move our Faith from the Cross to other things, and regrettably, he succeeds with many, if not most, Christians.

If he does succeed, the sin nature will once again begin to rule in that Believer's life. It won't rule as it did before he was Saved, but it will definitely rule in some way. He'll find himself just as unable to overcome sin as he was before being Born-Again.

In these cases, the Believer who is being ruled by the sin nature sets out to try harder than ever to live for God but, despite all of his efforts, finds himself losing the battle more and more. It leaves him in a confused state, not understanding what is happening, especially considering that he is trying so hard. This is what Paul was talking about when he said: *"For that which I do I allow (understand) not: for what I would, that do I not; but what I hate, that do I"* (Rom. 7:15).

As the Believer should understand, this is Paul's account of his struggle before the Lord gave him the interpretation of the New Covenant, which is the meaning of the Cross. Despite his trying so hard to live right, he found himself failing.

LACK OF UNDERSTANDING

If the reader should notice, we have the word, *"Understand,"* in parenthesis after the word, *"Allow."* Actually, the Greek word should have been translated, *"Understand,"* for that's what it actually means. So, it would then say:

"For that which I do I understand not." Regrettably, that characterizes most Christians.

In other words, they're struggling with everything within themselves and with all their might to live right, but continue to fail. This they don't understand.

So, what is wrong?

Satan has succeeded in pulling the Believer's Faith from the Cross of Christ to other things. If he does this, irrespective as to what these other things might be, the Believer has just been placed in a posture of failure. It doesn't matter how hard he tries, how hard he labors, or how hard he struggles, he is doomed to failure simply because no human being can get victory in this manner. The works of the flesh will begin to manifest themselves in one's heart and life, which will cause untold problems (Gal. 5:18-21).

The answer to this situation is for the Believer to put his Faith once again in the Cross of Christ, understanding that the Cross is the solution to all of his problems. He will find that, little by little, victory will once again be his. Even with this being done, and we speak of Faith properly placed, there still may be failures. If so, get up, spiritually speaking, and start back on the road of Faith with the Object being the Cross of Christ, and, ultimately, you will find that sin no longer has dominion over you (Rom.. 6:14).

REACTION TO THE SIN NATURE

The following presents to us the various ways in which the sin nature is addressed as it regards the modern church. The first four constitute wrong directions and will lead to nothing but failure and extreme trouble. It is only the last one which guarantees victory. Let's look at it carefully. I will use five headings:

1. IGNORANCE

Due to the fact that almost nothing is preached or taught on the sin nature from behind our pulpits, most Christians are ignorant of this which can cause them tremendous problems. When we consider that Paul took so much time and put forth so much effort to explain the sin nature, exactly as he did in Romans, Chapter 6, we are then made to realize just how important this subject actually is. Please look at it in this way:

When the Lord began to give the meaning of the New Covenant to Paul, which, incidentally, is the meaning of the Cross, the very first thing He did was to explain to Paul the meaning of the sin nature, which he gave to us in Romans, Chapter 6.

2. DENIAL

Some preachers claim that even though all of us had a sin nature before we were Saved (sometimes called the evil nature or the Adamic nature), now that we have come to Christ, we are new Creations, with old things having passed away and all things having become new (II Cor. 5:17). So, they deny the presence of a sin nature.

If, in fact, that is true, why did Paul take up so much time explaining something that no longer exists? We have to admit that Paul is addressing Believers and not unbelievers in these Passages.

The sin nature will be totally eradicated either when the Believer dies, or else, at the sound of the Trump. Paul also said:

"For this corruptible *(sin nature)* **must put on incorruption** *(a Glorified Body with no sin nature)*, **and this mortal** *(subject to death)* ***must*** **put on immortality** *(will never die)*" **(I Cor. 15:53)**.

Yes, we do have a sin nature, although Saved and even Spirit-filled; however, it will cause us little problem if we adhere to the Ways of the Lord, which is the Cross.

3. LICENSE

Of the few Christians who have at least a modicum of understanding respecting the sin nature, some claim that due to this fact, they simply cannot help but sin. It's called the *"sinning a little bit everyday"* religion. They claim the Grace of God covers all of their sins and, thereby, make little effort to obtain any type of victory.

Paul's answer to that is, *"God forbid. How shall we, who are dead to* (the) *sin, live any longer therein?"* (Rom. 6:2).

4. STRUGGLE

Not knowing God's Prescribed Order of Victory, many Christians are led to believe that this Christian experience is just a long series of struggles, with them fighting the sin nature on a daily basis. That is incorrect. That's not the more Abundant Life of which Jesus spoke (Jn. 10:10).

While we as Believers definitely are called upon to fight, it's not with the sin nature, but rather *"the good fight of Faith."* That's the only struggle we are to have. It's a good fight because if we fight it correctly, we're going to come out as the winner.

5. GRACE

The Grace of God is the only manner in which we can live this life, and live it as we should. What does this mean?

Grace is simply the Goodness of God extended to undeserving people. In other words, the Lord has many good things that He wants to give us, and all of it is made possible by the Cross of Christ and our Faith in that Finished Work. Then, the Holy Spirit, Who Alone can make us what we ought to be, and Who works entirely within the parameters of the Cross of Christ (Rom. 8:1-2), will work mightily on our behalf.

The Cross is the Means by which God gives us all things. In other words, it's the Cross that makes the Grace of God, which is the Goodness of God, possible in our hearts and lives.

When we look exclusively to the Cross, we are availing ourselves of the Grace of God, which guarantees the Help of the Holy Spirit and guarantees victory.

WHY DOES THE LORD ALLOW THE SIN NATURE TO REMAIN IN THE BELIEVER AFTER CONVERSION?

While there are, no doubt, many reasons, the primary reason is that it is for disciplinary reasons.

The weak link in man's triune makeup is his body.

In fact, the body is neutral. It need not cause us problems but can cause us severe problems. It is through the body that Satan works his evil passions, i.e., *"works of the flesh."* As a Believer, we have the ability and strength to yield the members of our physical body as instruments of Righteousness or unrighteousness (Rom. 6:13). As stated, the human body is neutral; however, the way that God provides our strength and ability is through the Cross and not through our own efforts. This is what causes problems with many Christians.

RIGHTEOUSNESS

Millions of Christians are trying to yield their physical bodies to Righteousness but, despite all of their efforts, are instead yielding themselves to unrighteousness. Now, that is tragic, but it happens to be true.

If the Believer looks to the Cross, and the Cross exclusively, for all that he receives from the Lord, including victory in his daily life and living, he will find himself being able to yield the members of his physical body to Righteousness. Otherwise, he cannot! That is the order that God has devised for us to live this life and to be what we ought to be in Christ. It might be summed up as:

• The Cross: it was there that Jesus paid the price for man's Redemption. He atoned for all sin and, thereby, broke the grip of sin on the human race, at least, for all who will believe (Jn. 3:16).

The Cross of Christ is the Means by which all of these good things are given to us.

• Our Faith: the Object of our Faith must ever be Christ and the Cross (I Cor. 1:17, 18, 23; 2:2; Gal. 6:14; Col. 2:10-15).

• The Holy Spirit: the Spirit works entirely within the framework of the Finished Work of Christ and will not work outside of that framework. In other words, it's the Cross of Christ which gives the Holy Spirit the legal means to do all that He does with us and for us (Rom. 8:1-11; Eph. 2:13-18).

So, to answer the question, the sin nature remains due to the fact that the human body is not yet glorified. Once the Trump sounds, and *"this corruptible shall have put on incorruption, and this mortal shall have put on immortality,"* there will be no more sin nature, but only then (I Cor. 15:54).

So, the good fight of Faith, which is being carried out in our lives daily, guarantees us that the *"elder,"* i.e., *"the sin nature,"* will ultimately serve the younger, i.e., *"the Divine Nature."*

ESAU

"And when her days to be delivered were fulfilled, behold, there were twins in her womb.

"And the first came out red, all over like an hairy garment; and they called his name Esau" (Gen. 25:24-25).

Esau is a type of the sin nature which is *". . . enmity against God: for it is not subject to the Law of God, neither indeed can be"* (Rom. 8:7).

His name means, *"The hairy one,"* which speaks of sensuality. In other words, he was a man of the world and cared not at all, as we shall see, for the things of God although he was of the godly family. How can one be so close to the Things of God and yet be so devoid of Spiritual things?

JACOB

"And after that came his brother out, and his hand took hold on Esau's heel; and his name was called Jacob: and Isaac was threescore years old (60) when she (Rebekah) bore them" (Gen. 25:26).

Isaac was 40 years old when he and Rebekah married (Vs. 20). He was 60 years old when the two boys were born, showing that they had been some 20 years trying to have children and succeeded only when the Lord intervened.

Usually, there is a considerable interval — an hour or more — between the birth of twins, but here, Jacob appears without delay, following immediately after his brother. This means there was absolutely no interval between them. Though very rare, yet similar cases have been chronicled from time to time.

That being the physical explanation, there is a spiritual sense involved here, as well, even greatly so.

In later years, Esau would refer to this phenomenon of birth because of Jacob's own unworthy conduct (Gen. 27:36).

SANCTIFICATION

These boys were named by their mother. She was, no doubt, led by the Holy Spirit, especially considering that their names so very much characterized their dispositions once grown.

To be at a person's heel is to be his determined pursuer and one, who on overtaking, throws him down. This, in a sense, at least in the spiritual, characterizes Jacob. He wanted the birthright mostly for spiritual reasons, but he went about to get it in all the wrong ways.

To Abraham was given the great Doctrine of *"Justification by Faith,"* on which the entirety of the Salvation Plan is based. About thirteen and one-half Chapters are devoted to this Patriarch.

Jacob instead signifies Sanctification, with about twenty-five and one-half Chapters devoted to this Patriarch. This shows us that *"living the life"* is far more complicated than *"receiving the Life."*

Perhaps in Jacob, as no other personality of the Bible, we find the greatest illustration of the great quest for victory. We see ourselves in Jacob, and plainly so, even as intended by the Holy Spirit. If not, then you're not looking at yourself properly.

We find the motive of Jacob as being very good but his actions being very deplorable.

ISAAC'S LOVE FOR ESAU

"And the boys grew: and Esau was a cunning hunter, a man of the field; and Jacob was a plain man, dwelling in tents.

"And Isaac loved Esau, because he did eat of his venison: but Rebekah loved Jacob" (Gen. 25:27-28).

The original language proclaims the fact that Esau was a wild, undisciplined man, who lived a wild life, seeking sport and adventure. In contrast to him, Jacob was a quiet, mature individual. The Hebrew, *"Tam,"* also means that he was sensible, diligent, dutiful, and peaceful. He could be counted on to carry out the duties of life. He was orderly and paid attention to business.

But yet, Isaac loved Esau while Rebekah loved Jacob.

While Isaac certainly should have loved Esau, the type of love he manifested toward him was in opposition to the Word of God. He was determined to give the Blessing of the birthright to Esau even though his oldest son cared not at all for Spiritual things.

At this stage, Isaac seems to have forgotten his very purpose and reason for living.

Regrettably and sadly, Isaac is a symbol of the Church. If left to its own devices, it will give the birthright to Esau every time. What was Isaac thinking? What is the modern church thinking? What do I mean by the modern church?

I mean that the modern church all too often places its hand of approval upon an Esau while altogether ignoring or even opposing Jacob. In other words, it will place its seal of approval on one not chosen by God. When I say the church, I am primarily speaking of organized religion, but it really goes for any type of religion.

And yet, if one is not led exclusively by the Spirit, this is what one is liable to do. Even the mighty Samuel would have chosen one of the other brothers in place of David simply because he looked on the outward appearance, as do most (I Sam. 16:6-7).

> *"'Tis the grandest theme through the ages rung;*
> *"'Tis the grandest theme for a mortal tongue;*
> *"'Tis the grandest theme that the world ever sung,*
> *"Our God is able to deliver thee."*
>
> *"'Tis the grandest theme in the Earth or main;*
> *"'Tis the grandest theme for a mortal strain;*
> *"'Tis the grandest theme, tell the world again,*
> *"Our God is able to deliver thee."*
>
> *"'Tis the grandest theme, let the tidings roll,*
> *"To the guilty heart, to the sinful soul;*
> *"Look to God in Faith, He will make you whole;*
> *"Our God is able to deliver thee."*

JACOB

Chapter Two

THE BIRTHRIGHT

THE BIRTHRIGHT

"And Jacob sod pottage: and Esau came from the field, and he was faint:

"And Esau said to Jacob, Feed me, I pray you, with that same red pottage; for I am faint: therefore was his name called Edom.

"And Jacob said, Sell me this day your birthright" (Gen. 25:29-31).

Even though Esau was hungry, this had little, if anything, to do with his trading the birthright for a bowl of stew.

The first emphasis is on Jacob wanting the birthright.

Exactly what was the birthright?

• Succession to the earthly inheritance of Canaan.

• Possession of the Covenant Blessing, which included his seed being as the stars of the sky and all the families of the Earth being blessed in him.

• Progenitorship of the Promised Seed, which was the greatest Blessing of all and, of course, spoke of Christ.

The firstborn (a male) was to receive the birthright, and Esau was the firstborn, but only by a few minutes.

As it can be seen, the birthright then dealt primarily with Spiritual things, of which Esau had no regard or concern.

Under the Mosaic Law, which would come about 400 years later, the privileges of the firstborn were clearly defined:

• The official authority of the father.

• A double portion of the father's property.

• The functions of the domestic priesthood.

More than likely, the birthright in Isaac's time included these same privileges.

Jacob, deplorable as was his character, valued Divine and Eternal Blessings. Had he placed himself in God's Hands, the Prophecy made to his mother before he was born would have been fulfilled to him without the degradation and suffering, which his own scheming brought upon him. But yet, if we had been placed in the same circumstances, would we have done any better, or even as well?

The domestic priesthood meant that the eldest son acted as Priest for the family and offered the sacrifices which God had commanded Adam and his sons to offer. Of course, this was all before the Law was given to Moses.

PROPHET?

"And Esau said, Behold, I am at the point to die: and what profit shall this birthright do to me?

"And Jacob said, Swear to me this day; and he swore unto him: and he sold his birthright unto Jacob.

"Then Jacob gave Esau bread and pottage of lentiles; and he did eat and drink, and rose up, and went his way: thus Esau despised his birthright" (Gen. 25:32-34).

The natural heart places no value on the Things of God, as we see evident in the choices made by Esau. To the natural heart, God's Promises are a vague, valueless, and powerless thing simply because God is not known, hence it is that present things carry such weight and influence in man's estimation. Anything that man can *"see,"* he values because he is governed by sight and not by faith. To him, the present is everything; the future is a mere uninfluential thing — a matter of the merest uncertainty. Thus it was with Esau.

His question, *"What profit shall this birthright do to me?"* characterizes the majority of the human race, and always has. The *"present"* is everything while the *"future"* is nothing. As a result, they abandon all interest in eternity, and mostly because of unbelief.

The Things of God did not interest the eldest son of Isaac, so he despised his birthright; thus Israel despised the pleasant land (Ps. 106:24); thus they despised Christ (Zech. 11:13); and thus those who were bidden to the marriage despised the invitation (Mat. 22:5).

Think about it! To Esau, a mess of pottage was better than a title to Canaan.

Esau knew exactly what he was denying. He wanted no part of anything that was Spiritual. He disdained it, thought little of it, if anything at all, and passed it off as nothing — good only to get a bowl of soup. Untold millions, even billions, follow in his footsteps.

They have no desire for Spiritual things.

Heaven is a far off place that they don't really even know if it exists. They joke about going to Hell when the truth is, Hell is no joke. As stated, it is all because of unbelief.

THE THOUGHTS OF FAITH

When a person truly knows God, he will have a true worth of eternal things. As well, he will see present things for what they really are, temporal, vague, slippery, and, therefore, of little consequence. The clearer one can see the vanity of man's present, the more he can cleave to God's Future. Look at the Judgment of Faith:

The Scripture says, *"Seeing then that all these things shall be dissolved, what manner of persons ought you to be in all Holy conversation* (lifestyle) *and Godliness, looking for and hasting unto the Coming of the Day of God, wherein the Heavens being on fire shall be dissolved, and the elements shall melt with fervent heat? Nevertheless we, according to His Promise, look for new heavens and a new Earth, wherein dwells Righteousness"* (II Pet. 3:11-13). These are the Thoughts of God and, therefore, the thoughts of Faith.

The things which are seen shall soon be dissolved, and we say that in the light of eternity.

THE CROSS

We must seek to judge things as the Lord judges things, and this can only be done by Faith. In fact, *"Faith"* is the key to all things. However, as we have stated, and due to its great significance, we will continue to repeat, proper Faith, that is, the Faith that God recognizes, can only be found in our understanding of the Cross. If we attempt to understand the Word of God without putting the Word in its proper perspective of the Cross of Christ, then we will have a false understanding of what the Word teaches.

The Story of the Word of God is the Story of Christ and the Cross. The entirety of its warp and woof is centered up in the Cross of Christ. In fact, the Cross was the first Promise given after the Fall. The Lord said to Satan through the serpent:

"And I will put enmity (hatred) between you (Satan) and the woman, and between your seed (humanity without God) and her Seed (the Lord Jesus Christ); it (Christ) shall bruise your head (the Victory of the Cross), and you shall bruise His Heel (the sufferings of the Cross)" (Gen. 3:15).

THE SYMBOLISM OF THE CROSS

Immediately, even beginning in Genesis, Chapter 4, we find the symbolism of the Cross given plainly in the substitutionary offering of the sacrifices. The lamb was to serve as a substitute until Christ would come. In fact, the head of each family was to serve as a Priest regarding that family, and was commanded by God to offer up sacrifices. Hence, in essence, Esau was saying that he had no interest in such things, didn't see any use in any of it, and had little, if any, qualms in trading the birthright, which included the domestic priesthood, for a bowl of soup. How cheaply he sold out! Isn't it the same with the world today?

As we presently view the situation, we cannot help but come to the conclusion that mankind is doing the identical same thing presently. It really doesn't matter if he sells his soul for a bowl of soup or one billion dollars, the end result is the same. Compared to the worth of the soul and the degree of eternity, what is one billion dollars?

The sad truth is, the far greater majority of the world gets only what Esau got, a little soup for the belly, and that's about it.

The offering up of sacrifices by the head of each family, and this was before the Law was given, was meant by God to be continued until the Law would be given. This would include the Sacrificial system, and in a much more pronounced way, is that which was given to Moses some 2,400 years after the Fall. All of it typified Christ and what Christ would do on the Cross as it regards the Redemption of humanity.

BELIEVERS AND THE CROSS

It should be understood that Esau was in the Covenant, but yet, he wasn't of the Covenant. In other words, he was like multiple millions of modern Christians who are, in fact, in the church but are not in the Lord.

It is my contention that if the Believer doesn't understand the Cross, then he will not truly understand the Things of the Lord, with many going in the same direction as Esau. The sadness is, most modern Christians have little understanding of the Cross of

Christ beyond the fact that Jesus died for them, and great numbers in the modern church are even denying that.

By that statement, I'm referring to the fact that they claim that the Cross is of little consequence, in fact, of no consequence at all. They teach that man's Salvation comes in other ways.

THE JESUS DIED SPIRITUALLY DOCTRINE

This, *"The Jesus Died Spiritually doctrine,"* is only one of many ways that men teach which eliminates the Cross.

In this particular doctrine, they teach that Jesus took upon Himself the satanic nature while He hung on the Cross, thereby, dying as a sinner and going to the burning side of Hell, as all Christ rejecters do. They teach that He suffered three days and nights in Hell, with Satan and all the demon hordes thinking that He was defeated. They claim that this, the three days and nights of suffering in the burning side of Hell, is the Atonement. At the end of the three days and nights of suffering, they then claim that God said, *"It is enough,"* with Jesus then being *"Born-Again,"* as any sinner is Born-Again, and then raised from the dead.

In spite of the fact that there is not a shred of Biblical evidence to support such contentions, this is what millions believe. It is called, *"The Jesus Died Spiritually doctrine."* It means that He not only died physically on the Cross, which they account for nothing, but, as well, that He died spiritually, which means that He died without God.

All of this is done through a twisting of Scripture. It is as Peter said: *". . . which they who are unlearned and unstable wrest . . . the . . . Scriptures, unto their own destruction"* (II Pet. 3:16). Let's look at some of the Scriptures which they use to support their fallacious doctrine.

FIRSTBORN

Concerning Jesus being *"Born-Again"* in Hell, their basic Scripture is Romans 8:29. It says, *"For whom He did foreknow, He also did predestinate to be conformed to the Image of His Son, that He might be the Firstborn among many brethren."*

The Greek word for *"Firstborn"* is, *"Prototokos."* It means, *"The foremost, the beginning, the chief, the best."*

It doesn't mean that Jesus was *"Born-Again,"* but rather that He is the One Who makes it possible for all sinners to be Born-Again.

For instance, Paul also said: *"Who (Christ) is the Image of the invisible God, the Firstborn of every creature"* (Col. 1:15).

This doesn't mean that the Lord of Glory is a created being such as all other things, but rather that He is the One Who has created all things. In other words, He is the Creator.

Again Paul said: *"And He (Christ) is the Head of the Body, the Church: Who is the beginning, the Firstborn from the dead; that in all things He might have the preeminence"* (Col. 1:18).

Once again, this doesn't mean that Jesus was Born-Again, but rather that He is the One Who has made the Resurrection possible. In fact, He is the Resurrection.

The Greek scholars tell us that there is no English word which can adequately explain the Greek word, *"Prototokos."* The word, *"Firstborn,"* is the closest they can get, but it does not adequately explain what it really is.

MY GOD, MY GOD, WHY HAVE YOU FORSAKEN ME?

Jesus was put on the Cross at about 9 a.m., and died at about 3 p.m. The Scripture says that there was *"darkness over all the land,"* from the sixth hour to the ninth hour. And at *"about the ninth hour Jesus cried with a loud voice, saying, 'Eli, Eli, lama sabachthani?' that is to say, 'My God, My God, why have You forsaken Me?'"* (Mat. 27:46).

There is evidence that during this three-hour period, from noon until 3 p.m., God actually turned His Face from Christ because He was bearing the penalty of the sin of the world. To fully carry out that penalty, He would have to die.

This doesn't mean that God forsook Christ because He was now a sinner, but because He was bearing the sin penalty, and the thrice-Holy God could not look at sin in that fashion in any manner.

However, moments before He died, He said, *"It is finished"* (Jn. 19:30). This meant that He was about to die and, therefore, the sin penalty would be satisfied. He then said, and this is very, very important: *"Father, into Your Hands I commend My Spirit."* This Scripture then says, *"And having said thus, He gave up the ghost"* (Lk. 23:46).

As is obvious here, He commended His Spirit to God, certainly not to Satan and, thereby, to Hell.

While after His Death Jesus did go to Hell, it was only to the Paradise part of Hell and not to the burning side (Eph. 4:8-9). The whole underground religion is referred to as Hell.

He also *"preached unto the spirits in prison,"* referring to fallen Angels (I Pet. 3:19-20). There is no record whatsoever of His going into the burning side of Hell, much less suffering there for three days and nights, burning in the flames, etc.

Those who believe this are actually repudiating the Cross and, therefore, must be put in the category of *"enemies of the Cross of Christ"* (Phil. 3:18).

No, it's the Cross, and the Cross Alone, which guarantees our Salvation and our Sanctification (Eph. 2:13-18; I Pet. 1:18-20).

"I will sing the wondrous Story,
"Of the Christ Who died for me,
"How He left His Home in Glory,
"For the Cross of Calvary."

"I was lost, but Jesus found me,
"Found the sheep that went astray,
"Threw His Loving Arms around me,
"Drew me back into His Way."

"Soon He'll come the Lord of Glory,
"Come the Church His Bride to claim,
"And complete the wondrous Story,
"Come Lord Jesus, come again."

"He will keep me till the river
"Rolls its waters at my feet;
"Then He'll bear me safely over,
"Where the loved ones I shall meet."

JACOB

Chapter Three

DECEPTION

DECEPTION

THE BIRTHRIGHT AGAIN COMES INTO VIEW

"And it came to pass, that when Isaac was old, and his eyes were dim, so that he could not see, he called Esau his oldest son, and said unto him, My son: and he said unto him, Behold, here am I.

"And he said, Behold now, I am old, I know not the day of my death:

"Now therefore take, I pray you, your weapons, your quiver and your bow, and go out to the field, and take me some venison;

"And make me savoury meat, such as I love, and bring it to me, that I may eat; that my soul may bless you before I die.

"And Rebekah heard when Isaac spoke to Esau his son. And Esau went to the field to hunt for venison, and to bring it" (Gen. 27:1-5).

As the record will show, if Esau was ready to sell the birthright for a mess of pottage, his father was prepared to sell it for a dish of venison! Concerning this, Williams said: *"Humbling picture of a man of God under the power of his lower sensual nature!"*

Isaac had been told by God at the time of Jacob's birth that he (Jacob) was to possess the birthright. But yet, he ignores this Word from the Lord and proceeds in his determination to give this birthright to Esau, despite the fact that Esau knew the Lord not at all!

REBEKAH

So, Rebekah overhears the intention of Isaac and proceeds to manage the affairs herself; therefore, she steps outside the path of Faith.

We may wonder about all of this, considering that these people were the Church of that particular time;

however, the Lord definitely had, and has, a purpose in setting before us all the traits of man's flawed character. We will find that it serves two means. It is to magnify God's Grace and to serve as a warning for you and me.

The truth is, all of this is done not at all to perpetuate the memory of sins, which, in fact, are forever blotted out from His Sight. In fact, all the flaws, sins, and wrong directions of Abraham, Isaac, and Jacob, plus every other Believer who has ever lived, have been perfectly washed away, with each of these individuals taking their place amid *"the spirits of just men made perfect."*

In all of this we see that God has not been dealing with perfect men and women but with those of *"like passions as we are,"* and that He has been working and bearing with the same failures, the same infirmities, and the same errors as those over which we mourn everyday.

THE POWER OF SIN

In all of this, and most assuredly, we should see the terrible power of sin which shows up in the flaws of humanity, irrespective of the Blessings of God upon our lives. If we forget this, we need only look at the pages of the Bible, and the case is made.

In fact, all of this stands in striking contrast to the way in which the great majority of human biographies are written, in which, for the most part, we find not the history of men but of beings devoid of error and infirmity. Such flatteries have the effect of discouraging us rather than edifying us. They are rather histories of what ought to be than of what they really are, and they are, therefore, useless to us. Not only are they useless but, for the most part, harmful.

Thus, the Word of God in no way glosses over the flaws, faults, and failures of even its champions. They are laid out in all of their ugliness with nothing held back. This shows us the terrible degree of man's depravity and lostness and, as well, the weakness of even the strongest Believer.

THE CROSS

Consequently, we see, or most definitely should see, the terrible need for the Cross. In fact, the Cross of Christ is the answer, and the only answer, for man's dilemma, whatever that dilemma might be.

When it's all said and done and the last roll call has been given, when all the façade is stripped away and we've tried to explain Justification and Sanctification by Faith, and when we add our understanding of God's Grace coupled together with His Love, we finally see that really the only thing that is left is the Cross. Maybe we can say that all of these great Doctrines are bound together in one symbol, and that symbol is the Cross of Christ. It alone stands between us and eternal Hell! It alone stands between us and eternal darkness! The Cross alone stands as the beacon of Light in the midst of a darkened world!

Such is the power of sin, but make no mistake about it, the Cross is greater! If sin has dragged down the entirety of the human race, and done so in all of its putrid ugliness, the Cross has lifted man out of this morass of evil. Of course, when we speak of the Cross, we speak of Christ.

THE NEW CHURCH

The new church in its modern doctrine strikes at the very Foundation of the Faith. It understands Christ's

Death on the Cross as merely God's Way of showing how much He loves us. In this view, Christ does not atone for our sins since our sins, as one preacher put it, are merely nothing more than our individual acts of individual wills. Consequently, they teach that Jesus is not at all our Sacrifice, rather He is our Example. He shows us how to love each other. His Death on the Cross makes us feel sorry for Him, and when we really realize how much He suffered, it makes us feel God's Love. This motivates us, they say, to change our lives and to love others.

So, the new church does not involve itself in proclaiming God's Judgment against sinners and His Gracious Offer of Salvation through Faith in Jesus Christ and what He did for us at the Cross. Rather, the new church simply educates people as to how much God loves them. According to the way of thinking of the new church, God really does not want to punish anyone. He wants all to feel good about themselves, to lead a full life, and to be happy. Although this theology of the new church turns God into a warm, fuzzy therapist, it is essentially a teaching of moralism and despair, focusing on human works. It gives no comfort to tormented souls and includes no provision for the forgiveness of sin. In fact, the words of Paul scream out against this nonsense. He said, *"If Righteousness could be gained through the Law, Christ died for nothing!"* (Gal. 2:21).

EXPOSITORS

Concerning all of this, Michael Horton said: *"Before, God existed for His Own happiness, but this new god exists for ours. Instead of sinners having to be justified before a good and holy God, we are now ourselves the good guys who demand that God justify Himself before us. Why should we believe in Him? How will believing in Him make me happier and more fulfilled than believing in karma or the latest ideological bandwagon?"*

Gene Veith also said: *"Throughout its history the Church has always had two options — to go along with the times or to counter them. One could argue that the most vital theological movements in Church history have been those that went against the trends of their time."*

RESPONSE TO THE CROSS

In 1997, the Lord began to give to this Evangelist a Revelation of the Cross of Christ. It was not something new, actually, the teaching of the Apostle Paul as the Holy Spirit gave it to him. However, the difference in my own situation was that the Lord helped me to understand this which the great Apostle had taught.

It revolutionized my life exactly as it has revolutionized the lives of untold millions of others. In fact, there is no deliverance, no victory, and no salvation outside of the Cross of Christ. As the song says, *"All else is sinking sand."*

However, I have been amazed at the response of many, even when they were proverbially hanging on by their fingertips, if that! Staring destruction in the face, they say, *"I suppose that's alright for some (speaking of the Cross), but it's definitely not for all."*

What could they mean by such thinking?

Does God have 10, five, or even two ways of Salvation and Sanctification? The answer to that is quite simple: no, He doesn't! He has only one Way, and that is the Cross. That's why Paul said:

"But God forbid that I should glory, save in the Cross of our Lord Jesus Christ, by Whom the world is crucified unto me, and I unto the world" (Gal. 6:14).

Therefore, this brings us to the reason that the Cross is rejected.

THE CROSS IS NEVER REJECTED FOR THEOLOGICAL REASONS, BUT ALWAYS FOR MORAL REASONS

What do we mean by that?

Despite its dire cost, the great Plan of Redemption is, in reality, a simple provision. A person doesn't have to be a scholar, a theologian, a genius, or any such like in order to understand God's Plan of Redemption. He just simply has to believe (Jn. 3:16; Rom. 10:9-10, 13; Rev. 22:17).

So, if a person rejects the Cross, he must do so on the basis of moral reasons. This means that the problem is pride, self-will, stubbornness, rebellion against God, or some such sin, which, as is obvious, all fall into the morality problem.

When the Lord first began to open up this great Truth to me after some six years of soul-searching prayer, I first thought that Scriptural ignorance was the problem. However, after nearly 16 years of observing people, I have now come to the conclusion that while ignorance definitely does abound, the greatest problem of all is *"unbelief."* In other words, the great mass of the modern church, and again we speak of the *"new church,"* no longer believes in the Cross. The striking thing about all of this is we are not speaking of modernists but, in reality, those who claim to be fundamentalists or Pentecostal, etc. In other words, many who are presently rejecting the Cross claim at the same time to be Spirit-filled. I have to wonder, *"Filled with what spirit?"* The Holy Spirit will always lead to the Cross.

PAUL SAID

"For the Law of the Spirit (Holy Spirit) of Life in Christ Jesus (what Jesus did for us at the Cross) has made

me free from the Law of Sin and Death" (Rom. 8:2).

We learn from this Passage plus scores of others that the Holy Spirit works exclusively within the parameters of the Finished Work of Christ, so, despite the claims, the truth is, the Holy Spirit has nothing to do with the direction of the new church.

The problem is the new church tries to dress up the *"old man"* when, in reality, he must be killed (Rom. 6:6-8).

REBEKAH

"And Rebekah spoke unto Jacob her son, saying, Behold, I heard your father speak unto Esau your brother, saying,

"Bring me venison, and make me savoury meat, that I may eat, and bless you before the LORD before my death.

"Now therefore, my son, obey my voice according to that which I command you" (Gen. 27:6-8).

As we shall see, Jacob's history teaches the lesson, which the natural will is so unwilling to learn, that planning for self instead of resting in the Hand of God brings sorrow. Rebekah schemes in order to get Jacob the birthright exactly as Sarah schemed to give Abraham a son. Both were on the path of self-will.

Abraham and Sarah attempted to deceive Pharaoh; Isaac and Rebekah attempted to deceive Abimelech; Jacob and Rebekah attempted to deceive Isaac. Again we say, *"Such is the path of self-will."*

Here we have the aged Patriarch Isaac standing, as it were, at the very portal of eternity with the Earth and nature fast fading away from his view. Yet, he was occupied about *"savoury meat,"* and about to act in direct opposition to the Divine council by blessing the elder instead of the younger.

Rebekah reasons that if Isaac will do this thing, which is against God, she is justified in her actions of deception. However, wrongdoing is never justified! It always reaps a bitter result, exactly as it did here.

DECEPTION

"Go now to the flock, and fetch me from thence two good kids of the goats; and I will make them savoury meat for your father, such as he loves:

"And you shall bring it to your father, that he may eat, and that he may bless you before his death.

"And Jacob said to Rebekah his mother, Behold, Esau my brother is a hairy man, and I am a smooth man:

"My father peradventure will feel me, and I shall seem to him as a deceiver; and I shall bring a curse upon me, and not a blessing" (Gen. 27:9-12).

Rebekah's plan is one of deception and not pleasing at all to the Lord. However, such is the path of the flesh; it always seems right to the natural heart and mind.

We may look at this and think that such chicanery died with Jacob and his mother; however, regrettably, that is not the case.

My following statements may be strong, but I feel them to be absolutely correct:

I have lived for the Lord almost all of my life and as the writer of *"Amazing Grace"* said, *"Through many dangers, toils, and snares, I have already come."* In this, I've learned a few things:

From experience, and above all, my study of the Word of God and the Revelations given to me by the Lord concerning the Word, I personally believe that if one doesn't walk the path of Faith, one will practice the life of spiritual deception. There are only two paths, *"Faith"* and *"flesh."*

To walk the path of Faith, one must ever understand what Faith actually is. The Holy Spirit through Paul defined it very ably. He said:

"I am crucified with Christ: nevertheless I live; yet not I, but Christ lives in me: and the life which I now live in the flesh (our natural walk before God) I live by the Faith of the Son of God, Who loved me, and gave Himself for me" (Gal. 2:20).

Notice the way that Paul used the term, *"The Faith of the Son of God."*

This refers to what Jesus did for us at the Cross, which was the great Sacrifice of Himself. In fact, Christianity is often referred to as *"the Faith,"* with that latter term always referring to what Christ did at the Cross.

So, it's the Cross, it's the Cross, or it is deception!

THE CURSE

"And his mother said unto him, Upon me be your curse, my son: only obey my voice, and go fetch me them.

"And he went, and fetched, and brought them to his mother: and his mother made savoury meat, such as his father loved.

"And Rebekah took goodly raiment of her eldest son Esau, which were with her in the house, and put them upon Jacob her younger son:

"And she put the skins of the kids of the goats upon his hands, and upon the smooth of his neck:

"And she gave the savoury meat and the bread, which she had prepared, into the hand of her son Jacob" (Gen. 27:13-17).

It should be understood that Rebekah wanted the Blessing for Jacob not just because he was her favorite son, but because she knew this was the Will of the Lord. However, her means of obtaining this showed a lack of trust and, thereby, constituted a work of the flesh. In essence, by resorting to trickery, she was doing the same thing that Sarah did as it regarded a son being born to Abraham. Both women would seek to *"help"* God, but it was that which the Lord could never accept, irrespective as to whom the people might be.

We are observing here the greatest hindrance to the Christian experience. We do not trust the Lord, or else, we do not know how to trust the Lord, which is more often the case than many would realize.

If the Believer doesn't understand the following three things, he will invariably seek to do exactly what Rebekah here sought to do. He will resort to the flesh because, as stated, if the path of Faith is not properly trod, there's nowhere else to go but the way of the flesh.

These three things are:

1. THE CROSS

Even though we've already said these very same things in this Volume, due to the fact that we're dealing with the very heart of the Christian experience, we dare not say the following too little, with it being virtually impossible to say it too much.

The Believer must understand that everything he receives from the Lord from the time that he is brought to Christ, throughout the entirety of his life and living, comes by the means of the Cross of Christ (Rom. 6:3-14; I Cor. 1:17-18, 21, 23; 2:2, 5; Gal. 6:14; Eph. 2:13-18; Col. 2:10-15; I Pet. 1:18-20).

2. OUR FAITH

The problem is not faith, but rather the proper object of our faith. In fact, every one in the world has faith. Even the scientist, who boasts that he would never think of basing his claims on Faith, is, in fact, carrying on his work and life by and through faith. Every experiment he performs is done on the basis of faith, whether he realizes it or not.

The nations of the world, which have a free market economy, are operating on the principle of faith, hence, it producing the greatest prosperity in the world because it's God's Way. The nations of the world, which have a controlled economy and stifle faith, can scarcely feed their people.

However, although faith, none of that is the type of faith which God recognizes. The only type of Faith that HE will recognize is that which pertains solely to the Cross, i.e., *"the Sacrifice of Christ."* It is Faith in Christ and His Finished Work, i.e., *"the Cross,"* which God recognizes, and that alone! As previously stated, that's why Paul referred to it as, *"The Faith"* (Rom. 1:5, 8, 17; 3:3, 22, 25, 27-28; 4:5, 11; I Cor. 2:5; II Cor. 5:7; Gal. 2:16, 20; 3:23).

3. THE GOOD FIGHT OF FAITH

In fact, the only fight the Christian is supposed to engage is *"the good fight of Faith"* (I Tim. 6:12). We are not told to fight the Devil, sin, or demon spirits. We are told to *"fight the good fight of Faith."* This means that every struggle, every effort, and all the wrestling (Eph. 6:12) are in the realm of Faith. Satan tries to move our Faith from the Cross of Christ to other things, and it really doesn't matter how good the other things are or even how Scriptural in their own right. If we are depending on those things, whatever they might be, to give us victory, we will fail simply because that's not God's Way. It is Faith and Faith alone, but more particularly, Faith in Christ and what Christ did at the Cross. If your faith is not anchored in Jesus Christ and Him Crucified, then again allow me to state, *"It's not faith which God will recognize."*

THE HOLY SPIRIT

The Believer must understand that it is the Holy Spirit Who makes possible to us all the great things which Jesus did at the Cross. It really doesn't matter how much Faith we have; it's the Holy Spirit Who carries out the task. However, the secret is this:

He will not work except within the parameters of the Sacrifice of Christ. This is what makes it legally permissible for Him to do all the things which He Alone can do.

Before the Cross, the Holy Spirit could work with Believers and, even at times, work within them, at least to help them perform a task which God had called them to do. However, as far as His Abiding in them, even the great Patriarchs and Prophets, as He does presently, that He couldn't do. The reason He couldn't do those things is simply because the sin debt still hung over the heads of the entirety of the human race. Although functioning as a stopgap measure, the blood of bulls and goats still couldn't take away sins (Heb. 10:4). So, the Holy Spirit was then limited as to what He could do as it regarded Old Testament Saints.

SINCE THE CROSS

However, since the Cross, and because all sin has been taken away (Jn. 1:29), the Holy Spirit can now come into the heart and life of the Believer, which He does immediately at Conversion, and abide there forever (Jn. 14:16-17).

So, it is the Cross which makes possible the great Work the Holy Spirit does within our hearts and lives.

Paul said: *"For the Law (the Law devised by the Godhead) of the Spirit (Holy Spirit) of Life (all Life comes from the Son by the Spirit) in Christ Jesus (what Jesus did for us at the Cross) has made me free from the Law of Sin and Death"* (Rom. 8:2).

So, now you have it:
• The Cross of Christ.
• Our Faith, with its Object being the Cross of Christ.
• The Holy Spirit, Who works exclusively within the framework of the Cross of Christ.

This little diagram is God's Way and, in fact, His Way for everything.

THE DECEPTION

"And He came unto his father, and said, My father: and he said, Here am I; who are you, my son?

"And Jacob said unto his father, I am Esau your firstborn; I have done according as you bade me: arise, I pray you, sit and eat of my venison, that your soul may bless me.

"And Isaac said unto his son, How is it that you have found it so quickly, my son? And he said, because the LORD your God brought it to me" (Gen. 27:18-20).

One sin, if not repented of, is always followed by a worse sin. As Jacob falsely claimed the Help of the Lord, all religious deception does such. A Believer's sin is worse than the sin of an unbeliever simply because it makes the Lord, in essence, a part of the sin, so to speak. Thus, blasphemy is added to disobedience.

Jacob brings the Lord into his perfidiousness, but so it is with all Believers who fail God. It's bad enough to do wrong, but to attempt to make the Lord a part of our wrong makes it infinitely worse.

Inasmuch as our very bodies are Temples of the Holy Spirit (I Cor. 3:16), then the Third Person of the Triune Godhead must observe all we do, whether good or bad. In a sense, even though never touched by sin Himself, it never fails to grieve Him, and to do so to a degree perhaps we will never understand (Eph. 4:30).

THE DEED

"And Isaac said unto Jacob, Come near, I pray you, that I may feel you, my son, whether you be my very son Esau or not.

"And Jacob went near unto Isaac his father; and he felt him, and said, The voice is Jacob's voice, but the hands are the hands of Esau.

"And he discerned him not, because his hands were hairy, as his brother Esau's hands: so he blessed him.

"And he said, Are you my very son Esau? And he said, I am.

"And he said, Bring it near to me, and I will eat of my son's venison, that my soul may bless you. And he brought it near to him, and he did eat: and he brought him wine and he drank" (Gen. 27:21-25).

The depth of Rebekah's sin carried out by her son Jacob is labeled very correctly, I think, by Matthew Henry. He said: *"Rebekah wronged Isaac by practicing an imposition upon him; she wronged Jacob by using her authority and persuasion to tempt him to wickedness; she sinned against the Lord, and dishonored His power and faithfulness, by supposing He needed such means of affecting His Purpose, and fulfilling His Promise.*

"She put a stumbling block in Esau's way, and furnished him with a pretext for enmity, both against Jacob and against the Salvation of the Lord, by putting Jacob upon acting such a treacherous part.

"It was one of those crooked measures which have too often been adopted to accomplish the Divine Promises; as if the end would justify, or at least excuse the means."

The entirety of this transaction speaks of fraud. All the parties are to be blamed: Isaac is to be blamed for endeavoring to set aside the Divine Will; Esau for wishing to deprive his brother of the Blessing he had himself relinquished to him; and Rebekah and Jacob for wishing to secure it by fraudulent means, not trusting wholly in the Lord.

As an aside, how remarkable it is in this wonderful Creation of God that of all the billions of people in this world, every voice is different.

THE BLESSING

"And his father Isaac said unto him, Come near now, and kiss me, my son.

"And he came near, and kissed him: and he smelled the smell of his raiment, and blessed him, and said, See, the smell of my son is as the smell of a field which the LORD has blessed:

"Therefore God give you of the dew of Heaven, and the fatness of the Earth, and plenty of corn and wine:

"Let people serve you, and nations bow down to you: be lord over your brethren, and let your mother's sons bow to you: cursed be everyone who curses you, and blessed be he who blesses you" (Gen. 27:26-29).

It is observed by Matthew Henry that the blessing given by Isaac is expressed in very general terms. He went on to say that no mention is made of those distinguishing Mercies included in the Covenant with Abraham.

The first part of the blessing is a generalization. It speaks of the blessings of the Earth belonging to the recipient.

However, in Verse 29, it becomes much more particular, with even the entirety of the Earth bowing down to him. The idea pertains to Christ.

The Incarnation would bring the Son of God into the world. So, this Blessing would pass through Jacob and many others, and be realized only in Christ. And, even yet, it hasn't been fulfilled in totality, but most definitely shall be at the Second Coming. It is ironic: the Blesser is Christ, and the Blessing is also Christ!

ESAU

"And it came to pass, as soon as Isaac had made an end of blessing Jacob, and Jacob was yet scarce gone out from the presence of Isaac his father, that Esau his brother came in from his hunting.

"And he also had made savoury meat, and brought it unto his father, and said unto his father, Let my father arise, and eat of his son's venison, that your soul may bless me.

"And Isaac his father said unto him, Who are you? And he said, I am your son, your firstborn Esau" (Gen. 27:30-32).

Does not Jacob realize that Esau will soon come upon the scene? Perhaps he thought that Esau cared so little for the birthright that he would raise no objection. However, if he thought all of this, why did he not say such to his father without trying to deceive the old man?

The truth is, Esau did want the blessing, but not for the right purpose and reason. As well, he would treat the transaction made between him and his brother, as it regards the birthright, as no more than a joke. However, he finds to his dismay that he has been outtricked!

Esau represents those in the church who would walk the path of self-will. Jacob represents those who know the path of Faith but would leave that path and suffer greatly. Isaac represents those who are in positions of leadership and know so little of the Mind of God that they would give the birthright to the Devil instead of to Christ. What an ignominious mess! However, I wonder how much the church has really changed, if any at all?

A JUST FEAR

"And Isaac trembled very exceedingly, and said, Who? where is he who has taken venison, and brought it to me, and I have eaten of all before you came, and have blessed him? yes, and he shall be blessed.

"And when Esau heard the words of his father, he cried with a great and exceeding bitter cry, and said unto his father, Bless me, even me also, O my father.

"And he said, Your brother came with subtilty, and has taken away your blessing" (Gen. 27:33-35).

Concerning this, Ellicott says, *"The trembling of Isaac was not from mere vexation at having been so deceived, and made to give the blessing contrary to his wishes. What Isaac felt was that he had been resisting God. Despite the prophecy given to Rebekah, and Esau's own unspiritual character and heathen marriages, he had determined to bestow on him the birthright by an act of his own will; and he had failed. But he persists no longer in his sin, 'although he does acknowledge the subtilty of Jacob.'"*

Isaac trembles at what he had almost done, which would have given the Blessing of Abraham to this ungodly, unspiritual son, whom the Holy Spirit refers to as a *"fornicator"* (Heb. 12:16).

THE PATH OF ESAU

"The will of the flesh" made Isaac wish to bless Esau, but Faith in the end conquered (Heb. 11:20), and he cries respecting Jacob: *"I have blessed him, and he shall be blessed."*

Hebrews 12:17 recalls Esau's bitter weeping when he found that he had lost the birthright, and now he failed with his tears to cause his father to change his mind. He found no place of repentance in his father's will.

As Paul describes this *"repentance"* (Heb. 12:17), he is not speaking of true Repentance, for Esau manifested no such thing. He is referring to Esau attempting to change the mind of his father, Isaac. Esau wanted the material part, but he had no interest whatsoever in the Spiritual part, which was, in reality, the substance of the birthright. In fact, Esau little desired the birthright, if at all, but wanted the blessing. How so similar to many in the modern church!

Millions today are presently being led down the path of Esau. Of the Spiritual aspect of the birthright, they have no desire. They only want the so-called double portion of material goods that went with the birthright.

BLESSING

Sometime ago, I overheard one of the leading gurus of the *"Word of Faith"* movement claim that the *"Blessing of Abraham"* had nothing to do with Spiritual things, but only with money. It's the only time in my life that I found myself standing on the floor in front of the TV set screaming at the absolute absurdity of such a statement. The tragedy is, this man pastors a church in California, which numbers several thousands of people, and has wide influence over untold thousands through television.

However, let it be known, the real *"Blessing"* cannot come to Esau, who desires only material things, but rather to Jacob, even though he is a sad illustration of the destructive power of fallen human nature. Therefore, Psalm 46:11 is very dear to the hearts of all true Believers:

"The LORD of Hosts is with us; the God of Jacob is our refuge. Selah."

Here are brought together into the one Verse the two great titles, *"The LORD of Hosts"* and *"God of Jacob."* The one title presents Him as the God of countless Hosts of sinless Angels; the other title proclaims Him as the God of one stumbling, sinning, scheming, planning, and broken man! These Divine titles link Almighty Power with infinite Grace.

JACOB

"And he said, Is not he rightly named Jacob? for

he has supplanted me these two times: he took away my birthright; and, behold, now he has taken away my blessing. And he said, Have you not reserved a blessing for me?

"*And Isaac answered and said unto Esau, Behold, I have made him your lord, and all his brethren have I given to him for servants; and with corn and wine have I sustained him: and what shall I do now unto you, my son?*

"*And Esau said unto his father, Have you but one blessing, my father? bless me, even me also, O my father. And Esau lifted up his voice, and wept.*

"*And Isaac his father answered and said unto him, Behold, your dwelling shall be the fatness of the Earth, and of the dew of heaven from above:*

"*And by your sword shall you live, and you shall serve your brother; and it shall come to pass when you shall have the dominion, that you shall break his yoke from off your neck*" (Gen. 27:36-40).

Only one son could inherit the spiritual prerogatives of the birthright and the temporal lordship which accompanied it (Ellicott).

Concerning Verse 39, the actual Hebrew reads, "*Your dwelling shall be of the fat places of the Earth,*" but most expositors consider that the preposition, "*Of,*" should be translated, "*From.*" Thus it would read, "*Behold your dwelling shall be away from the fat places of the Earth, and away from the dew of heaven from above, and by your sword you shall live.*"

This is closer to the original intent of the Hebrew language and, as well, more aptly describes the descendants of Esau, the Arabs. For the most part, their domicile or dwelling has been the desert and not otherwise. As well, they have been, and are, a violent people, thereby, fulfilling Verse 40, "*And by your sword you shall live.*"

NO BLESSING

The Edomites were the descendants of Esau, and the Prophecy was fulfilled in that they were in subjection to Israel for many, many years. However, in the first days of Joram and then of Ahaz, Edom revolted and recovered its freedom exactly as Isaac had prophesied in Verse 40.

So, in reality, there was no blessing for Esau, as there can never be a blessing for those who would demean the Ways of God, thereby, setting their own course.

As we have stated, the Blesser is the Lord Jesus Christ, and the Blessing, as well, is the Lord Jesus Christ. In fact, Christ being born into this world and, thereby, redeeming lost humanity by going to the Cross is what all of this is about. God had to have a lineage of Faith through whom He could come as a Man, and the lineage of Abraham produced these people. It is Jesus Christ, or it is nothing! He said of Himself:

"... *I am the Way, the Truth, and the Life: no man comes unto the Father, but by Me"* (Jn. 14:6).

THE LORD JESUS CHRIST

In essence, Jesus Christ is the coin, so to speak, of the Spiritual realm. It is not the Church, not good works, and not good deeds, but Faith in Christ and what Christ has done for us at the Cross.

Jesus Christ Alone was and is the Son of God, and Jesus Christ Alone went to the Cross and paid the price for man's Redemption (Jn. 3:16; Gal. 1:4). So, everyone in this world who places their Faith and trust in Muhammad, Buddha, the Pope, the Church, denominations, or good works will be eternally lost. Let no one think that faith in the church, or whatever, equates with Faith in Jesus Christ. It must be Christ, and Christ Alone; and more so, it must be *"Christ and Him Crucified"* (I Cor. 2:2), or else, one will find oneself worshipping *"another Jesus"* (II Cor. 11:4).

REBEKAH

"And Esau hated Jacob because of the blessing wherewith his father blessed him: and Esau said in his heart, The days of mourning for my father are at hand; then will I kill my brother Jacob.

"And these words of Esau her elder son were told to Rebekah: and she sent and called Jacob her younger son, and said unto him, Behold, your brother Esau, as touching you, does comfort himself, purposing to kill you.

"Now therefore, my son, obey my voice; and arise, flee thou to Laban my brother to Haran;

"And tarry with him a few days, until your brother's fury turn away;

"Until your brother's anger turn away from you, and he forget that which you have done to him: then I will send, and fetch you from thence: why should I be deprived also of you both in one day?" (Gen. 27:41-45).

Esau had no cause to hate Jacob. He knew that the Prophecy had given the birthright to Jacob. As well, he knew that his profligate lifestyle did not warrant such. He had no desire to be the Priest of the family, in fact, no desire whatsoever for the things of God. So, his hatred was fueled by ungodliness and not for any imagined wrong.

It must be remembered that Esau was in the Covenant but actually not part of the Covenant. Although he was in the sacred family, he was not really a spiritual part of the sacred family. As previously stated, so are millions of modern church members. They are in the Church but not really of the Church. They claim the Lord, but they aren't really of the Lord.

FALLEN HUMAN NATURE

As we have stated, Jacob himself was a sad illustration of the destructive power of fallen human nature. But yet, he truly loved the Lord and truly wanted the things of the Lord. In fact, Jacob is a type of the consecrated Child of God who tries by self-will to attain from the Lord what can only be attained through and by the Holy Spirit. However, as Jacob, we have to learn that lesson the hard way, also.

How so much his life mirrors my own and yours! However, even though it will take some time and pass through many dangers, toils, and snares, ultimately, Jacob, the deceiver, the supplanter, and the heel-catcher will become *"Israel,"* the *"Soldier of God."*

MORE DECEPTION

"And Rebekah said to Isaac, I am weary of my life because of the daughters of Heth: if Jacob take a wife of the daughters of Heth, such as these which are of the daughters of the land, what good shall my life do me?" (Gen. 27:46).

There is no doubt that Rebekah was concerned about *"the daughters of the land"* and none of them being a suitable wife for Jacob. She, of course, is the very recipient of this which Abraham demanded concerning a wife for his son, Isaac. However, at this time, her real reason for sending Jacob away was not that which she told Isaac, but rather because she feared for Jacob's life as it regarded the anger of Esau.

So, we cannot exonerate Rebekah altogether from a charge of duplicity in this. This is what she wanted Isaac to believe, but it is not the real reason.

The *"few days"* of Verse 44 would turn into some 20 years, and she, in fact, would never see Jacob again. She would die before his return to the Land of Promise.

Such is the path of self-will. How it must have broken her heart a thousand times over that she never saw her son again.

I think there is no doubt that Rebekah ultimately made all of this right with God, but there was no way she could undo the results of her act. This would haunt her for the rest of her life.

THE FRUITS OF OUR OWN DEVICES

How different it would have been had she left the matter entirely in the Hands of God! This is the way in which Faith manages instead of us trying to do it ourselves. Jesus said concerning these very things, *"Which of you by taking thought can add to his stature one cubit?"* We gain nothing by our anxiety and planning; we only shut out God, and that is no gain.

It is always a just Judgment from the Hand of God to be left to reap the fruits of our own devices. I know of few things sadder than to see a Child of God so entirely forgetting his proper place and privilege as to take the management of his affairs into his own hands. The birds of the air and the lilies of the field may well be our teachers when we so far forget our position of unqualified dependence upon God.

Out of this Text we also learn what a profane person actually is, even as the Holy Spirit described Esau (Heb. 12:16). It is one who would like to hold both worlds, one who would like to enjoy the present without forfeiting his title to the future. It is the person who attempts to use God instead of God using him. Please understand, we're not speaking here of those of the world but those in the church, those who claim Divine privilege.

"Wonderful birth, to a manger He came,
"Made in the likeness of man,

"To proclaim God's Boundless Love,
"For a world sick with sin,
"Pleading with sinners to let Him come in."

"Wonderful life, full of service so free,
"Friend to the poor and the needy was He;
"Unfailing goodness on all He bestowed,
"Undying Faith in the vilest He showed."

"Wonderful death, for it meant not defeat,
"Calvary made His Great Mission complete,
"Wrought our Redemption, and when He arose,
"Banished forever the last of our foes."

"Wonderful hope, He is coming again,
"Coming as King over the nations to reign;
"Glorious promise, His Word cannot fail,
"His Righteous Kingdom at last must prevail!"

JACOB

Chapter Four

THE BLESSING

THE BLESSING

ISAAC

"And Isaac called Jacob, and blessed him, and charged him, and said unto him, You shall not take a wife of the daughters of Canaan.

"Arise, go to Padan-aram, to the house of Bethuel your mother's father; and take you a wife from thence of the daughters of Laban your mother's brother" (Gen. 28:1-2).

Now we have the commencing of God's Special Dealings with Jacob. Now begins the *"making of a man."*

God will accomplish His Own Purpose no matter by what instrumentality. However, if His Child, in impatience of spirit and unbelief of heart, takes himself out of God's Hands, he must expect much sorrowful exercise and painful discipline. Thus it was with Jacob, and thus it is with us.

Isaac now seems to have fully returned to the path of Faith. There is now no attempt to substitute Esau for Jacob or to lessen the privileges of the latter, but with hearty cheerfulness, he blesses the younger son and confirms him in the possession of the whole Abrahamic Blessing.

It was not the Will of God for Esau or Jacob to marry *"the daughters of the land."* However, now that Jacob was the recipient of the Blessing, thereby, the chosen one as it regarded the birthright, which had to do with the coming of the Redeemer into the world, it was imperative that he not marry one of the Canaanite girls as had his brother Esau. These people were idolaters, and even above that, their lineage was of the cursed line of Canaan. So, the command by Isaac, and rightly so, was emphatic, *"You shall not take a wife of the daughters of Canaan."* He was rather to take a wife of one of the daughters of Laban, his mother's brother.

THE BLESSING

"And God Almighty bless you, and make you fruit-
ful, and multiply you, that you may be a multitude of
people;
"And give you the Blessing of Abraham, to you,
and to your seed with you; that you may inherit the
land wherein you are a stranger, which God gave
unto Abraham.
"And Isaac sent away Jacob; and he went to Padan-
aram unto Laban, son of Bethuel the Syrian, the brother
of Rebekah, Jacob's and Esau's mother" (Gen. 28:3-5).

The appellative, *"God Almighty,"* means, *"El-Shaddai,"*
and promises guardianship and companionship. Concerning this, Williams says: *"This great title, declaring*
God to be the Almighty One, assured Jacob beforehand
of the sufficiency and ability of God to meet and provide
for all his needs. This is the more instructive, when
it is noticed that God promises to bless him in going
obediently to Haran just as He had promised to bless
his grandfather Abraham if obediently leaving Haran.
This illustrates how the life of Faith appears a life of
contradictions to human wisdom."

THE BLESSING OF ABRAHAM

The *"Blessing of Abraham"* is mentioned by Paul
(Gal. 3:14). It means *"Justification by Faith."* Paul also
said: *"And the Scripture, foreseeing that God would*
justify the heathen through Faith, preached before the
Gospel unto Abraham, saying, In you shall all nations
be blessed" (Gal. 3:8; Gen. 12:3).

In its most simplistic form, it simply means that a
believing sinner is justified before God by simply having Faith in Christ and what Christ has done for us at
the Cross.

The word, *"Justify,"* or, *"Justification,"* is a legal term. It refers to one being declared *"innocent,"* *"not guilty,"* or *"accepted."*

The Salvation process is instant, but yet, is broken down into three parts, which, one might say, is done simultaneously. The Scripture says: *"And such were some of you: but you are "washed," but you are "sanctified," but you are "justified" in the Name of the Lord Jesus, and by the Spirit of our God"* (I Cor. 6:11).

To be *"washed"* refers to the accomplishment of the Blood, which was shed by Christ on the Cross. It is not a physical experience, but rather a Spiritual experience. The moment the sinner evidences Faith in Christ, the Precious Blood of Christ cleanses (washes) from all sin (I Jn. 1:7). The believing sinner is then sanctified. This means to be set apart, which means to be *"made clean."* He is then declared, *"Justified,"* and all *"in the Name of the Lord Jesus, and by the Spirit of our God."* This means that all of this was done for us in Christ and brought about in our lives by the Holy Spirit.

The *"Blessing of Abraham"* was promised not only to Jacob but, as well, *"to your seed with you,"* which includes every single Believer who has ever lived, both Jews and Gentiles.

THE LAND

The *"land"* he was promised, of course, refers to the land area of Canaan, which would later be named Israel, and would be the home of the Jewish people, Jacob's *"seed."* All of this was for the purpose of bringing the Redeemer into the world, i.e., *"the Lord Jesus Christ."* A people would have to literally be created, which they were, who would have Faith in God. To these people God could give His Word, and, as well, they would serve as the womb of the Messiah, so to speak. However, when this Redeemer would come, which He did about 1,800 years later, He would come for the entirety of the world and not for the Jews only (Jn. 3:16).

Whereas the word, *"Land,"* then referred to an exact geographical location, it now has a Spiritual connotation. The *"land"* we now possess is a Spiritual Inheritance. However, it is just as real in the spirit world as the actual taking of the physical land by Joshua when the children of Israel finally possessed that place. Concerning the present time, the song says:

"We are able to go up and take the country.
"And possess the land from Jordan unto the Sea.
"Though the giants may be there our way to hinder,
"Our God has given us the victory."

JESUS HAS WON EVERY VICTORY

However, there is a vast difference in the taking of the land by Joshua, which would take place about 300 years into the future, than the taking of the land presently, to use a metaphor.

Jesus Christ, our Heavenly Joshua, has already taken the land for us, which means that He has won every victory, defeated every foe, and has done it all for us. For us to have this great possession and to occupy it totally and completely, which refers to having victory over the world, the flesh, and the Devil, all we have to do is to trust in Christ and what He has already done for us in the Sacrifice of Himself. In fact, it is at the Cross where He won this great Victory and did so in totality (Eph. 2:13-18; Col. 2:14-15).

The biggest mistake the Christian can make is to try to do all over again what Christ has, in fact, already done. That's why Jesus said: *"Come unto Me, all you who labor and are heavy laden, and I will give you rest"* (Mat. 11:28). This life of Faith, for that's what it is, is now a resting or reposing in Him, for He has already won the battle and has done so in totality. In other words, the land is yours right now! All you have to do is believe it, enjoy it, and rest in it. It is truly a land of *"milk and honey,"* spiritually speaking.

ESAU

"When Esau saw that Isaac had blessed Jacob, and sent him away to Padan-aram, to take him a wife from thence; and that as he blessed him he gave him a charge, saying, You shall not take a wife of the daughters of Canaan" (Gen. 28:6).

Esau, understanding spiritual things not at all, now tries to rectify his situation concerning marriage to Canaanite girls by taking yet another wife of the family of Ishmael.

The world, as Esau, who is a type of the world, does religious things and thinks that constitutes spirituality. It doesn't!

Esau knew nothing of the life of Faith, only that of self-will. To know the life of Faith, one must know Jesus Christ and His Power to save.

Esau, knowing nothing of the path of Faith, concludes erroneously that the reason Isaac gave Jacob the Blessing is because he (Esau) had married Canaanite women.

Esau was like millions in the modern church presently. He wanted the Blessing, but he understood the Blessing not at all in spiritual terms but only in material terms. That Jacob now had the Blessing, which he obtained by Faith, rankles Esau to no end, and he will now try to obtain the Blessing by self-will.

THE MODERN CHURCH

All of this is a perfect picture of the modern church. We have those who trust in Christ and His Cross symbolized by Jacob, and we have those who trust in other things symbolized by Esau. However, as Cain hated Abel and murdered him, Esau also hated Jacob and would have murdered him if the opportunity had presented itself.

None of this is meant to excuse Jacob's wrongdoing, but the wrongdoing he committed is a wrong that most every single Christian commits in attempting to rightly walk the path of Faith. In fact, the Seventh Chapter of Romans describes it perfectly, even as Paul gave there his own Testimony. However, the wrongdoing on Jacob's part was in not understanding the path of Faith, while the wrongdoing on Esau's part was his efforts to ignore the path of Faith altogether.

JACOB

"And that Jacob obeyed his father and his mother, and was gone to Padan-aram" (Gen. 28:7).

The *"obedience"* mentioned here of Jacob was the opposite of that concerning Esau. While Jacob's going to Syria to obtain there a wife of the family of Abraham was the right thing to do, the way it was brought about was not the right thing. However, that is laid aside for the moment as the Holy Spirit shows us the difference, or, at least, one of the many differences, between Jacob and Esau.

Concerning disobedience on the part of Esau, the Scripture says, *"And Esau was forty years old when he took to wife Judith the daughter of Beeri the Hittite, and Bashemath the daughter of Elon the Hittite."*

It then says, *"Which were a grief of mind unto Isaac and to Rebekah"* (Gen. 26:34-35).

The path of Faith, which in its total conclusion is Faith in Christ and what He did for us in His Sufferings, has as its interesting strength the principle of obedience. The obedience presently demanded is that we not resort to self-will in any capacity but ever trust Christ for all things, understanding that everything we receive from God comes to us exclusively through the Cross because it was there that every Victory was won. All of this is referred to as *"the good fight of Faith"* (I Tim. 6:12).

THE DAUGHTERS OF CANAAN

"And Esau seeing that the daughters of Canaan pleased not Isaac his father" (Gen. 28:8).

The truth is, Esau had little understanding as to why the daughters of Canaan did not please Isaac. He had no comprehension of the Spiritual issues involved or his own spiritual lack.

How typical Esau is of millions of so-called modern Christians who seek to please man even as Esau sought to please Isaac, but have no understanding whatsoever of trying to please God. They are two different things altogether! How so similar all of this is to untold numbers of modern preachers who seek to please denominational heads, but have no thought of attempting to please God.

Let it be understood that we can please God, or we can please man. The simple truth is, we cannot please both.

ISHMAEL

"Then went Esau unto Ishmael, and took unto the wives which he had Mahalath the daughter of Ishmael Abraham's son, the sister of Nebajoth, to be his wife" (Gen. 28:9).

In fact, Ishmael had been dead now for some years, so it refers to Esau going to the family of Ishmael.

The truth is, Ishmael was no closer to acceptance than the daughters of Canaan. He had long before been rejected by the Holy Spirit and had been thrust out of the family of Abraham, even though he was the son of Abraham, but, in reality, a work of the flesh.

If the modern Believer doesn't understand the true path of Faith, he will always try to build his case on a work of the flesh.

Regrettably, the modern church has many works of the flesh exactly as did Abraham have this work of the flesh. Sadder still, it little knows or understands what is or isn't a work of the flesh exactly as Esau didn't understand. To him, this would surely please Isaac who, at this time, was a Type of Christ. His modern contemporaries do the same. Little do they know and realize that anything outside of the parameters of *"Jesus Christ and Him Crucified"* is unacceptable to God.

HARAN

"And Jacob went out from Beer-sheba, and went toward Haran" (Gen. 28:10).

A lonely wanderer, hated by his brother and obliged to flee from his home in order to save his life, Jacob learns the very first night of his exile that he is the object of Heaven's love and care, and that the Angels of God were busily employed passing and repassing from Heaven to Earth in ministering to him.

He learned that Earth and Heaven were united in his interest and for his temporal and eternal welfare.

This wondrous *"ladder"* united him to Jehovah, the God of his grandfather and the God of his father. In essence, one might could say that Jacob merited nothing, but God promised him everything. Such is Grace!

Now we might say that this is the beginning of *"the making of a man."* Jacob is alone, but yet, God and all the Holy Angels are with him, even as we shall see. Only now where he is totally dependent on the Lord, which means he had no other resources, could God reveal Himself to the Patriarch.

What a lesson for us!

That's why the great Apostle Paul said: *"Therefore I take pleasure in infirmities, in reproaches, in necessities, in persecutions, in distresses for Christ's sake: for when I am weak, then am I strong"* (II Cor. 12:10).

This is said by the Apostle because the Lord had said to him: *"My Grace is sufficient for you: for My strength is made perfect in weakness."* The Apostle then said in answer to that: *"Most gladly therefore will I rather glory in my infirmities, that the Power of Christ may rest upon me"* (II Cor. 12:9).

While God definitely was not the author of this manner in which Jacob was to go to Haran, he would definitely use this time to *"make the man."*

SLEEP

"And he stopped at a certain place, and tarried there all night, because the sun was set; and he took of the stones of that place, and put them for his pillows, and lay down in that place to sleep" (Gen. 28:11).

Nothing could possibly be more expressive of helplessness and nothingness than Jacob's condition as set before us here.

Cut off from his family, running from a murderous brother, and going to a place of which he knew nothing, it is here that God will begin to reveal Himself to the Patriarch.

In fact, the sun was setting on stage one of his life, with stage two about to begin.

The *"sleep"* represents his ceasing from his personal activity and God beginning His Personal Activity. Jacob had much to learn, and it will begin here.

That's exactly where the Lord has to bring most of us, and perhaps all of us. We have to be brought to the place where our own resources are dried up; therefore, we must now depend totally upon God. The *"sleep"* represents this dependence. We seldom come willingly to this place, but spiritually, the Holy Spirit must bring us to this place.

> *"Ring the bells of Heaven! There is joy today,*
> *"For a soul, returning from the wild!*
> *"See! The Father meets him out upon the way,*
> *"Welcoming His weary, wandering child."*
>
> *"Ring the bells of Heaven! There is joy today,*
> *"For the wanderer now is reconciled!*
> *"Yes, a soul is rescued from his sinful way,*
> *"And is born anew a ransomed child."*
>
> *"Ring the bells of Heaven! Spread the feast today!*
> *"Angels swell the glad triumphant strain!*
> *"Tell the joyful tidings, bear it far away!*
> *"For a precious soul is Born-Again."*

JACOB

Chapter Five

THE DREAM

THE DREAM

"And he dreamed, and behold a ladder set up on the Earth, and the top of it reached to Heaven: and behold the Angels of God ascending and descending on it" (Gen. 28:12).

Concerning this, Macintosh said: *"The ladder 'set on the Earth' naturally leads the heart to meditate on the display of God's Grace, in the Person and Work of His Son, The Lord Jesus Christ. On the Earth it was that the wondrous Work was accomplished, which forms the basis — the strong and everlasting basis — of all the Divine councils in reference to Israel, the Church, and the world at large. On the Earth it was that Jesus lived, labored, and died; that through His death He might remove out of the way every obstacle to the accomplishment of the Divine purpose of blessing to man."*

The *"top of the ladder reaching to Heaven"* proclaims the medium of communication between Heaven and Earth. It, in fact, would, in essence, show the way from Earth to Heaven. That *"Way"* would be Jesus Christ.

In fact, Christ alluded to this when Nathaniel said to Him: *"Rabbi, You are the Son of God; You are the King of Israel"* (Jn. 1:49).

Jesus then said to him: *"Verily, verily, I say unto you, Hereafter you shall see Heaven open, and the Angels of God ascending and descending upon the Son of Man"* (Jn. 1:51).

In essence, one could say that Jesus Christ was and is that ladder.

The *"Angels of God ascending and descending on it,"* proclaim all the resources of God, which are now at the disposal of Jacob. It is the same for every modern Believer, that is, if we properly understand Jesus Christ and look to Him exclusively according to what He has done for us in the Sacrifice of Himself on the Cross.

THE LORD

"And, behold, the LORD stood above it, and said, I am the LORD God of Abraham your father, and the God of Isaac: the land whereon you lie, to you will I give it, and to your seed" (Gen. 28:13).

The words, *"Above it,"* in the original Hebrew, actually should read, *"Beside him."* Not only did the Angels descend by it to him, but God Himself descended this stairway of Glory, and standing beside him said: *"Behold, I am with you, and will keep you in all places where you go"* (Vs. 15).

When He said to Jacob, *"I am the LORD God of Abraham your father, and the God of Isaac,"* He was, in essence, telling Jacob that as He had been with them, He would be with Jacob, also. As well, the Promises that He gave to both, He now gives to Jacob.

The Patriarch, destitute and with a stone for a pillow, and literally having to leave this land, is now told by the Lord, *"To you will I give it, and to your seed."*

Only Faith could accept such a Promise, especially considering the condition in which Jacob presently found himself. However, most of the time, the great Promises given to us by the Lord come when they seem the most unlikely.

THE BLESSING

"And your seed shall be as the dust of the Earth, and you shall spread abroad to the west, and to the east, and to the north, and to the south: and in you and in your seed shall all the families of the Earth be blessed" (Gen. 28:14).

The first portion of this Verse speaks not only of Israel but, as well, of every single person who has ever been Born-Again. Considering that this seed would be *"as the dust of the Earth,"* we are speaking here of a tremendous multitude.

The spreading abroad in all directions tells us that *"this Gospel of the Kingdom shall be preached in all the world for a witness unto all nations; and then shall the end come"* (Mat. 24:14).

The *"seed"* expressed in the last phrase of this Verse speaks of Christ (Gal. 3:16), and to Him and Him Alone *"shall all the families of the Earth be blessed."*

Thank God my family got in on this great Blessing.

THE WORD OF GOD

"And, behold, I am with you, and will keep you in all places where you go, and will bring you again into this land; for I will not leave you, until I have done that which I have spoken to you of" (Gen. 28:15).

Several things are said in this Verse:

- I am with you.
- I will keep you.
- I will bring you again into this land.
- I won't leave you until I have done all that of which I have spoken to you.

As the Lord spoke these great Promises to Jacob, through Christ, He has spoken the same thing to us.

Concerning my own personal life and Ministry, I claim these Promises exactly as given to Jacob. I believe I have the Spiritual right to do this, and I believe that you do, as well, at least in the context of that which the Lord wants you to do.

If the Lord has spoken anything to you, irrespective as to what it might be, and you are sure of that Voice, if you will only walk in obedience and continue to look to Christ and His Cross, *"He will not leave you"* until this thing comes to pass.

As we understand the terminology as given to

Jacob, he wasn't personally, at least at that time, to own all of Israel, but his seed definitely would. In fact, this is at least one of the reasons that he charged his sons to *"bury him with his fathers in the cave that is in the field of Ephron the Hittite"* (Gen. 49:29).

THE PLACE OF THE LORD

"And Jacob awaked out of his sleep, and he said, Surely the LORD is in this place; and I knew it not" (Gen. 28:16).

How happy and free from care would Jacob's life have been had he let God plan for him! Yet, I'm not so sure but that all of us have to take the same course in some way as did Jacob.

Incidentally, the *"vow"* which Jacob vowed is the first recorded vow in the Bible.

For the first time, Jehovah reveals Himself to Jacob. Quite possibly, one might say, on this very night Jacob was born from above.

Isaac and Esau refused subjection to God; Rebekah and Jacob refused cooperation with God. The rebellion of the human will is seen in the first pair and its wickedness in the second pair.

What *"place"* was this?

It was not the geography that counted, but rather Jacob's present condition. He was at his weakest here. Whatever the material blessing from his father's flocks would have been, it is now lost. In fact, financially, he is, for all practical purposes, destitute. As well, he doesn't have the comfort of his family on which to lean.

Once again, the fact is, his brother is seeking to kill him. In this lonely, destitute condition the Lord meets Jacob and gives him the greatest Promises that could ever be given to any man.

This tells us, as previously stated, that all hopes of the flesh must die before the Spirit can properly be revealed to us. As long as Christian man has a frail arm of flesh on which to lean, that he will do. So, the Lord has to bring us to a place to where there are no more arms on which to lean, and our dependence is now totally in Him. Regrettably, we do not come to this place and position quickly or easily.

The gist of this particular Verse is, at the very time, moment, and place where and when Jacob least expects the Lord is when the Lord appears to him.

PUNISHMENT OR BLESSING?

It is ironic; the Lord never mentions here the wrongdoing of the Patriarch. There is no reprimand, no upbraiding, and definitely no punishment. But yet, I think if this situation was brought into the present, the modern church would think of nothing but punishment.

It thinks in this vein simply because it little knows the path of Faith, but rather functions mostly in the realm of law. Of course, law demands punishment while Faith demands Grace.

The modern church, as well, would never even dream of admitting that God would speak to someone who, just a few days before, had practiced great deception on his father Isaac and his brother Esau, and who plainly lied. Once again, such thinking is because the church functions mostly in law. As it regards God speaking to such an individual, such would shut the door, but Faith builds a ladder, and on that ladder, God descends, along with all His Holy Angels.

As we have previously stated, Jacob merited nothing, and God promised him everything. Such is Grace!

THE HOUSE OF GOD AND
THE GATE OF HEAVEN

"And he was afraid, and said, How dreadful is this place! this is none other but the House of God, and this is the Gate of Heaven" (Gen. 28:17).

"How dreadful is this place!" could have been translated, *"How awe-inspiring is this place!"*

Jacob was afraid and in such a case, rightly so; so were Moses (Ex. 20:18-19), Job (Job 42:5-6), Isaiah (Isa. 6:5), Peter (Lk. 5:8), and John (Rev. 1:17-18), at similar discoveries of the Divine Presence.

Considering what Jacob had experienced, it is no wonder that he refers to this place as *"Beth-el,"* i.e., *"the House of God"* and *"the Gate of Heaven."*

Presently, under Christ, *"the House of God"* is Believers. Paul said, *"Don't you know that you are the Temple of God, and that the Spirit of God dwells in you?"* (I Cor. 3:16).

Now the *"Gate of Heaven"* is Jesus Christ, as it always has been. However, due to the Incarnation and what Jesus has done for us at the Cross, the *"Gate of Heaven"* can be found almost anywhere, for Christ can be accepted anywhere.

THE STONE

"And Jacob rose up early in the morning, and took the stone that he had put for his pillows, and set it up for a pillar, and poured oil upon the top of it" (Gen. 28:18).

I think the *"stone"* would have been looked at by the Lord as a Type of Christ, with the *"oil"* serving as a Symbol of the Holy Spirit.

Incidentally, the stone claimed by British Israelism to be the stone which served as a pillow for Jacob could not be such. That particular stone is *"Scottish sandstone,"* and all the stone around Beth-el in Israel is *"limestone."*

BETHEL

"And he called the name of that place Beth-el: but the name of that city was called Luz at the first" (Gen. 28:19).

The place that Jacob named as *"Beth-el,"* which means, *"House of God,"* was a little ways from the town then called *"Luz."* It was then a Canaanite town but came to be called, *"Beth-el,"* after the conquest by Israel (Judg. 1:26). *"Beth-el"* is actually a suburb of Jerusalem at present. The last time I was there, a Jewish army base was the principle part of the area.

THE VOW

"And Jacob vowed a vow, saying, If God be with me, and will keep me in this way that I go, and will give me bread to eat, and raiment to put on," (Gen. 28:20).

This is the first recorded vow in the Bible. Williams says concerning these statements by Jacob: *"There is much to make it appear that the word 'if' in this Passage means 'since.' Personal Salvation is not a matter of education, but of Revelation (Mat. 11:27). And Jacob no doubt had received a good religious education from his parents; but, now, for the first time, Jehovah reveals Himself to him."*

The path of Faith has now been opened up to Jacob, and he, for all practical purposes, understands what it is. There is every evidence, as stated, that Jacob truly was *"Born-Again"* this particular night.

In fact, millions are in the modern church who have never been Born-Again. They have received some religious education exactly as did Jacob, but they've never had a Revelation from the Lord. What would that Revelation be?

REVELATION

In its most simplistic form, Revelation is the Holy Spirit dealing with the heart, even as the Word of God is preached or proclaimed in some way, creating alarm in the sinner's soul and, as well, bringing about the need for Christ. In fact, such *"Revelation"* is a must if an individual is to be Saved. Otherwise, he merely has an education, which definitely will not suffice.

Such a Revelation will always come, providing the Word of God is faithfully preached, and the Anointing of the Holy Spirit accompanies such a Word. Without fail, if the heart is open at all, the Revelation will then come!

As well, this Passage proves that Jacob had basically forfeited the double portion which came to the one having the birthright, at least when the father died. In fact, both Jacob and Esau were expecting Isaac to die at this particular time. He didn't, incidentally!

In Jacob's mind, all of this inheritance was gone. So, he asked the Lord to provide for him. As stated, he was now totally dependent on the Lord for everything.

PEACE

"So that I come again to my father's house in peace; then shall the LORD be my God" (Gen. 28:21).

The Patriarch is asking two things:

1. Would he ultimately be able to come home?

2. Could he come in peace, i.e., *"free from Esau's avenging threats"*?

The Lord did all of this with Jacob, plus much more. He gave him far more than *"bread to eat"* and *"raiment to put on."*

TITHE

"And this stone, which I have set for a pillar, shall be God's House: and of all that You shall give me I will surely give the tenth unto You" (Gen. 28:22).

Jacob set up the stone for a *"pillar"* and designated the place as *"God's House."*

In fact, this definitely was one of the greatest Revelations thus far that God had given to any man. From this tremendous experience, Jacob claimed his part in the great appellative, *"The God of Abraham, of Isaac, and of Jacob."*

His vow is that he would *"give the tenth,"* or tithe, unto God.

Just exactly as to whom he would give this, we aren't told. So, more than likely, when he came into possessions of herds, no matter how large those herds, Jacob gave a tenth unto God, which he, no doubt, offered in sacrifice. If that was the case, and it, no doubt, was, we now find Jacob offering up sacrifices to a degree as no one else. This would have greatly glorified God, with all the sacrifices being a Symbol of the coming Redeemer Who would die on the Cross, shedding His Life's Blood (Eph. 2:13-18).

JESUS CHRIST AND HIM CRUCIFIED

In effect, if the tithe we now give to the Work of God doesn't go to proclaim the Message of Jesus Christ and Him Crucified, then, in reality, we are not giving to God but to something else entirely.

This is the second time that giving to the Lord in the form of tithes is mentioned in the Bible. On the first occasion, Abraham paid tithes to Melchizedek, who was a Type of Christ as our Great High Priest. Jesus would become this by dying on the Cross as a Sacrifice. So, both occasions of paying tithes speak to the Cross; therefore, our tithes presently must go for the same benefit, to proclaim the grand Message of *"Jesus Christ and Him Crucified"* (I Cor. 1:23; 2:2). Otherwise, we really aren't paying tithes!

THE JOURNEY

"Then Jacob went on his journey, and came into the land of the people of the east" (Gen. 29:1).

Grace forgave Jacob and confirmed to him the Promises. We will find in this scenario that even though Jacob has had a great Revelation from the Lord, still, spiritually speaking, he has yet a ways to go.

Self is the culprit; no one can really enjoy God until he gets to the bottom of self.

This *"journey,"* even as we shall see, was to last for some 20 years. In it, Jacob would learn much but would still need another Revelation before the total change would come. More than anything else, these 20 years were to make him see the need for change.

God will not really begin to reveal Himself until the end of the flesh is seen. If, therefore, I have not reached the end of my flesh in the deep and positive experience of my soul, it is morally impossible that I can have anything like a just apprehension of God's Character. Regrettably, it takes a long time to come to the end of self-will.

This is what this *"journey"* is all about!

We will find in the coming scenario that the problem of deception is still with Jacob, and an old sin is an easy sin!

Jacob was now in Mesopotamia, about 450 miles from Beer-sheba.

THE WELL

"And he looked, and behold a well in the field, and, lo, there were three flocks of sheep lying by it; for out

of that well they watered the flocks: and a great stone was upon the well's mouth" (Gen. 29:2).

As we shall see, it is obvious that this well could only be used at fixed times. A great stone covered its mouth, which probably required two or three men to remove it.

From the way the scenario unfolds, more than likely, Laban, the father of Rachel, owned this well because immediately upon her arrival with the sheep, the stone was rolled away. Her sheep were watered first while the rest yet had to bide their time until her sheep were watered though they had been there long before her.

Considering the value of wells of that particular time, this is probably the truth of the matter.

Jacob comes upon this well and sees sheep and shepherds gathered by it. They are evidently waiting for the stone to be rolled away so their sheep can be watered.

WATER

"And there were all the flocks gathered: and they rolled the stone from the well's mouth, and watered the sheep, and put the stone again upon the well's mouth in his place" (Gen. 29:3).

This Verse plainly tells us how the sheep were watered at this particular well. As stated, it probably belonged to Laban and was only opened at certain times.

Jacob is now coming to the end of his journey, but yet, spiritually speaking, it is a journey that will continue.

To be brought to the place where the Lord desires that we be is not done quickly or easily. As it regards the Child of God, every action plays a part in the Sanctification process. Wells with their water always presented a place of refreshment, especially in a climate such as that in which Jacob now found himself. Thank God the Lord always has a *"well"* at the desired place.

HARAN

"And Jacob said unto them, My brethren, where do you live? And they said, Of Haran are we" (Gen. 29:4).

In those days, signs were not on every corner giving directions, etc. As well, one did not ask just anyone concerning distances or directions. Robbers were lying in wait for those who were lost or disoriented.

So, when Jacob asked these shepherds where they were from, with their reply being, *"Haran,"* which was actually his destination, he knew he was close. This, no doubt, reminded him of God's Promise to guide him on his journey.

For the Lord to be with one, to guide, to lead, to give direction, and to help in that which at first seems to be but small things, but which quickly leads to large things, is the greatest Blessing that one could ever know. This which the Lord promised to do for Jacob, as wonderful as it was, is available to every single Believer, irrespective as to whom they might be. Paul quotes the Master when He said: *". . . I will never leave you, nor forsake you.*

"So that we may boldly say, The Lord is my Helper, and I will not fear what man shall do unto me" (Heb. 13:5-6).

However, such relationship is not automatic with the Believer. The Believer must actively want and desire such relationship and must ask the Lord to provide such. It is a prayer that the Lord will definitely answer. However, He will not push His Way in but, most of the time, is waiting for the initiative to be taken by the Believer.

LABAN

"And he said unto them, Do you know Laban the son of Nahor? And they said, We know him" (Gen. 29:5).

Laban, it is remembered, is Rebekah's brother. He is the one who primarily dealt with Eliezer, the servant of Abraham, who had come to find a bride for Isaac, which took place approximately 80 to 90 years before (Gen., Chpt. 24). This would mean that Laban was over 100 years of age, which was not uncommon in those days.

The language spoken then by the shepherds was probably Chaldean. Jacob, who spoke Hebrew, was evidently able to converse with them either because he had learned Chaldean from his mother or, as is more probable, because the dialects were not then greatly dissimilar.

He called Laban the son of Nahor though he was actually the grandson. In both Hebrew and Aramaic, there is no separate word for grandson. *"Son"* means any descendant down the line.

RACHEL

"And he said unto them, Is he well? And they said, He is well: and, behold, Rachel his daughter comes with the sheep" (Gen. 29:6).

This is the first mention of Rachel in the Bible. She will figure very prominently in the great Plan of God, being the mother of Joseph and Benjamin. She was the ancestress of three of the great Tribes of Israel, Benjamin, Ephraim, and Manasseh, the latter two being the sons of Joseph. She and her sister Leah were honored by later generations as those *"who together built up the house of Israel"* (Ruth 4:11).

The evidence is that Laban was not so well-to-do financially. His daughter was serving as a shepherdess. She was evidently raised to do her part in the family and, thereby, was taught responsibility and industry. From such, the Lord drew the mothers of Israel.

In all of this we see the Hand of the Lord working, which is a pleasure to behold. Jacob, who must have a wife in order for the great Plan of God to be brought forth, is led to this particular well even at the exact time that Rachel appears. What a mighty God we serve!

THE SHEEP

"And he said, Lo, it is yet high day, neither is it time that the cattle should be gathered together: water the sheep, and go and feed them.

"And they said, We cannot, until all the flocks be gathered together, and till they roll the stone from the well's mouth; then we water the sheep" (Gen. 29:7-8).

Knowing that the shepherds have brought the sheep for water, Jacob wonders as to why they are not attending to the task but seemingly waiting.

More than likely, as stated, the reason was that Laban owned the well, and the flocks could not be watered until Rachel had watered her flock.

Wells in those days were very valuable, especially in the places of hot, dry climates, which this was. So, a system for watering undoubtedly was worked out with the various different flocks in the area.

The stone at the well's mouth, which is so often mentioned here, was to secure the water; for water was scarce — it was not there for everyone's use.

RACHEL, THE SHEPHERDESS

"And while he yet spoke with them, Rachel came with her father's sheep: for she kept them" (Gen. 29:9).

We readily see the Hand of the Lord working in this situation regarding the meeting of Jacob with Rachel. I think the Holy Spirit immediately informed Jacob that this young lady was to be his wife. However, as we shall see, Jacob's way was fraught with difficulty.

At this point, Laban had no sons, although later, he would have. As the younger daughter, Rachel was assigned to the task of keeping the sheep, which she did. How old Rachel was at this time, we have no way of knowing; however, she was probably in her late teens.

LOVE AT FIRST SIGHT

"And it came to pass, when Jacob saw Rachel the daughter of Laban his mother's brother, and the sheep of Laban his mother's brother, that Jacob went near, and rolled the stone from the well's mouth, and watered the flock of Laban his mother's brother" (Gen. 29:10).

Three times the Holy Spirit has Moses to repeat the term, *"His mother's brother."* It is not done unintentionally. The idea is, Jacob has met with his own relations, with *"his bone and his flesh."*

This is some proof that Laban owned this well in that Rachel waters her sheep first, or at least Jacob waters them for her.

It is highly unlikely that Jacob would have acted here as he did had he not learned from Rachel, or possibly the waiting shepherds, that the well belonged to Laban and that no sheep were to be watered until Rachel had first watered hers.

The Scripture says, *"When Jacob saw Rachel. . . ."* Every evidence is that it was love at first sight.

RACHEL AND THE SPIRIT OF GOD

"And Jacob kissed Rachel, and lifted up his voice, and wept" (Gen. 29:11).

The Patriarch is overcome with emotion, and I think mostly at the joy of seeing the Hand of God working in his life. Truly, the Lord was with him. While he was very happy to have met his relatives, which means that his long journey was now over, I think the greatest joy of all was that of a Spiritual note. As well, he may have known at that very moment, and informed by the Spirit of God, that Rachel would be his wife. He, of course, would not have told her that then, but more than likely, the Spirit of the Lord definitely informed him of such, at least at some point.

RELATIONS

"And Jacob told Rachel that he was her father's brother, and that he was Rebekah's son: and she ran and told her father" (Gen. 29:12).

Jacob was actually the nephew of Laban. Terms of relationship were used in a very indefinite way among the Hebrews.

We will find that Jacob's love for Rachel is one of the Bible's outstanding examples of human love — seven years *"seemed to him but a few days because of the love he had for her"* (Gen. 29:20).

When she told her father Laban about Jacob, I wonder if he did not recall when his sister Rebekah, those many years before, had come to him when Eliezer had come on behalf of Abraham as it regarded a bride for Isaac?

LABAN AND JACOB

"And it came to pass, when Laban heard the tidings of Jacob his sister's son, that he ran to meet him, and embraced him, and kissed him, and brought him to his house. And he told Laban all these things" (Gen. 29:13).

Laban now did almost exactly what he had done those many years before when he was told by Rebekah of Eliezer. As he ran then to meet Abraham's servant, he now runs to meet Jacob.

The Patriarch now relates to Laban all the things which had happened between him and Esau. No doubt, he especially gave all the information which Laban required about his mother Rebekah, who was Laban's sister.

Laban would have been well over 100 years of age at this time.

THE BEGINNING

"And Laban said to him, Surely you are my bone and my flesh. And he abode with him the space of a month" (Gen. 29:14).

Jacob is now about to begin to reap the bitter fruit of his sin. At the outset, he is deceived exactly as he deceived his father, and was deeply wounded in the deepest affections of his heart.

It is a popular mistake to suppose that Jacob did not marry Rachel till the end of the seven years, or even the second seven years. Every evidence is, however, that he took her immediately for his wife, serving the term after the wedding.

After Jacob related everything to Laban, the uncle admitted that Jacob was indeed who he had said he was, for the simple reason that no one else would have had the knowledge of so many details.

Jacob abiding with Laban for the space of a month means that he lived with Laban for this particular period of time, and then went out and obtained his own place after that.

WAGES

"And Laban said unto Jacob, Because you are my brother, should you therefore serve me for nought? tell me, what shall your wages be?" (Gen. 29:15).

Jacob, the dealer, meets now with Laban, the dealer, and they both are seen, as it were, straining every nerve to outwit each other.

Evidently, during the month that Jacob spent in the house of Laban, he applied himself to serve his uncle even as he had begun when he watered his flock. So, Laban wanted to strike up a bargain with him that Jacob might be in his employ.

Due to the manner in which Jacob had to leave his home, he was destitute of money of any nature and so was at the mercy of Laban to a great degree.

THE BARGAIN

"And Laban had two daughters: the name of the elder was Leah, and the name of the younger was Rachel.

"Leah was tender eyed; but Rachel was beautiful and well favored.

"And Jacob loved Rachel; and said, I will serve you seven years for Rachel your younger daughter.

"And Laban said, It is better that I give her to you, than that I should give her to another man: abide with me.

"And Jacob served seven years for Rachel; and they seemed to him but a few days, for the love he had to her" (Gen. 29:16-20).

Would the deception that Laban was now planning to carry out on Jacob have been carried out if, in fact, Jacob had not tried to practice deception on his father Isaac?

I think not! The Scripture emphatically states that, *"We reap what we sow"* (Gal. 6:7-8). Even though the Passage in Galatians is speaking of sowing to the flesh or sowing to the Spirit, still, the principle is the same.

SOWING TO THE FLESH

In its most simplistic form, this refers to trying to live this Christian life by means other than Faith in

Christ and what Christ has done for us at the Cross.

Even though Believers were not referred to as *"Christians"* during Jacob's time, the principle was the same. Jacob all too often was trying to follow the Lord by the means of self-will instead of trust in the Lord.

However, we have far less excuse today than did Jacob. The Cross through which everything comes to the Believer from the Lord is now historical. In other words, it's a fact. The Cross with Jacob was prophetic, meaning that it was yet in the future. Still, as we receive everything presently from the Lord by looking back to the Cross, in Old Testament Times, everything was received from the Lord by looking forward to that coming time of the Cross. In fact, the sacrifices of old represented Christ and His Cross. Faith in those sacrifices per se would have done little good; however, Faith in Who and What they represented was the secret of all victory and power. Let's say it another way:

Any effort made other than Faith in Christ and the Cross is *"sowing to the flesh,"* which means that such will never bring forth the desired result.

SOWING TO THE SPIRIT

Sowing to the Spirit refers to the Holy Spirit, and refers to placing our Faith and confidence totally and completely in Christ and the Cross through which the Holy Spirit works (Rom. 8:1-11).

Many Christians have the idea that *"sowing to the Spirit"* refers to doing spiritual things. It really doesn't! While those things we do might be good, helpful, instructive, and informative; still, our walk with God is not so much in what we *"do,"* but rather what we *"believe"* (Jn. 3:16).

As we look at Jacob, we might possibly think that we would never do such a thing as Jacob did as it regards the practicing of deception. While deception may not be our direction, to be sure, some other wrong is. In other words, we don't come to the place of *"walking after the Spirit"* very quickly or very easily. As well, we can't come there at all if someone doesn't teach us the Truth.

That's the reason the material in this Book is so very, very important. Jesus said: *"You shall know the Truth, and the Truth shall make you free"* (Jn. 8:32).

While it's not possible to eliminate the growing process in the heart and life of the Believer, we can save ourselves much grief if we are blessed enough to come under correct teaching.

So, Jacob loved Rachel and agreed to serve Laban some seven years for her hand, so to speak.

It would seem from these statements that Jacob served Laban for seven years before Rachel became his wife; however, the terminology employed rather refers to a contract or agreement. Jacob married both Leah and Rachel immediately, the first in which he was deceived into doing so, and the second by intention. Now he must serve 14 years, which he did.

> *"I've a Message from the Lord, hallelujah!*
> *"The Message unto you I'll give;*
> *"'Tis recorded in His Word, hallelujah!*
> *"It is only that you 'look and live.'"*

> *"I've a Message full of love, hallelujah!*
> *"A Message, O my friend, for you;*
> *"'Tis a Message from above, hallelujah!*
> *"Jesus said it and I know it's true."*

> *"Life is offered unto you, hallelujah!*
> *"Eternal Life your soul shall have,*
> *"If you'll only look to Him, hallelujah!*
> *"Look to Jesus Who Alone can save."*

"I will tell you how I came, hallelujah!
"To Jesus when He made me whole:
"'Twas believing on His Name, hallelujah!
"I trusted and He saved my soul."

JACOB

Chapter Six

THE BEGINNING OF THE NATION OF ISRAEL

THE BEGINNING OF THE NATION OF ISRAEL

THE AGREEMENT IS MADE

"And Jacob said unto Laban, Give me my wife, for my days are fulfilled, that I may go in unto her" (Gen. 29:21).

His *"days being fulfilled"* simply means that the contract had been agreed upon that he was to serve Laban seven years for Rachel. This is proven by Verse 30.

We shall see that as Jacob had deceived his father Isaac, he will now be deceived. The deception he practiced upon Isaac cost him at least 14 years of servitude.

THE BARGAIN SEALED

"And Laban gathered together all the men of the place, and made a feast" (Gen. 29:22).

After everything had been agreed upon as it regarded Jacob serving Laban for seven years, Laban would now make a great feast and invite all the notables of the area to the wedding. However, as we shall see, Laban had something else in mind altogether.

LEAH

"And it came to pass in the evening, that he (Laban) took Leah his daughter, and brought her to him (brought her to Jacob); and he (Jacob) went in unto her.

"And Laban gave unto his daughter Leah Zilpah his maid for an handmaid.

"And it came to pass, that in the morning, behold, it was Leah: and he (Jacob) said to Laban, What is this you have done unto me? did I not serve with you for Rachel? wherefore then have you beguiled me?" (Gen. 29:23-25).

When Leah went into Jacob, she, no doubt, was wearing a veil, and, as well, the room was probably dark.

She evidently said nothing that night, but the next morning, to Jacob's surprise, it was not Rachel who had been given to him, but rather Leah.

The question, *"Did not I serve with you for Rachel?"* could have been translated, *"Did not I agree to serve with you for Rachel?"* In this is *"Election."*

ELECTION

In Romans, Chapter 9, we have the Doctrine of *"Election."* Jacob and Esau are mentioned in this scenario. Concerning Election, Mackintosh has, I think, an excellent statement. He said:

"It is deeply interesting to the spiritual mind to mark how sedulously the Spirit of God in Romans Nine, and indeed throughout all Scripture, guards against the inference which the human mind draws from the Doctrine of God's Election. When He speaks of 'vessels of wrath,' He simply says, 'fitted to destruction;' He does not say that God 'fitted' them. Whereas, on the other hand, when He refers to 'vessels of mercy,' He says, 'whom He had afore prepared unto Glory.' This is most marked.

"If the Reader will turn for a moment to Matthew 25:34-41, he will find another striking and beautiful instance of the same thing."

Mackintosh continues: *"When the King addresses those on His Right Hand, He says, 'Come, you blessed of My Father, inherit the Kingdom prepared for you from the foundation of the world' (Vs. 34). But when He addresses those on His Left, He says, 'Depart from Me you cursed.' He does not say, 'Cursed of My Father.' And further, He says, 'Into everlasting fire, prepared (not for you but) for the Devil and his Angels'"* (Vs. 41).

And then: *"In a word, then it is plain that God has 'prepared' a Kingdom of Glory. And 'vessels of mercy' to inherit the Kingdom; but He has not prepared 'everlasting fire' for men, but for 'the Devil and his Angels;' nor has He fitted the 'vessels of wrath,' but they have fitted themselves.*

"The Word of God as clearly establishes 'Election' as it sedulously guards against 'reprobation.' (The idea is) Everyone who finds himself in Heaven will have to thank God for it, and everyone who finds himself in Hell will have only himself to thank."

SEVEN OTHER YEARS

"And Laban said, It must not be so done in our country, to give the younger before the firstborn.

"Fulfill her week, and we will give you this also for the service which you shall serve with me yet seven other years.

"And Jacob did so, and fulfilled her week: and he gave him Rachel his daughter to wife also.

"And Laban gave to Rachel his daughter Bilhah his handmaid to be her maid.

"And he went in also unto Rachel, and he loved also Rachel more than Leah, and served with him yet seven other years" (Gen. 29:26-30).

Concerning Laban's contention that the custom in his country was that the younger must not be married before the firstborn, of that, there is no proof. It seems to be something that Laban concocted on his own. There is some evidence of such in India but not in his part of the world.

Laban now offers Rachel to Jacob for seven more years, making 14 total; however, Jacob did not complain about the situation, perhaps seeing that he had little choice in the matter. His actions seem to suggest that he knew that he was now paying for his deception regarding Isaac and his brother. Consequently, he accepts the situation.

CHASTISEMENT

The Lord doesn't actually punish His Children, but He definitely does chastise His Children. What is the difference?

Chastisement is designed to teach us something while punishment contains no instruction, only hurt. Jacob is being chastised. He seems to recognize this and accepts it.

This in no way meant that Laban was right in what he did. To be sure, the Lord would deal with him as the Lord deals with all. However, Jacob suffered such, with there being no evidence that he sought to take matters into his own hands.

WHAT THE LORD SAW

"And when the Lord saw that Leah was hated, He opened her womb: but Rachel was barren" (Gen. 29:31).

All of this, as we shall see, was to prove that *"the origin of Israel was to be a work not of nature but of Grace."*

The word, *"Hated,"* as used in Verse 31, here means, *"Loved less."*

There is no indication that Jacob mistreated Leah, but there is indication that Rachel did. The Lord saw all of this, and as a result, He made Leah fruitful, and at the same time, He made Rachel barren.

In fact, Leah was the ancestress of both David and Jesus, and there could have been no greater honor than that!

We learn from all of this the minute Involvement of the Lord in all things. He knows all, sees all, and involves Himself in all!

All of this shows that whatever Laban did, Leah was not a party to the deception. She had no choice but to do as she did, but none of this was her idea.

It certainly wasn't Rachel's idea, but, as well, she had no say in the matter either. Her wrong comes in by taking out the situation on Leah, who was not to blame. In fact, the situation had to be very difficult for all three, Jacob, Rachel, and Leah. However, it seems that Leah unjustly suffered the brunt of this scenario. As noted, the Lord didn't take kindly to what was happening.

REUBEN

"And Leah conceived, and bore a son, and she called his name Reuben: for she said, Surely the LORD has looked upon my affliction; now therefore my husband will love me" (Gen. 29:32).

Reuben means, *"See, a son."*

Considering that in those days being barren was a reproach and that having children was a great blessing, she evidently hoped that her having this child, in effect, giving Jacob his firstborn, would increase his affection for her. To be unloved or even loved less presents a very unsavory situation. It's very hard for anyone to function in such a climate. From the information given in the next Verse, it doesn't seem that the situation was ameliorated.

SIMEON

"And she conceived again, and bore a son; and said, Because the LORD has heard I was hated, He has therefore given me this son also: and she called his name Simeon" (Gen. 29:33).

Simeon means, *"Hearing."* She is functioning from the position that the Lord has heard her petition; however, at the moment, it didn't change, but ultimately it would.

LEVI

"And she conceived again, and bore a son; and said, Now this time will my husband be joined unto me, because I have born him three sons: therefore was his name called Levi" (Gen. 29:34).

Levi means, *"Joined."*

She names her son accordingly in the hopes that her husband will be joined to her with greater love. There is evidence that this ultimately did happen (Gen. 31:4, 14; 49:31).

JUDAH

"And she conceived again, and bore a son: and she said, Now will I praise the LORD: therefore she called his name Judah; and left bearing" (Gen. 29:35).

Judah means, *"Praise."* From this Tribe would come both David and, above all, Christ.

Throughout, in the midst of her melancholy, there is a tone of fervent piety and Faith, and that not merely to God but to the Covenant Jehovah. Now, she slowly parts with her hope of human affection and finds comfort in Jehovah Alone.

This time she says, *"I will praise Jehovah."* It was this son of the despised one, whose birth called forth from her this hymn of simple thanksgiving, who was foreordained to be the ancestor of the promised two more sons and a daughter.

In her six sons, we find the Plan of Salvation outlined so dramatically, as well as these men being Types of Christ. In fact, all of the sons of Leah and Rachel were Types of Christ, with each son portraying a particular Ministry of our Lord to Believers. In other words, He was our Substitute in all things. We will look first at the six sons of Leah and how their names draw out the Plan of Salvation.

THE SIX SONS OF LEAH

1. Reuben: *"See, a son."* This represents the child that is born into the world, whomever that child may be.

2. Simeon: *"Hearing."* When the child is old enough, it is to hear the Gospel.

3. Levi: *"Joined."* The child is born, it hears the Gospel, and it is joined to Christ.

4. Judah: *"Praise."* The child is born, it hears the Gospel, it is joined to Christ, and it praises the Lord.

5. Issachar: *"Reward."* The son is born, it hears the Gospel, it is joined to Christ, it praises the Lord, and the Lord gives the reward of Eternal Life.

6. Zebulun: *"Dwelling."* The child is born, it hears the Gospel, it is joined to the Lord, it then praises the Lord, it has a reward, and now it will dwell with the Lord forever and forever.

Thus is the Plan of Salvation wrought out in the six sons of Leah.

The names of all of these sons also portray Christ and a particular Work and Ministry which He has carried out for Believers, which we will address in the body of the next Chapter.

All of these children born to Leah, her maid Zilpah, Rachel, and her maid Bilhah, including the two sons of Joseph, were the heads of the Thirteen Tribes of Israel, which were recipients of the Word of God and, as well, served as the Womb of the Messiah. So, we're seeing here the birth of a people totally unlike any other people on the face of the Earth who has ever been or ever will be. As Christians, we are a part of Israel, but only in the spiritual sense.

GIVE ME CHILDREN, OR ELSE I DIE

Rachel pictures Israel; Leah pictures the Church. Rachel is first loved but not possessed — sorrowful and childless; Leah, blessed with children and triumphant.

Rachel has children afterwards, Joseph and Benjamin. Joseph, a beauteous Type of Christ, rejected by his brethren but glorified among the Gentiles. Benjamin, a Type also of Christ, the son of his mother's sorrow but of his father's right hand. That is, the Messiah was to be born of Israel, and that is why Israel had to drink so great a cup of sorrow. However, He becomes the Lord Messiah, reigning in Power in the Heavens at the Right Hand of God.

"And when Rachel saw that she bore Jacob no children, Rachel envied her sister; and said unto Jacob, Give me children, or else I die.

"And Jacob's anger was kindled against Rachel: And he said, Am I in God's Stead, Who has withheld from you the fruit of the womb?" (Gen. 30:1-2).

Concerning this situation, Keil said: *"If not warranted to infer that Rachel's barrenness was due to lack of prayer on her part and Jacob's, we are at least justified in asserting that her conduct in breaking forth into angry reproaches against her husband was unlike that of Jacob's mother Rebekah, who in similar circumstances sought relief in prayer."*

BLAME!

The brief period of some four or five years that had elapsed since Rachel's marriage, in comparison with the 20 years of Rebekah's barrenness, signally discovers Rachel's sinful impatience.

In this thing, she seems to blame Jacob, but she should have known that God Alone could remove sterility. However, jealousy of Leah appears for the moment to have blinded her to this fact.

As we have stated, Rachel here pictures Israel while Leah pictures the Church. In a sense, Paul addressed this very thing, even though he actually is writing about Sarah.

The Apostle said: *"For it is written, Rejoice, you barren who bears not; break forth and cry, you who travail not: for the desolate has many more children than she who has an husband"* (Gal. 4:27).

Leah was not loved very much by her husband, but she had many more children than the one who had the greater love of the husband. The Church, of which Leah is a type, has many more children than Israel, of which Rachel is a type.

Jacob's anger is kindled against Rachel because she should have been taking the matter to the Lord instead of blaming him.

BILHAH

"And she said (Rachel said), Behold my maid Bilhah, go in unto her; and she shall bear upon my knees, that I may also have children by her.

"And she gave him Bilhah her handmaid to wife: and Jacob went in unto her.

"And Bilhah conceived, and bore Jacob a son" (Gen. 30:3-5).

All of this shows little Faith in God. Jealousy, envy, and superstition seem to have guided these affairs. To be sure, as sinful as it was, Sarah's resorting to Hagar was much more understandable than Rachel resorting to Bilhah.

Both of these women, Rachel and Leah, seemed to trust God, but only to a certain degree. It was somewhat a mixture of Faith and fancy, not unlike the modern church.

Trust in Christ, at least to a certain degree, and trust in other things mark the modern church. It leans partly on God and partly on the world!

At this stage, I'm not certain that Leah and Rachel properly understood the significance of all that was going on. They somehow understood that the bearing of a goodly number of children was of great significance, but there is little indication that they fully understood why.

DAN

"And Rachel said, God has judged me, and has also heard my voice, and has given me a son: therefore called she his name Dan" (Gen. 30:6).

Dan means, *"To judge, or one decreeing justice."*

Calvin said, *"Jacob began with polygamy, and is now drawn into concubinage. Though God overruled this for the development of the Seed of Israel, He did not thereby condone the offence of either Jacob or Rachel."*

Calvin went on to say: *"So God often strives to overcome men's wickedness through kindness, and pursues the unworthy with His Grace."*

Exactly what Rachel meant by naming the child Dan, which means, *"Judging,"* is open to question. The indication seems to be that she felt that God had vindicated her, that is, had judged her righteous by giving this son to Bilhah, her maid. Whether God saw it that way is also open to question.

As someone has well said, *"Men rule, while God overrules."* While He in no way ever condones evil or wrongdoing, not even to the slightest degree, at times, He does use such to bring about His Will. There had to be 13 sons born to Jacob in order to found the Nation of Israel. Twelve would be for the regular Tribes while one would be for the Priestly Tribe.

To be sure, God had many ways of doing this, but at the same time, He has purposely limited Himself to work through human instrumentation. Consequently,

He is either limited or expanded according to the faithlessness or Faith of the individual or individuals. Many years later, He would say of Israel: *"Yes, they turned back and tempted God, and limited the Holy One of Israel"* (Ps. 78:41).

NAPHTALI

"And Bilhah Rachel's maid conceived again, and bore Jacob a second son.

"And Rachel said, With great wrestlings have I wrestled with my sister, and I have prevailed: and she called his name Naphtali" (Gen. 30:7-8).

Naphtali means, *"Wrestling."*

The contention between Rachel and Leah evidently was great. Rachel likens it as to a *"wrestling match."* Due to the births of both Dan and Naphtali, she considers herself to have prevailed.

Concerning this, Ellicott says: *"Rachel's was a discreditable victory, won by making use of a bad custom, and it consisted in weaning her husband still more completely from unloved Leah. Now that Bilhah and children were added to the attractiveness of her tent, her sister, she boasts, will be thought of no more."*

GAD AND ASHER

"When Leah saw that she had left bearing, she took Zilpah her maid, and gave her Jacob to wife.

"And Zilpah Leah's maid bore Jacob a son.

"And Leah said, A troop comes: and she called his name Gad.

"And Zilpah Leah's maid bore Jacob a second son.

"And Leah said, Happy am I, for the daughters will call me blessed: and she called his name Asher" (Gen. 30:9-13).

Gad means, *"Good fortune,"* while Asher means, *"Happy."*

Ellicott said: *"By ceasing to bear, Leah had lost her one hold upon Jacob's affection, and to regain it, she follows Rachel's example."*

The struggle of these two women gives us an idea of their Faith, or the lack of such. It seems that neither one actually understood, at least as they should have, what the path of Faith actually was. In other words, their Faith was riddled with self-will. They had a great tendency to *"help God"*! Of course, when they helped Him, it was always from the vantage point of jealousy, envy, malice, or some other passion gone awry. As previously stated, this picture drawn out here before us is not totally unlike our modern actions. Despite the Lord appearing to Jacob and giving him great Promises, we find that the Patriarch still has a long way to go.

And yet, placed in his same position, I wonder, *"Would we have done any better, or even as well?"* From our sanctimonious perches, we far too often ask with a sneer, *"Would you buy a used car from Jacob?"*

We must never make the mistake of judging the work before it is finished, and that we far too often do! We must not forget that one of the greatest appellatives in history belongs in part to Jacob, *"The God of Abraham, of Isaac, and of Jacob."*

MANDRAKES

"And Reuben went in the days of wheat harvest, and found mandrakes in the field, and brought them unto his mother Leah. Then Rachel said to Leah, Give me, I pray you, of your son's mandrakes.

"And she said unto her, Is it a small matter that you have taken my husband? and would you take away

my son's mandrakes also? And Rachel said, Therefore he shall lie with you tonight for your son's mandrakes.

"And Jacob came out of the field in the evening, and Leah went out to meet him, and said, You must come in unto me; for surely I have hired you with my son's mandrakes. And he lay with her that night" (Gen. 30:14-16).

These Passages present a perfect picture of prayer mixed with superstition. Let not the reader think that this foolish practice died with the wives of Jacob.

These two women were mostly functioning from the position of jealousy or envy. God's purposes were considered, but less than their own passions. The idea of true Faith is that we think like God instead of on the far lower level of our own passions.

At this time, Reuben was probably four or five years old. According to oriental superstition, the mandrake possessed the virtue of promoting fruitfulness and fertility. It was an apple-like fruit.

Somehow Rachel found out about the situation and asked for some of the mandrakes.

The request seemingly didn't sit well with Leah. So, Rachel, who held the dominant hand, made a bargain with Leah. For some of the mandrakes she would not stand in the way of Leah spending the night with Jacob.

ISSACHAR AND ZEBULUN

"And God hearkened unto Leah, and she conceived, and bore Jacob the fifth son.

"And Leah said, God has given me my hire, because I have given my maiden to my husband: and she called his name Issachar.

"And Leah conceived again, and bore Jacob the sixth son.

"And Leah said, God has endued me with a good dowry; now will my husband dwell with me, because

I have born him six sons: and she called his name Zebulun" (Gen. 30:17-20).

Issachar means, *"Reward,"* while Zebulun means, *"Dwelling."*

From Verse 17, we know that Leah sought the Lord as it regarded her conceiving another son, which she did. The Lord heard and answered her prayer, and this was despite the fact that superstition had been involved regarding the mandrakes. How so much the Lord overlooks in answering prayer for all of us.

THE THINGS OF THE LORD

Rachel and Leah, it seems, were not as knowledgeable of the Things of the Lord as they should have been. Still, it seems that they were influenced by the Promises of God to Abraham on whose posterity were entailed the richest Blessings, and from whom the Messiah in the fullness of time was to descend. It was the belief of these Promises that rendered every pious female in those times desirable of being a mother.

Little did Leah realize at this time that the child who had been born to her two or three years earlier, Judah, would head up the Tribe from whom the Messiah would come. Near Jacob's dying day, the great Patriarch prophesied: *"The sceptre (ruling power) shall not depart from Judah, nor a Law-Giver from between His Feet until Shiloh (another name for the Messiah) come; and unto Him shall the gathering of the people be"* (Gen. 49:10).

Leah thinks that God has heard her prayer regarding her fifth conception because she had given her maid Zilpah to Jacob, who had brought forth two sons for Jacob, Gad and Asher.

Leah conceived again and brought forth a sixth son, whom she thought would give her preeminence over Rachel. This would mean that Jacob would look at her as the favorite wife, especially considering that Rachel personally had not been able to conceive at all.

DINAH

"And afterwards she bore a daughter, and called her name Dinah" (Gen. 30:21).

Even though Dinah is the only daughter mentioned in the entirety of this family, there is a possibility that Jacob had other daughters as well. It seems to be evidenced in Genesis 37:35, although, the word, *"Daughters,"* here could, in fact, refer to grandchildren, etc.

At any rate, Dinah is mentioned here because of the incident in her history afterwards related (Gen. 34:1).

JOSEPH

"And God remembered Rachel, and God hearkened to her, and opened her womb.

"And she conceived, and bore a son; and said, God has taken away my reproach:

"And she called his name Joseph; and said, The LORD shall add to me another son" (Gen. 30:22-24).

The Lord demonstrated that the mandrakes could not remove sterility by allowing Rachel's barrenness to continue at least two years longer, though she had made use of this supposed remedy, and by opening Leah's womb without them.

We should learn from all of this how useless superstition is and that the Lord rules in all things. As well, I think it is obvious here that Rachel only exacerbated her situation instead of helping it.

I wonder how much superstition is presently involved in the prayers and faith of many modern Christians? Let me give you at least one example:

CONFESSION

Memorizing Scriptures and confessing the Word of God are good things and should be practiced by all Christians. Still, if we think that by confessing certain Scriptures over and over, such will work some type of favor with God or some type of magic, we are doing nothing less than engaging in superstition exactly as Rachel used her mandrakes in order to bring about conception, which, of course, didn't work. But yet, many in the modern Charismatic world have been taught that endless repetition will bring about things from God, etc.

I happened to be with a man sometime back who was a dear friend. He had some problems, which I will not now relate. Another well-meaning brother gave him two or three particular Scriptures, told him to memorize them and quote them over and over, and this would address the problem.

Pure and simple, even though the Scriptures definitely are the Word of God, quoting them over and over, thinking that such will bring about some type of help, is the wrong type of faith and actually, as stated, is no more than superstition.

THE CROSS

I will emphasize again that every Christian ought to memorize Scriptures constantly and quote them constantly, *"For the Word of God is quick* (alive)*, and powerful, and sharper than any two-edged sword, piercing even to the dividing asunder of soul and spirit, and of the joints and marrow, and is a discerner of the thoughts and intents of the heart"* (Heb. 4:12). However, we must be careful that we do not reduce the Word to superstition.

Believers receive from the Lord, which is always according to His Word, due to what Christ has done for us at the Cross. It is the Cross that makes it all possible, and it is the Cross which must always be the Object of our Faith (I Cor. 1:17-18, 21, 23; 2:2; Col. 2:10-15). With our Faith rightly placed, then the Word functions in our lives as it should.

Let me say it again: the use of the Word in this wrong manner is not new. It was used by the Jews in such a way during the time of Christ and even long before. Of this practice, Jesus said: *"But all their works (Pharisees) they do for to be seen of men: they make broad their phylacteries, and enlarge the borders of their garments"* (Mat. 23:5).

The *"phylacteries"* were sort of a little leather case worn around the wrist or the forehead. In the small case, they placed particular Scriptures printed on pieces of leather, or even the Ten Commandments. They thought of these things as amulets or charms which would bless them, especially considering that it was the Word of God. As is obvious, Jesus condemned this practice.

RACHEL

Ultimately, God answered Rachel's petition and *"opened her womb."*

She named her son *"Joseph,"* which means, *"He shall add,"* which, in effect, was a Prophecy referring to the birth of another son, who, in fact, would be Benjamin.

It seems by now that Rachel had advanced somewhat in the Spirit and had forsaken human devices, such as resorting to mandrakes, etc. She now evidenced a complete dependence on the sovereign Grace of the Covenant God of Abraham, Isaac, and Jacob.

Concerning this, Horton says of her: *"When God remembers it does not mean He has forgotten. Rather it means that it was God's time and He actively entered the situation to do something about it. This intervention was to answer Rachel's prayers that He had been listening to the entire time of Leah's childbearing years. God, not the mandrakes, made it possible for Rachel to have a son. Barrenness was considered a disgrace. Now that disgrace was removed by the birth of a son. But she was not satisfied, since Leah had six sons. So she named the boy Joseph, meaning 'He shall add,' and she asked for another son. Unfortunately the fulfillment of that prayer would cause her death"* (Gen. 35:16-19).

TYPES OF CHRIST

The following shows how these sons are Types of Christ:

- Reuben: Jesus is the *"Son of God."*
- Simeon: through Jesus we *"hear"* God.
- Levi: through Jesus we are *"joined"* to the Father.
- Judah: through Jesus God accepts our *"praises."*
- Dan: Jesus has taken the *"Judgment"* due us.
- Naphtali: Jesus has *"wrestled"* the powers of darkness, all on our behalf, and has defeated the foe.
- Gad: Jesus is the *"Troop"* who has fought on our behalf and has brought us *"good fortune."*
- Asher: Jesus has made us *"happy."*
- Issachar: Jesus is our *"Reward."*
- Zebulun: Jesus has made it possible for Believers to *"dwell"* in the House of the Lord forever.
- Joseph: Jesus has *"added"* all Believers to the Kingdom.
- Benjamin: Jesus is the Father's *"Strong Right Hand,"* and sits with Him in Heavenly Places.

FOURTEEN YEARS

"And it came to pass, when Rachel had born Joseph,

that Jacob said unto Laban, Send me away, that I may go unto my own place, and to my country.

"Give me my wives and my children, for whom I have served you, and let me go: for you know my service which I have done you" (Gen. 30:25-26).

The principles of Grace may be professed, but the real measure of our experience of the Power of Grace is quite another thing.

Jacob's Vision portrayed to him the story of Grace; but God's Revelation at Beth-el takes time to act. It's called, *"Progressive Sanctification."* Character and conduct prove the real measure of the soul's experience and conviction, whatever the profession may be.

Jacob's terminology, *"For whom I have served you, and let me go,"* proves that both Leah and Rachel became his wives immediately, and then he served the 14 years for them.

It is highly unlikely that 11 sons and one daughter could have been born to this family in just seven years as some claim. No, this number of children played out over the last 14 years.

Having served the 14 years which had been agreed upon, he tells Laban that he now wants to go back to Canaan.

"A ruler once came to Jesus by night,
"To ask Him the way of Salvation and Light;
"The Master made answer in words true and plain,
"'You must be Born-Again.'"

"You children of men, attend to the Word
"So solemnly uttered by Jesus the Lord;
"And let not this Message to you be in vain,
"'You must be Born-Again.'"

"Oh you who would enter that glorious rest,
"And sing with the ransomed the song of the blest;

"The Life Everlasting if you would obtain,
"'You must be Born-Again.'"

"A dear one in Heaven your heart yearns to see,
"At the beautiful gate may be watching for thee;
"Then list to the note of your solemn refrain;
"'You must be Born-Again.'"

JACOB

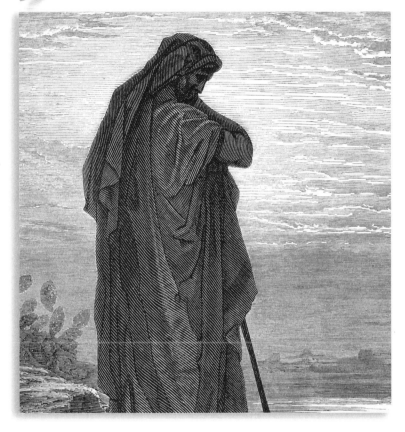

Chapter Seven

THE LEADING
OF THE LORD

THE LEADING OF THE LORD

"And Laban said unto him, I pray you, if I have found favor in your eyes, tarry: for I have learned by experience that the LORD has blessed me for your sake.

"And he said, Appoint me your wages, and I will give it" (Gen. 30:27-28).

Laban doesn't at all desire that Jacob leave. He readily admits that since Jacob had been with him, the Lord has blessed the entirety of all that he was and all that he had. He admits this! So, in order to keep Jacob and, as well, to keep the Blessing, he tells Jacob to name his wages, and he will pay it.

While Laban knew about the Lord, there is no evidence that he really knew the Lord. However, he did know that Jehovah was real and that the Blessings of God were definitely upon Jacob. This he readily observed and recognized. So, for material benefits alone, he desired that the Patriarch remain with him as long as possible.

We should learn a lesson from all of this.

Any person who is truly a Believer is a Blessing to all who are in his employ, or else, whoever employs him. The only time that possibly wouldn't hold true is when the Believer is out of the Will of God, as was Jonah.

A PERSONAL EXAMPLE

I call to mind an event similar to this which took place when I was but a boy.

Our little church was very small, perhaps averaging 30 to 35 people. There was a dear sister in the church who loved the Lord supremely. She had a large family. Her husband was in prison, so it was very difficult to make ends meet. This was before the government welfare net, etc.

She had a job in a local five-and-dime store.

At a particular point in time, the manager of this store requested of her that she stop talking to people about their problems, in other words, talking to them about the Lord during her working hours.

She tried to conduct herself in that fashion but soon found that she was unable to do so. People kept coming to her for counsel and advice. After two or three warnings, the manager of the five-and-dime terminated her.

After about 30 days, if that, he came to her house requesting that she come back to work. His reason was as follows:

Whenever he terminated her, his business was cut about one-half. He found out that many of the people were coming into the store, and while they would buy something, sometimes purchase quite a few things, they mainly wanted to talk to this dear lady. She was always kind and gracious and had a word for each one, whomever the person may have been. As she gently and kindly talked to them, especially about their problems, she witnessed to them about the Lord and how He was able to save.

This man realized that this woman, in fact, was his business.

So, when he hired her back, he told her explicitly to conduct herself as she felt like she ought, and nothing else would be said.

Pure and simple, this dear lady, who was very godly, to say the least, was a great blessing to this business establishment. That's the way the Lord intends for it to be. Unfortunately, there are many who profess to know Christ but really have very little relationship with Him, if any. These people are not a blessing to anyone, but rather a curse.

So, what I'm speaking of and who I'm speaking of refers to those who truly love the Lord and the blessing they are to all concerned.

THE BLESSING RECALLED

"And he said unto him, You know how I have served you, and how your cattle was with me.

"For it was little which you had before I came, and it is now increased unto a multitude; and the LORD has blessed you since my coming: and now when shall I provide for my own house also?" (Gen. 30:29-30).

Jacob knows that the Hand of the Lord is upon him. He also knows, that being the case, the Lord will bless all that he touches. Inasmuch as he is now working for Laban, then Laban is the one who is the recipient of the Blessing. However, even as we have addressed, Jacob's time of servitude is now over, and a different arrangement must be entered into.

THE AGREEMENT

"And he said, What shall I give you? And Jacob said, You shall not give me anything: if you will do this thing for me, I will again feed and keep your flock:

"I will pass through all your flock today, removing from thence all the speckled and spotted cattle, and all the brown cattle among the sheep, and the spotted and speckled among the goats: and of such shall be my hire.

"So shall my Righteousness answer for me in time to come, when it shall come for my hire before your face: every one that is not speckled and spotted among the goats, and brown among the sheep, that shall be counted stolen with me.

"And Laban said, Behold, I would it might be according to your word" (Gen. 30:31-34).

Some have criticized Jacob as it regards this particular agreement. They have once again attributed such to devious ways, trickery, and even dishonesty; however, it would appear that he acted honestly in all of his dealings with Laban.

The tenor of this agreement seems to me that he is referring his cause to God rather than to enter into any stipulated agreement for stated wages with Laban, whose selfishness, one would have to acknowledge, was very great.

Laban selfishly concluded that his cattle would produce few different in color from their own, and in the natural, he would be correct. However, I think we may consider all of this, at least that which happened with Jacob, as a Miracle from God. This we do know:

The Lord will never bless sin and dishonesty or even the slightest hint of evil. So, if the Lord is involved, we must conclude that the acts, whatever they may have been, had been righteous.

THE PLAN GIVEN TO JACOB BY GOD

"And he removed that day the he goats that were ringstraked and spotted, and all the she goats that were speckled and spotted, and every one that had some white in it, and all the brown among the sheep, and gave them into the hand of his sons.

"And he set three days' journey between himself and Jacob: and Jacob fed the rest of Laban's flocks.

"And Jacob took him rods of green poplar, and of the hazel and chestnut tree; and pilled white strakes in them, and made the white appear which was in the rods.

"And he set the rods which he had pilled before the flocks in the gutters in the watering troughs when the flocks came to drink, that they should conceive when they came to drink.

"And the flocks conceived before the rods, and brought forth cattle ringstraked, speckled, and spotted" (Gen. 30:35-39).

Whenever Jacob proposed his plan, which would give him all of the spotted and mingled sheep and goats, Laban reasoned, and rightly so under normal circumstances, that the number of animals falling into this category would be small indeed. As he looked at his vast herd, even as Jacob made the proposal, he didn't see how he could lose.

It is my contention that the Lord told Jacob what to do in this situation.

It is said to have been frequently observed that, particularly in the case of sheep, whatever fixes their attention in copulation is marked upon the young. That Jacob believed in the efficacy of the artifice he adopted is apparent; but for the multiplication of part-colored animals, it will be safer to ascribe such to Divine Blessing than to human craft.

INCREASE

"And Jacob did separate the lambs, and set the faces of the flocks toward the ringstraked, and all the brown in the flock of Laban; and he put his own flocks by themselves, and put them not unto Laban's cattle.

"And it came to pass, whensoever the stronger cattle did conceive, that Jacob laid the rods before the eyes of the cattle in the gutters, that they might conceive among the rods.

"But when the cattle (sheep) were feeble, he put them not in: so the feebler were Laban's, and the stronger Jacob's.

"And the man increased exceedingly, and had much cattle (sheep), *and maidservants, and menservants, and camels, and asses"* (Gen. 30:40-43).

Incidentally, the term, *"Cattle,"* as used in the Old Testament, can refer to all domestic animals, such as lambs, goats, oxen, heifers, etc. In the Passages of our study, it seems to refer to all types, but for the most part being sheep.

I think we must conclude that the proposal of such a singular condition on the part of Jacob was an act not of folly but of Faith, being tantamount to a committal of his cause to God instead of Laban. The acceptance of it on the part of Laban was a display of greed and a proof that the bygone years of prosperity had only increased that greed.

That impressions made upon the minds of sheep at rutting time affect the unborn animal seems a well-established fact; but the extraordinary rapidity with which brown and speckled animals were produced appears to point to the intervention of a special providence on Jacob's behalf. There was nothing fraudulent in what Jacob did and may be inferred from the fact that he acted under Divine approval (Gen. 31:12). I don't see how we can do anything but come to this conclusion.

Increase in the best sense is God's Promise. It will be sent as He wills and when He wills, but will be found the true answer to prayer and the true manifestation of love. On all that belongs to us, the Blessing rests. We must understand that and treat it accordingly.

THE ATTITUDE OF LABAN

"And he heard the words of Laban's sons, saying, Jacob has taken away all that was our father's; and of that which was our father's has he gotten all this glory.

"And Jacob beheld the countenance of Laban, and, behold, it was not toward him as before" (Gen. 31:1-2).

The Lord told Jacob that it was now time to return to the land of Canaan. I think we must conclude from Verses 10 through 12 that Jacob's actions here were of the Lord as it regards his acquiring the great number of lambs and goats.

Two factors are involved here:

1. As long as Jacob was increasing the wealth of Laban, and he (Jacob) remained poor, Laban had no problem with that. However, once Jacob began to prosper, which, incidentally, was ordained by the Lord, and began to do so in a grand way, this created jealousy in Laban. He thought in his mind that everything Jacob acquired was actually his. He wanted all the Blessings of the Lord which rested upon Jacob to fall out totally to his increase and not Jacobs.

2. It was time for Jacob to leave. He had spent 20 years away from Canaan, and it was now time, according to the Lord, for him to go home. The Lord had other plans for Jacob, and those plans did not include Laban.

The Lord now lifts His Hand from the attitude of Laban as it regards Jacob. In other words, the Lord did not restrain him in any way in this situation, which would prove what the man really was.

While the Lord certainly was not the cause of the anger toward Jacob, due to the Hand being lifted, the natural heart of Laban began to show itself. The Lord can cause even our enemies to be at peace with us, but He can also lift His Hand to where the peace is dissolved (Prov. 16:17).

COMMAND OF THE LORD

"And the LORD said unto Jacob, Return unto the land of your fathers, and to your kindred; and I will be with you" (Gen. 31:3).

The Lord now moves upon Jacob's heart that it is time to return to Canaan.

It is so pleasing to the heart to note the minute Leading of the Lord in the life of the Patriarch. At this stage, I'm not certain how much Jacob actually knew regarding his part in the great Plan of God, which would more and more unfold as time went on. However, one can certainly see Spiritual progress in Jacob's life. In other words, these 20 years with Laban weren't wasted. He was a different man now than he was when God spoke to him at Beth-el those long years before. You can sense it in his demeanor, his manner, his attitude, and his spirit.

Exactly how the Lord appeared to the Patriarch, we aren't told. Perhaps it was in a Dream, as mentioned in Verse 10 concerning other matters.

The Promise of the Lord to be with him is the greatest Promise that anyone could ever have.

In fact, the Lord is always with every Believer; however, He is speaking here of being with Jacob in a special way, which does not hold true with everyone.

Jacob's role in the great Plan of God was to bring the necessary sons into the world who would head up the Tribes of Israel and would be the people of God in the world. In other words, they would be God's Special Chosen People. Of the 13 required sons, 11 had already been born. A little later, Benjamin would be born, which would be the last one as it regarded the sons of Jacob. However, even as we shall see, Joseph will be used in another context, actually as a Type of Christ, with his two sons, Ephraim and Manasseh, becoming a part of the Tribes of Israel, numbering 13, which was the desired number.

JACOB'S DECISION

Verses 4 through 9 read: *"And Jacob sent and called Rachel and Leah to the field unto his flock,*

"And said unto them, I see your father's countenance, that it is not toward me as before; but the God of my father has been with me.

"And you know that with all my power I have served your father.

"And your father has deceived me, and changed my wages ten times; but God suffered him not to hurt me.

"If he said thus, The speckled shall be your wages; then all the cattle bore speckled: and if he said thus, The ringstraked shall be your hire; then bore all the cattle ringstraked.

"Thus God has taken away the cattle of your father, and given them to me" (Gen. 31:4-9).

From these Passages we learn a little more concerning what had taken place between Jacob and Laban. For instance, the Patriarch says that Laban had changed his wages 10 times, which probably refers to *"many times,"* instead of the actual number 10. As used in the Old Testament, the number 10 contains the idea of completeness and not necessarily the exact amount unless accordingly specified.

CHANGING THE RULES

When Laban saw that Jacob's flocks were increasing according to the bargain originally made, he then changed the rules. However, as we see, God overruled that particular change. Whatever it was that Laban said that Jacob could have, which was reduced from the original agreement, the Lord had them all to turn out in that particular manner.

We should see from this that the Lord doesn't take kindly to His Children being put upon. Sometimes He will step in, even as He did with Jacob, and other times, He doesn't. Nevertheless, one can be doubly certain that the Lord knows all things and keeps account of all things. In other words, what we sow, that is what we will reap.

So that his conversation will not be overheard, the Patriarch asks both Rachel and Leah to come out into the field where he is in order that he might talk to them. His words to them consists of three parts:

1. He relates to them the change in Laban's manner toward him and his consequent fear of violence.

2. He justifies his own conduct toward their father and accuses him of repeated injustice.

3. Finally, he announces to them that he has received the Divine command to return to Canaan.

THE DREAM

"And it came to pass at the time that the cattle conceived, that I lifted up my eyes, and saw in a Dream, and, behold, the rams which leaped upon the cattle were ringstraked, speckled, and grisled.

"And the Angel of God spoke unto me in a Dream, saying, Jacob: And I said, Here am I.

"And He said, Lift up now your eyes, and see, all the rams which leap upon the cattle are ringstraked, speckled, and grisled: for I have seen all that Laban has done unto you.

"I am the God of Beth-el, where you anointed the pillar, and where you vowed a vow unto Me: now arise, you get out from this land, and return unto the land of your kindred" (Gen. 31:10-13).

I don't see how that one can look at these Passages and then come to the conclusion that what Jacob did regarding the animals was immoral, fraudulent, or dishonest.

The dream would be given to Jacob and was meant to be understood as a Divine intimation to Jacob that whatever would be done was not to be ascribed to the success of his own stratagems, but to the Blessings of God.

In the Dream that the Lord gave to the Patriarch, several things are said and done:

• The Lord told Jacob what to do about the spotted animals.

• He told him that He had seen all that Laban had done unto him.

• He reaffirmed that He was the God of Beth-el, which proclaimed the fact that every Promise given there to Jacob still held true.

• He reminded Jacob that He anointed the pillar, which spoke of the Holy Spirit and of Christ.

• He reminded Jacob of the *"vow"* which had been made about giving a tenth to the Lord. Most probably, these were animals which should be offered up in sacrifice.

• He now tells Jacob that it's time to leave Syria and go back to Canaan.

RACHEL AND LEAH

"And Rachel and Leah answered and said unto him, Is there yet any portion or inheritance for us in our father's house?

"Are we not counted of him strangers? for he has sold us, and has quite devoured also our money.

"For all the riches which God has taken from our father, that is ours, and our children's: now then, whatsoever God has said unto you, do" (Gen. 31:14-16).

There is a marked severity towards their father in the answer of Jacob's wives. They are recalling that they received no dowry whatsoever when they married Jacob.

So, they are upset with their father, not only as to how he has treated Jacob, but in the manner in which he has treated them as well. So, they tell Jacob, *"Whatsoever God has said unto you, do."*

It's a shame that Laban figures so prominently in the Gospel Message, but yet, never came to know the Lord. His sister and two daughters would be instrumental in bringing into the world those who would be the heads of the great Tribes of Israel, and to whom God would make all the Promises. He was so close, but yet, so far, far away. He saw the Hand of God move mightily but never came to know the Lord.

JACOB DEPARTS

"Then Jacob rose up, and set his sons and his wives upon camels;

"And he carried away all his cattle, and all his goods which he had gotten, the cattle of his getting, which he had gotten in Padan-aram, for to go to Isaac his father in the land of Canaan.

"And Laban went to shear his sheep: and Rachel had stolen the images that were her father's.

"And Jacob stole away unawares to Laban the Syrian, in that he told him not that he fled.

"So he fled with all that he had; and he rose up, and passed over the river, and set his face toward the mount Gilead" (Gen. 31:17-21).

The Scripture says that Jacob is leaving, *"For to go to Isaac his father in the land of Canaan."* These 20 years that Jacob has been gone are silent regarding Isaac. How so much he must have grieved for his son. While Esau, no doubt, provided some comfort, there was no Spiritual bond whatsoever between Isaac and his oldest son. Esau simply did not know God and had no desire to know God.

He knew, of course, that God had laid His Hand on Jacob, but these 20 years passed in silence. Did he hear from Jacob during this time? Did Isaac send any news to Jacob from home?

It is believed that Rebekah died while Jacob was away, but no one knows when. The Scriptures are silent regarding her death, only saying that she was buried with Isaac in the tomb of Abraham (Gen. 49:31).

The great Plan of God, regarding the formation of Israel as a Nation, will now begin. From the time of Abraham, when he arrived in Canaan, to Jacob, when he went into Egypt, was 215 years. When he left Syria, he was about 100 years old. When he went into Egypt, he was 130 (Gen. 47:9). So, he would spend about 30 years in Canaan before going into Egypt and about 20 years of that grieving for Joseph, whom he thought was dead.

THE IMAGES

From Verse 19, some have concluded that Rachel was an idol-worshipper because she had stolen the images which belonged to her father.

Concerning this, Horton says: *"Rachel had a reason for stealing the teraphim. These were small idols (like figurines) considered the family gods and were kept on a god-shelf, probably in the corner of the main room of the house.*

"When there was any question about the inheritance, the person who had the teraphim was considered to have the right to the double portion of the primary heir. When Jacob first came, he was welcomed into the family and adopted as the heir, since Laban had no sons at the time. But Laban had sons born shortly after, and that normally would invalidate Jacob's claim unless he possessed the teraphim. Rachel felt Jacob deserved more than he was getting, so she stole them for his benefit, and for the benefit of Jacob's family. There is no evidence she wanted to worship these images."

This was evidently sheepshearing time, and Laban was busy in this endeavor. Consequently, while Laban was busy, Jacob took his vast herds and fled. He passed over the Euphrates River and then set his face toward Mount Gilead.

THE DREAM

"And it was told Laban on the third day that Jacob was fled.

"And he took his brethren with him, and pursued after him seven days' journey; and they overtook him in the mount Gilead.

"And God came to Laban the Syrian in a Dream by night, and said unto him, Take heed that you speak not to Jacob either good or bad" (Gen. 31:22-24).

Laban, busy shearing the sheep, did not hear of Jacob's departure for some three days. He immediately set out, evidently with a group of armed men, to overtake the Patriarch. It took some seven days for Laban to overtake Jacob, covering approximately 100 miles.

Every indication is, Laban meant to do Jacob harm. The Lord would not have warned him in a Dream had that not been the case. He probably intended to take the herds, his two daughters, and all the children, and maybe even kill Jacob. However, what he doesn't know is that Jacob, no doubt, was surrounded by a band of Angels (Gen. 32:1-2). So, had he disregarded the admonition given to him by the Lord in the Dream, Laban, no doubt, would have met with a violent end. While it would not have been at the hand of Jacob, it would definitely have been at the hand of Angels.

THE CHASE

"Then Laban overtook Jacob. Now Jacob had pitched his tent in the mount: and Laban with his brethren pitched in the mount of Gilead.

"And Laban said to Jacob, What have you done, that you have stolen away unawares to me, and carried away my daughters, as captives taken with the sword?

"Wherefore did you flee away secretly, and steal away from me; and did not tell me, that I might have

sent you away with mirth, and with songs, with tabret, and with harp?

"And have not suffered me to kiss my sons and my daughters? you have now done foolishly in so doing.

"It is in the power of my hand to do you hurt: but the God of your father spoke unto me yesternight, saying, You take heed that you speak not to Jacob either good or bad.

"And now, though you would need be gone, because you sore longed after your father's house, yet wherefore have you stolen my gods?

"And Jacob answered and said to Laban, Because I was afraid: for I said, Peradventure you would take by force your daughters from me.

"With whomsoever you find your gods, let him not live: before our brethren discern for you what is yours with me, and take it to you. For Jacob knew not that Rachel had stolen them" (Gen. 31:25-32).

Laban accused Jacob of carrying away his daughters as captives, but that is totally untrue. Rachel and Leah voluntarily accompanied their husband in his flight.

The idea that Laban would have tendered a great going away party for Jacob is crassly hypocritical. More than likely, the Lord told Jacob to depart as he did because of Laban's hostile intentions.

One thing is certain: there is no way that Laban would have allowed Jacob to take the herds with him, and he probably would not have allowed his daughters or any of the children to go with Jacob. So, his accusations and his claims hold no merit.

He then accused Jacob of having stolen his gods, which Jacob vehemently denied, and rightly so. He had no idea that Rachel had taken these things, and as it would prove out, they were of no consequence anyway as far as the inheritance was concerned. After this meeting, Rachel would never see her father again.

THE IMAGES

"And Laban went into Jacob's tent, and into Leah's tent, and into the two maidservants' tents; but he found them not. Then went he out of Leah's tent, and entered into Rachel's tent.

"Now Rachel had taken the images, and put them in the camel's furniture, and sat upon them. And Laban searched all the tent, but found them not.

"And she said to her father, Let it not displease my lord that I cannot rise up before you; for the custom of women is upon me. And he searched but found not the images" (Gen. 31:33-35).

How foolish for Laban to call these things his gods which could be stolen! Could he expect protection from things that could neither resist nor discover their invaders? Happy are they who have the Lord for their God, for they have a God of Whom they cannot be robbed. Enemies may steal our goods but not our God.

To explain the significance of all of this, let us say it again: the idea was, whoever had the small image could, at a given point in time, claim the inheritance. This is at least one of, if not the most, important reasons for Laban's diligence in searching for this little idol. As well, it's the reason that Rachel had taken it, but which would do her no good. She would never see her homeland again, or her father, for that matter, after he left.

THE SITUATION

"The camel's furniture" actually was a saddle riding affair, made of wickerwork, and had the appearance of a basket or cradle. It was usually covered with carpet and was protected against wind, rain, and sun by means of a canopy and curtains, while light was admitted by

openings in the side. When riding a camel, this was the apparatus which served as a saddle-like affair, at least for women.

Rachel had hidden the images under this saddle and was sitting on it. She apologized for not standing, claiming that she was having her *"period."* Whether this was correct or not, we have no way of knowing, but there is a good possibility that it was.

She reasoned in her mind that her father surmised that she was having some type of problem and would not inquire further, which means he would not search under the camel's saddle. This proved to be correct. At any rate, Laban did not find these idols, so Rachel's ruse worked.

THE ANGER OF JACOB

"And Jacob was angry, and did chide with Laban: and Jacob answered and said to Laban, What is my trespass? what is my sin, that you have so hotly pursued after me?

"Whereas you have searched all my stuff, what have you found of all your household stuff? set it here before my brethren and your brethren, that they may judge between us both.

"This twenty years I have been with you; your ewes and your she goats have not cast their young, and the rams of your flock have I not eaten.

"That which was torn of beasts I brought not unto you; I bore the loss of it; of my hand did you require it, whether stolen by day, or stolen by night.

"Thus I was; in the day the drought consumed me, and the frost by night; and my sleep departed from my eyes.

"Thus have I been twenty years in your house; I served you fourteen years for your two daughters, and

six years for your cattle: and you have changed my wages ten times.

"Except the God of my father, the God of Abraham, and the fear of Isaac, had been with me, surely you had sent me away now empty. God has seen my affliction and the labor of my hands, and rebuked you yesternight" (Gen. 31:36-42).

CONTENTION

The contention between Jacob and Laban had gone on for many years. By now it had reached a fever pitch. No doubt, if the Lord had not spoken to Laban in a dream, he would have taken everything Jacob had, including his wives and children, and, as stated, would have possibly even killed him. However, he was afraid to lift a hand against him in any manner at this particular time because of what the Lord had told him.

Jacob was now very angry. Instead of the father being sad regarding his two daughters and all of his grandchildren leaving, and knowing that he would possibly never see them again, he was more interested in material things than anything else. It is interesting that Jacob referred to these images as *"stuff"* (Vs. 37).

Jacob then rehearsed his 20 years with Laban and, in effect, was saying that Laban had absolutely no reason to be angry with him. He had treated Laban fair in every respect, and, in fact, that was correct.

He then reminded Laban that he (Laban) knew that God was with him (with Jacob), and he had best conduct himself toward the Patriarch accordingly.

The loss of Laban's manufactured deities was a ridiculous commentary on the folly of worshipping or trusting in a god that could be stolen. What a spectacle of infinite humor, if it were not so sad — a man seeking for his lost gods! The Gospel presents us with the opposite picture — the Ever-present God seeking for His Lost Children.

THE PROTECTION OF GOD

"And Laban answered and said unto Jacob, These daughters are my daughters, and these children are my children, and these cattle are my cattle, and all that you see is mine: and what can I do this day unto these my daughters, or unto their children which they have born?" (Gen. 31:43).

At Beth-el, Jacob was to learn what God was; at Haran what man was, and what a difference! At Beth-el, God enriched him; at Haran, man robbed him!

The Lord speaking to Laban in a Dream should have told him that idols were vain and wicked inventions of man's folly, but yet, he clung to them!

The parting of Laban and Jacob sadly illustrates the mutual suspicion which grips men's hearts when governed by the spirit of the world.

So, Laban passes from the scene, not to be mentioned again except in passing (Gen. 46:18, 25). He had seen the Hand of God greatly so in the life of Jacob, with the Lord, as stated, even speaking to him in a Dream. However, he had no heart for God and, thereby, the opportunity of Heaven had been eternally lost.

Laban wrongly claims everything that Jacob has, but recognizes that due to the Power of God, there is nothing he can do regarding the taking of them. In fact, were he to try anything, he would, no doubt, forfeit his life. He knows this, but still doesn't relinquish claim.

How hard is the heart of man: how so difficult to turn, even in the face of the exhibition of the Power of God!

MEN RULE, BUT GOD OVERRULES!

This whole scenario tells us that God is always in charge.

Laban had little regard for Jacob despite the fact that, at this particular time, he was a very rich man, and all because of the Patriarch. His greed would not allow him to see that, and, as well, he only grudgingly gave God the glory. Instead of allowing Jacob to show him the One True God in service for Him, he saw only worldly wealth.

How similar this entire spirit is with many in the modern Charismatic movements, who claim the Word of Faith doctrine, etc. The emphasis is not at all on Righteousness and Holiness, but rather on material things. Let the reader hear and know: if we labor for the meat that perishes, we will perish along with it. That's why Jesus said:

"Labour not for the meat which perishes, but for that meat which endures unto Everlasting Life, which the Son of Man shall give unto you: for Him has God the Father sealed" (Jn. 6:27).

Without a doubt, the situation presented before us regarding Jacob and Laban is at least one of the greatest hindrances to the Child of God. Why do we serve God? Is it for worldly accoutrements, or is it for the Joy of Christ Himself?

THE COVENANT

"Now therefore you come, let us make a Covenant, I and you; and let it be for a witness between me and you.

"And Jacob took a stone, and set it up for a pillar.

"And Jacob said unto his brethren, Gather stones; and they took stones, and made an heap: and they did eat there upon the heap.

"And Laban called it Jegar-sahadutha: but Jacob called it Galeed.

"And Laban said, This heap is a witness between me and you this day. Therefore was the name of it called Galeed" (Gen. 31:44-48).

The Covenant was a suggestion of Laban, or even a demand. Jacob is the one who had been wronged, so if one of the two needed a Covenant, it was the Patriarch. However, the evidence is, Laban wanted this Covenant because he was afraid relative to what the Lord had told him in the Dream (Vs. 24). Jacob had a Dream as well (Vss. 10-13). In this Dream, God, in essence, had promised to be with Jacob. So, the Patriarch needed no Covenant because his trust was in the Lord to take care of him. However, evil men need covenants or contracts simply because their word is no good. So, Laban claimed that the heap of stones which they had erected, and over which they had broken bread, was to be a *"witness between me and you this day."*

THE GOD OF ISAAC

"And Mizpah; for he said, The LORD watch between me and you, when we are absent one from another.

"If you shall afflict my daughters, or if you shall take other wives beside my daughters, no man is with us; see, God is witness between me and you.

"And Laban said to Jacob, Behold this heap, and behold this pillar, which I have cast between me and you:

"This heap be witness, and this pillar be witness, that I will not pass over this heap to you, and that you shall not pass over this heap and this pillar unto me, for harm.

"The God of Abraham, and the god of Nahor, the god of their father, judge between us. And Jacob swore by the fear of his father Isaac.

"Then Jacob offered sacrifice upon the mount, and called his brethren to eat bread: and they did eat bread, and tarried all night in the mount.

"And early in the morning Laban rose up, and kissed his sons and his daughters, and blessed them:

and Laban departed, and returned unto his place" (Gen. 31:49-55).

At this stage, Laban makes a show of piety as it regards his daughters, but his actions have spoken much louder than his words. He is more concerned about material things than anything else.

Laban now adds an oath to the Covenant, calling on the God of Abraham and the gods of Nahor, the gods of their father, to judge between Jacob and Laban. All of this proves that Laban worships many so-called gods. He really doesn't know the God of Abraham but only puts him into the mix and on the same level as the gods of Nahor, etc. So, Verse 53 should have been translated:

"The God of Abraham, and the gods of Nahor, the gods of their father. . . ."

Jacob ignored the gods of Nahor and took his oath only in the Name of the One True God, Who was the *"Fear"* of, or *"The One Reverenced"* by Isaac.

THE SACRIFICE

As well, the Scripture says that *"Jacob offered sacrifice upon the mount, and called his brethren to eat bread"* (Vs. 54).

The sacrifice meant nothing to Laban, even though he was well acquainted with this practice, but everything to Jacob. In essence, he was saying that he was placing his Faith and confidence in what the sacrifice represented. The very purpose and reason for his grandfather Abraham being called out of Ur of the Chaldees, the actions of his father Isaac, and his own life, for that matter, were to bring the One into the world of Whom the sacrifices represented. As the lamb gave its life, pouring out its blood, with its carcass then being offered on the Altar, likewise, Christ would give His Life, offering up Himself on the Cross as a Sacrifice in order that man might be Saved. The terrible sin debt must be paid, and there was no other way to pay it, that is, if the fallen sons of Adam's lost race were to be redeemed. God would have to become man, whom Paul would refer to as the *"Last Adam"* and the *"Second Man"* (I Cor. 15:45, 47).

Verse 55 says that *"Laban departed, and returned unto his place."*

Regrettably and sadly, that *"place,"* at least as far as we know, was eternal darkness, forever without God. In essence, he sold his soul for a few flocks and herds. What a sorry trade!

THE ANGELS OF GOD

"And Jacob went on his way, and the Angels of God met him" (Gen. 32:1).

The second Vision concerning the Angels corresponds to that at Beth-el in Chapter 28 of Genesis. Then, Jacob's possessions consisted of a staff, but now, he has become a host, and he calls this place Mahanaim, i.e., *"two camps — his feeble camp and the encircling camp of God's Mighty Angels."*

Jacob was now about to cross over the brook into the Promised Land to where God had called him. There would be many dangers, toils, and snares. However, for a few moments, and the Holy Spirit does not inform us as to exactly how, He pulled back the cover of the spirit world and allowed Jacob to see the Angelic host which was ready to accompany him. And yet, strangely enough, as wonderful as this was and as much as it should have spoken unto Jacob, he seemingly did not recognize its significance. Despite the fact of being surrounded by Angels, he began to scheme and plan as it regarded the coming of Esau. He had wronged his brother some 20 years before, and now he must face him.

The Angels appearing and Jacob not quite realizing their significance point to the fact that all the great Manifestations, as wonderful as they might be, cannot bring us to the place where we ought to be in the Lord. That can only come when the sentence of death is written on the flesh, which only the Power of the Cross can bring about. That's one of the great problems of the modern church.

The Pentecostal arm of the Church at times looks for Manifestations. Mostly what they see has not been anything, and in some cases, it has literally been the powers of darkness. However, even if the Manifestations are real, which means they are genuinely of God, just as the Angels which made themselves visible to Jacob, that within itself will not bring about the victory for which we seek.

The following is a short article written by A.W. Tozer. It is titled, *"The Old Cross and the New."*

THE OLD CROSS AND THE NEW

All unannounced and mostly undetected, there has come in modern times a new cross into popular evangelical circles. It is like the old Cross, but different: the likenesses are superficial, the differences fundamental.

From this new cross has sprung a new philosophy of the Christian life, and from that new philosophy has come a new evangelical technique — a new type of meeting and a new kind of preaching. This new evangelism employs the same language as the old, but its content is not the same and its emphasis not as before.

THE WORLD

The old Cross would have no truck with the world. For Adam's proud flesh, it meant the end of the journey.

It carried into effect the sentence imposed by the Law of Sinai. The new cross is not opposed to the human race; rather, it is a friendly pal, and if understood aright, it is the source of oceans of good clean fun and innocent enjoyment. It lets Adam live without interference. His life motivation is unchanged; he still lives for his own pleasure, only now he takes delight in singing choruses and watching religious movies instead of singing bawdy songs and drinking hard liquor. The accent is still on enjoyment though the fun is now on a higher plain morally, if not intellectually.

A NEW APPROACH

The new cross encourages a new and entirely different evangelistic approach. The evangelist does not demand abnegation of the old life before a new life can be received. He preaches not contrast but similarities. He seeks to key into public interest by showing Christianity makes no unpleasant demands; rather it offers the same thing the world does, only on a higher level. Whatever the sin-mad world happens to be clamoring after at the moment is cleverly shown to be the very thing the gospel offers, only the religious product is better.

ACCEPTABLE TO THE PUBLIC

The new cross does not slay the sinner; it redirects him. It gears him into a cleaner and jollier way of living and saves his self-respect. To the self-assertive it says, *"Come and assert yourself for Christ."* To the egotist it says, *"Come and do your boasting in the Lord."* To the thrill-seeker it says, *"Come and enjoy the thrill of Christian fellowship and entertainment."*

The Christian message is slanted in the direction of the current vogue in order to make it acceptable to the public.

FALSE

The philosophy back of this kind of thing may be sincere, but its sincerity does not save it from being false. It is false because it is blind. It misses completely the whole meaning of the Cross.

A SYMBOL OF DEATH

The old Cross is a symbol of death. It stands for the abrupt, violent end of a human being. The man in Roman times who took up his cross and started down the road had already said good-bye to his friends. He was not coming back. He was not going out to have his life redirected; he was going out to have it ended. The Cross made no compromise, modified nothing, spared nothing; it killed all of the man, completely and for good. It did not try to keep on good terms with its victim. It struck cruel and hard, and when it had finished its work, the man was no more.

A DEATH SENTENCE

The race of Adam is under a death sentence. There is no commutation and no escape. God cannot approve any of the fruits of sin, however innocent they may appear or beautiful to the eyes of men. God salvages the individual by liquidating him and then raising him again to Newness of Life.

That evangelism which draws friendly parallels between the Ways of God and the ways of men is false to the Bible and cruel to the soul of its hearers. The Faith of Christ does not parallel the world; it intersects it. In coming to Christ we do not bring our old life up onto a higher plain; we leave it at the Cross. The corn of wheat must fall into the ground and die.

PUBLIC RELATIONS AGENTS?

We who preach the Gospel must not think of ourselves as public relations agents sent to establish good will between Christ and the world. We must not imagine ourselves commissioned to make Christ acceptable to big business, the press, the world of sports, or modern education. We are not diplomats, but rather Prophets, and our Message is not a compromise but an ultimatum.

LIFE

God offers Life, but not an improved old life. The Life He offers is Life out of death. It stands always on the far side of the Cross. Whoever would possess it must pass under the rod. He must repudiate himself and concur in God's Just Sentence against him.

What does this mean to the individual, the condemned man who would find Life in Christ Jesus? How can this theology be translated into Life?

Simply, we must repent and believe. He must forsake his sins and then go on to forsake himself. Let him cover nothing, defend nothing, and excuse nothing. Let him not seek to make terms with God, but let him bow his head before the stroke of God's Stern Displeasure and acknowledge himself worthy to die.

JESUS CHRIST

Having done this, let him gaze with simple trust upon the Risen Saviour, and from Him will come Life, rebirth, cleansing, and Power. The Cross that ended the earthly life of Jesus now puts an end to the sinner; and the Power that raised Christ from the dead now raises him to a New Life along with Christ.

To any who may object to this or count it merely a narrow and private view of truth, let me say, *"God has set His Hallmark of Approval upon this Message from Paul's day to the present."* Whether stated in these exact words or not, this has been the content of all preaching that has brought Life and Power to the world through the centuries. The mystics, the reformers, and the revivalists have put their emphasis here, and Signs and Wonders and Mighty Operations of the Holy Spirit gave witness to God's Approval.

Dare we, the heirs of such a legacy of Power, tamper with the Truth? Dare we, with our stubby pencils, erase the lines of the blueprint or alter the pattern shown us in the Mount? May God forbid. Let us preach the old Cross, and we will know the Power.

This message by A.W. Tozer is that which is so desperately needed by the modern church. Let me say it again:

We can have all the manifestations in the world and as good as they might be, and as much of a blessing as they may be temporarily, if we do not understand the Cross of Christ, we will find ourselves in the same condition after the Manifestation as we were before. Only the Cross can change men, not Manifestations! Only the Cross can put an end to the terrible works of the flesh and bring forth the Fruit of the Spirit! Only the Cross can properly place self into Christ. As someone has well said, *"Jesus died on the Cross not only to save us from sin but, as well, from self!"*

THE TWO CAMPS

"And when Jacob saw them, he said, This is God's Host: and he called the name of that place Mahanaim" (Gen. 32:2).

There is some disagreement as to exactly what

Jacob meant by the name, *"Mahanaim."* It means, *"Two armies or camps."*

Some claim there were two camps of Angels, one directing him from Syria and the other into the Promised Land. Others suggest that Jacob was speaking of his camp or host, and the Angels as another camp, which was God's Host.

"God's Host," in the Hebrew is, *"Mahaneh Elohim,"* which means, *"The Army or Camp of the Lord,"* as opposed to the Mahanoth, or hosts, of Jacob himself. More than likely, the latter is what Jacob was meaning.

The statement from Verse 1, *"And the Angels of God met him,"* can mean, *"Appeared to him."* These Angels probably had been with Jacob ever since they appeared to him in Beth-el some 20 years before.

I think one can say without any fear of Scriptural contradiction or exaggeration that Angels surround every Believer in some capacity (Heb. 1:14; 12:1).

But again, allow me to emphasize that as wonderful as Manifestations may be, and as much as all of us desire to have them, and I speak, of course, of those which are truly from God, those things will not change us, as powerful as they may be in their own right. It is only the Cross which can change the Child of God.

The Believer must understand that he is baptized into the Death of Christ, buried with Him, and raised with Him in Newness of Life (Rom. 6:3-5). Until he understands that by understanding that the Cross is the key, not only to his Salvation, but, as well, to his Sanctification, he will never know a victorious life. God cannot give victory to the flesh, of which we will have more to say momentarily, but only to His Son, the Lord Jesus Christ.

At any rate, Jacob is shown that he has a host of Angels around him.

GRACE

"And Jacob sent messengers before him to Esau his brother unto the land of Seir, the country of Edom.

"And he commanded them, saying, Thus shall you speak unto my lord Esau; Your servant Jacob says thus, I have sojourned with Laban, and stayed there until now:

"And I have oxen, and asses, flocks, and menservants, and womenservants: and I have sent to tell my lord, that I may find grace in your sight.

"And the messengers returned to Jacob, saying, We came to your brother Esau, and also he comes to meet you, and four hundred men with him" (Gen. 32:3-6).

During this some 20 years that Jacob had been away from home, he must, from time to time, have received some word as to the happenings there for the simple reason that he knew Esau now lived in *"the land of Seir, the country of Edom."*

Incidentally, some believe that Esau was the founder of the ancient city of Petra and may have been there when Jacob sent for him.

Knowing that he has done Esau wrong, he feels that the first thing he must do is to address this situation. To be sure, if we have wronged anyone, it is absolutely imperative as a Christian that the matter be handled Biblically. It doesn't matter what they have done. Whatever that may have been gives us no excuse to wrong them. If we have wronged anyone for any reason, no matter how legitimate it may seem on the surface, if we want to be where God wants us to be, the wrong must be set aright, at least as far as lies within our power.

The messengers whom Jacob had sent to Esau now returned, and their news is not exactly positive. Esau is coming to meet Jacob, but he has 400 men with him. Common sense tells us that one doesn't bring that many men as it regards a mere greeting. It is almost positive that Esau had other things in mind, and they were not exactly meant to be pleasant.

Jacob has asked for grace, and in the immediate sense, this was not to be granted; however, the Lord, as we shall see, would beautifully and wondrously change things.

FEAR

"Then Jacob was greatly afraid and distressed: and he divided the people who were with him, and the flocks, and herds, and the camels, into two bands;

"And said, If Esau come to the one company, and smite it, then the other company which is left shall escape" (Gen. 32:7-8).

Upon hearing this news concerning his brother Esau, Jacob immediately begins to make plans, and then he prays. He should have prayed first.

Once again, we come back to the *"manifestation of Angels."* As wonderful as that was, it didn't have much effect on Jacob because Manifestations cannot change an individual. In other words, despite this great Vision, Jacob was unchanged, and, in reality, Jacob was the problem. In this problem of the flesh, he tries to manage Esau instead of leaning on God.

As we see the first years of Jacob's life, which, in fact, spanned over half, his first thought was always a plan. In this we have a true picture of the poor human heart. True, he turns to God after he makes his plan and cries to Him for Deliverance, but no sooner does he cease praying than he resumes the planning.

PRAYING AND PLANNING

Concerning this, Mackintosh said: *"Now, praying and planning will never go together. If I plan I am leaning more or less on my plans; but when I pray, I should lean exclusively upon God. Hence, the two things are perfectly incompatible, they virtually destroy each other. When my eyes fill with my own management of things, I am not prepared to see God acting for me; and, in that case, prayer is not the utterance of my need, but the mere superstitious performance of something which I think ought to be done, or it may be, asking God to sanctify my plans. This will never do. The life of Faith is not asking God to sanctify and bless my means, but it is asking Him to do it all Himself."*

In other words, we don't make our plans and then ask God to bless them, but rather ask God to make the plans, which are guaranteed then of Blessing.

VICTORY

A few paragraphs back we made the statement, *"God cannot give victories to the flesh but only to His Son, the Lord Jesus Christ."* Perhaps we could say it a little differently and make it a little more understandable:

"God cannot give victories to man but only to His Son, the Lord Jesus Christ."

Now, that statement is very simple, but if you, the reader, properly understand it, you will understand a great deal of the entirety of the New Covenant. In brief, it means this:

Jesus Christ was and is our Substitute, and that means our Substitute in all things. He did for us what we could not do for ourselves and undid all that was wrong, which we did do.

For instance, He kept the Law of Moses in every respect, which, of course, we did not do and, in fact, could not do. However, as our Substitute, He addressed every nuance of the Law, kept it perfectly, and as the Scripture says, *"Blotted out the handwriting of Ordinances that was against us, which was contrary to us, and took it out of the way, nailing it to His Cross"* (Col. 2:14).

When He did this, which He did by the giving of Himself in Sacrifice, this atoned for all sin, past, present, and future. By atoning for all sin, He took away Satan's legal right to hold man in captivity, at least for all who will believe (Jn. 3:16; Col. 2:15).

VICTORY IS ALL IN CHRIST AND WHAT HE DID AT THE CROSS

Consequently, all the victories were purchased and won by the Lord Jesus Christ, which was done at the Cross. Therefore, the way that we obtain victory is by simply trusting in what Christ has done for us at the Cross and placing all our Faith there. This then gives the Holy Spirit the latitude to work within our hearts and lives (Rom. 6:3-14; 8:1-2, 11; I Cor. 1:17-18, 21, 23; 2:2, 5; Gal. 6:14).

So, all victory has already been won by Christ, all done for us, and we obtain this victory by simply trusting in what Christ has done. Because He did all of this at the Cross, this is why the Cross is so very, very important.

Consequently, God will not give victories to man because such would have been and is impossible at any rate. The victories were given to Jesus Christ simply because He is the One Who paid the price for victory in every capacity. Therefore, we simply believe Him, trust in Him, and place our Faith in Him and what He did for us in His Sufferings, and His Victory becomes ours, which it is intended to do.

ACTIVITY OR POSITION?

Many Christians erroneously think that victory comes by activity. What do we mean by that?

Millions of Christians are constantly doing this and doing that, with many of these things being very good things. They think that all of this *"doing"* will gain them victory or whatever it is they seek. It won't!

Everything we have in Christ is not at all because of our religious activity, but is altogether ours because of our position in Christ, which we attain simply by Faith. I speak of Faith in Him and what He did for us in His Great Sacrifice. However, it's very hard for many Christians to accept that which I've just said. They want to think that their activity is what gives them place and position in Christ, but again I emphasize, it doesn't!

When we do all of these religious things, whatever they may be, then, whether we realize it or not, we are, in effect, saying that what Jesus did at the Cross did not suffice, and we have to add something to His Work. These religious things we do may even be good in their own respect. However, if our faith and trust is in that, and this is the key, then we are tying to add something to His Work. Now, we can't have it both ways. What He did is either a *"Finished Work,"* or it isn't, and if it isn't, then we really have nothing at all.

To be frank, whenever we place our faith and confidence in our activity, we are insulting Christ to the highest degree. We may not think of such as doing that, but that's exactly what is happening. The writer of the following song is right:

"Nothing in my hands I bring,
"Simply to the Cross I cling!"

WHAT DO WE MEAN BY POSITION?

I am what I am in Christ, and I have what I have in Christ because of my position in Christ. I gained this position by simply believing Him and what He did for me at the Cross. That's why we constantly speak of the Cross, constantly extol the Cross, and constantly lift up the Cross. That's why Paul said: *"But God forbid that I should glory (boast), save in the Cross of our Lord Jesus Christ, by Whom the world is crucified unto me, and I unto the world"* (Gal. 6:14).

I lift up the Cross or boast of the Cross exactly as Paul because that's where I was able to attain my position as it regards Christ. I place my Faith and trust in Him and what He did, never divorcing Him from the Cross, and, thereby, am granted instant position in our Lord. Of course, as you understand, Christ is not still on the Cross. At this moment He is seated by the Right Hand of the Father at the Throne of God actually making intercession for all Saints. So, when we speak of the Cross, we are speaking of what Jesus there did.

Now, once again, that's very difficult for most Christians to accept. They want to think they have earned their place, or else, they have attained this position, whatever it is they think they have in the Lord, simply because they belong to a certain church, denomination, etc. For them to be told that none of that has anything to do with place and position in Christ doesn't sit well. As we have previously stated, it was very grievous for Abraham to have to give up Ishmael; likewise, it's very grievous for most Christians to have to give up their *"works religion."* However, please understand this:

As a Believer, there is no position in Christ attained by *"works"* of any nature. It simply cannot be done. It is all by Faith. Paul also said:

"Christ has become of no effect unto you, whosoever of you are justified by the Law; you are fallen from Grace" (Gal. 5:4). He has just said that if the Believers in Galatia, or anywhere else for that matter, trusted in circumcision or anything else of that nature, *"Christ shall profit you nothing"* (Gal. 5:2). So, Jacob makes

his plans and then prays, typical of most modern Christians, but little solving anything.

THE PRAYER

"And Jacob said, O God of my father Abraham, and God of my father Isaac, the LORD which said unto me, Return unto your country, and to your kindred, and I will deal well with you:

"I am not worthy of the least of all the Mercies, and of all the truth, which you have showed unto your servant; for with my staff I passed over this Jordan; and now I am become two bands.

"Deliver me, I pray you, from the hand of my brother, from the hand of Esau: for I fear him, lest he will come and smite me, and the mother with the children.

"And You said, I will surely do you good, and make your seed as the sand of the sea, which cannot be numbered for multitude" (Gen. 32:9-12).

There is no fault with Jacob's prayer. It is sincere, honest, straight forward, and, as well, puts self into its proper place and God in His Proper Place.

However, as we have stated, it is often hard to detect what is the real ground of the heart's confidence. We think that we are leaning upon the Lord and trusting exclusively in Him when, in reality, we are leaning on some scheme of our own devising.

Jacob asked the Lord to deliver him but then turned right around and tried to appease Esau with a present. Was he placing more confidence in a few lambs than he did Jehovah, to Whom he had just been committing himself?

LOOKING IN OUR OWN HEART

These are the questions which naturally arise out of Jacob's actions in reference to Esau. However, the hurtful part is that we can more readily answer them by looking into the glass of our own hearts. There we learn, as well as on the page of Jacob's history, how much more apt we are to lean on our own management rather than on that of God.

However, it's not that simple. We must be brought to see the end of our own efforts, that they are perfect folly, and that the true path of wisdom is to repose in full confidence upon God. As previously stated, we do not come there readily, quickly, easily, or without price. This fits perfectly with what Paul said in his second Letter to the Corinthians:

"And lest I should be exalted above measure through the abundance of the Revelations, there was given to me a thorn in the flesh, the messenger of Satan to buffet me, lest I should be exalted above measure.

"For this thing I besought the Lord thrice, that it might depart from me.

"And He said unto me, My Grace is sufficient for you: for My Strength is made perfect in weakness" (II Cor. 12:7-9).

Having made the above statements, we find Jacob closer now than he had been 20 years earlier at Beth-el. By him addressing the Lord as the *"God of my father Abraham, and God of my father Isaac,"* it portrays the fact that he understood the tremendous responsibility that was upon him, which included greatly his grandfather and his father. He claims, and rightly so, that his journey back to Canaan was in obedience to the Lord, even as it was.

THERE IS MORE TO BE LEARNED

Jacob then disavows all self-worthiness, rightly claiming that he did not deserve even the least of the Mercies of God. Despite his present problems, this is plainly not the same Jacob of 20 years before. He thanks God for the Truth and claims that the Lord has shown him great things, which was, no doubt, true. However, there was still more to be learned, as there is always more to be learned.

The *"two bands"* of which he speaks was his own doing and not that which the Lord had told him to do. That's what we meant by trying to manage the situation instead of letting the Lord take care of what needed to be done.

He asked for deliverance from the hand of his brother and gave us the greatest reason, *"The mother with the children."* He knew that these children were the beginning of this great Nation which God would raise up. This was a part of the Truth that God had revealed to him. Consequently, he realized their significance.

He closes his prayer by reminding the Lord of the Promises which Jehovah had made. In fact, and as stated, the prayer was excellent; however, even though the Patriarch had come a long way, he still had a way to go as it regarded his Faith.

A PRESENT FOR ESAU

"And he lodged there that same night; and took of that which came to his hand a present for Esau his brother;

"Two hundred she goats, and twenty he goats, two hundred ewes, and twenty rams,

"Thirty milk camels with their colts, forty cattle, and ten bulls, twenty she asses, and ten foals.

"And he delivered them into the hand of his servants, every drove by themselves; and said unto his servants, Pass over before me, and put a space between drove and drove.

"And he commanded the foremost, saying, When Esau my brother meets you, and asks you, saying, For

Whom do you work? and where are you going? and whose are these before you?

"Then you shall say, They be your servant Jacob's; it is a present sent unto my lord Esau: and, behold, also he is behind us.

"And so commanded he the second, and the third, and all that followed the droves, saying, On this manner shall you speak unto Esau, when you find him.

"And say you moreover, Behold, your servant Jacob is behind us. For he said, I will appease him with the present that goes before me, and afterward I will see his face; peradventure he will accept of me.

"So went the present over before him: and himself lodged that night in the company.

"And he rose up that night, and took his two wives, and his two womenservants, and his eleven sons, and passed over the ford Jabbok.

"And he took them, and sent them over the brook, and sent over that he had" (Gen. 32:13-23).

The idea was that there would be a space between the droves and when Esau came upon a drove, he was to be told that this was a present from Jacob. One-half mile or so further on he would meet another drove and would be told the same thing. Thus, Jacob hoped to appease his brother.

As stated, considering the number of animals which Jacob gave Esau as a gift, it tells us how large his flocks must actually have been.

The brook Jabbok crosses the Jordan about 30 miles north of the Dead Sea.

THE BROOK JABBOK

On a trip to Israel some years past, we visited the country of Jordan as well. Coming up on the eastern side of the Jordan River, intending to cross near the

Sea of Galilee over into Israel, which we did, we, of course, had to pass over the brook Jabbok. I asked the driver if he would stop, which he did, with all of us getting out of the bus.

Most of the people with us had little idea as to why we had stopped or the significance of this brook.

From where the modern road runs, at least where we crossed, is approximately five or six miles west toward the Jordan River. This is where Jacob would have crossed and, as well, would have had the wrestling match with the Lord.

As I stood there that day looking at this brook, which, incidentally, is quite large, at least as brooks go, my mind went back to that moment which took place about 3,700 years ago. Jacob figures so prominently in the great Plan of God that everything he did was of vast spiritual significance. This which took place by the side of the brook Jabbok was one of the most important events of all.

> *"I can see far down the mountain*
> *"Where I have wandered many years.*
> *"Often hindered on my journey*
> *"By the ghosts of doubts and fears.*
> *"Broken vows and disappointments*
> *"Thickly strewn along the way*
> *"But the Spirit has led unerring,*
> *"To the land I hold today."*

JACOB

Chapter Eight

THE WRESTLING

THE WRESTLING

*"And Jacob was left alone; and there wrestled a Man
with him until the breaking of the day"* (Gen. 32:24).

In the *"making of a man,"* we find here a turning
point in the history of this very remarkable person. To
be left alone with God is the only true way of arriving at
a just knowledge of ourselves and our ways. We could
never get a true estimate of nature and all its operations until we have weighed them in the balance of the
Sanctuary, so to speak, and there we ascertain their real
worth. No matter what we may think about ourselves,
or yet, what man may think about us, the great question is, *"What does God think about us?"* The answer
to this question can only be heard when we are *"left
alone,"* away from the world, away from self, away from
all the thoughts, reasonings, imaginations, and emotions
of mere nature, and *"alone"* with God. Thus, and thus
alone, can we get a correct judgment about ourselves.

Please note that it was not Jacob wrestling with a
man, but a Man wrestling with Jacob. My wrestling
with a man and a Man wrestling with me presents two
totally different ideas to the mind. In the former case,
I want to gain some object from him; in the latter he
wants to gain some object from me. In Jacob's case,
the Divine Object was to bring him to see what a poor,
feeble, worthless creature he was.

This *"Man"* Who wrestled with Jacob was none other
than Jehovah, i.e., *"a preincarnate appearance of the
Lord Jesus Christ."*

THE WRESTLING OF GOD WITH US

Two things are brought into play here:
1. The struggle, whatever direction it might take
as it regards the Believer, is always on the part of

God with us. This we must never forget. The initiative is always with Him, and it begins immediately at Conversion.

2. This struggle is to bring us to a particular place in the spiritual sense. In other words, we must come to the end of self to where our trust and Faith for everything is always in God. While most all Believers think of themselves in this capacity, the truth is, the *"flesh"* is far more predominant in us than even the best of us realize, whomever that might be. So, the purpose is away from self-reliance to total reliance on God. To be sure, the Believer is not brought to that place quickly or easily.

As we have stated, the Holy Spirit through Abraham showed us *"Justification by Faith."* It took 12 Chapters in this great Book of Genesis to do that. Jacob showed us *"Sanctification by Faith,"* and it took about 25 Chapters, a little over double the amount of the former. This means that it's much easier to *"receive this life"* than it is to *"live this life."* I sense the Presence of God even as I dictate these words. How so much all of us have found this out, and for most of us, the hard way.

THE FLESH

"And when He saw that He prevailed not against him, He touched the hollow of his thigh; and the hollow of Jacob's thigh was out of joint, as He wrestled with him" (Gen. 32:25).

The sentence of death must be written on the flesh — the Power of the Cross must be entered into before we can steadily walk with God.

We have followed Jacob so far amid all the windings and workings of his extraordinary character. We have seen him planning and managing during his 20 years of sojourn with Laban. However, not until he *"was left alone"* did he get a true idea of what a perfectly helpless thing he was in himself.

This dislocating of Jacob's hip reduced his strength to little more than zero. This is what it was meant to do. All of his life Jacob had depended on his scheming and ability. By the Lord crippling him, this was to serve as a symbol of the eradication of the flesh and total dependence on the Lord. As Jacob was left a cripple, so must the flesh in all of us be crippled to the extent that it can no longer be leaned upon.

WHAT IS THE FLESH?

Paul uses this term, *"Flesh,"* very often (Rom. 3:20; 6:19; 7:5, 18, 25; 8:1, 3, 5, 8).

When Paul speaks of the *"flesh,"* he is speaking of our own personal ability, strength, acumen, will power, talent, etc. In other words, it is what we can do as a human being apart from the Holy Spirit.

Of course, as human beings, we are made of flesh, and we have to live our lives in the flesh, even as Paul said (Gal. 2:20).

However, when it comes to living for God, which refers to Holiness, Righteousness, and Christlikeness in every respect, such cannot be produced by our own strength, ability, etc. All of these things are Works of the Holy Spirit and can accordingly be carried out exclusively by Him.

However, this is the hardest thing for the Believer to learn. We keep trying to make ourselves holy and to make ourselves righteous, all by our efforts, actions, and ability. It's hard for us to learn that it cannot be done. Regrettably, probably about ninety percent of all the actions of Believers present that which are functions of the flesh.

So, if we do not attain to Holiness and Righteousness by our own efforts and ability, whatever that might be, how, in fact, do we come to these places and positions in Christ?

WALKING AFTER THE SPIRIT

Paul said: *"There is now no condemnation to them who are in Christ Jesus, who walk not after the flesh, but after the Spirit"* (Rom. 8:1).

So, how does one *"walk after the Spirit,"* which alone can bring the person to the desired place in Christ?

Let us give the answer first. Walking after the Spirit is simply looking totally and completely to Christ and what He has done for us at the Cross, which is always the domain of the Holy Spirit. In other words, the Holy Spirit works exclusively within the parameters, so to speak, of the Finished Work of Christ. The Cross made it possible for Him to function within us as He does. He demands that we have Faith in that Finished Work, which, of course, is the Sacrifice of Christ and is referred to as, *"His Sufferings."* To explain this, Paul said: *"For the Law (a Law devised by the Godhead in eternity past) of the Spirit (Holy Spirit) of Life (all life comes from Christ through the Spirit) in Christ Jesus (meaning that everything the Spirit does within our lives is all done through and by what Jesus did at the Cross) has made me free from the Law of Sin and Death"* (Rom. 8:2).

In fact, the only way that one can have victory over *"the Law of Sin and Death,"* is by and through the *"Law of the Spirit of Life in Christ Jesus."*

Unfortunately, many Believers think that doing spiritual things constitutes walking after the Spirit. It doesn't!

While doing spiritual things may be very good, and I speak of reading the Bible, witnessing to the lost, engaging in prayer, giving money to the Work of the Lord, etc., these things, in fact, should be a result of walking after the Spirit but do not, within themselves, constitute walking after the Spirit.

DEAD TO THE FLESH

Since the Early Church, I suppose Christians have been trying to *"die to the flesh,"* or whatever type of terminology one would like to use. While growing up, as a child I heard this statement I suppose untold numbers of times.

Any Christian who is trying to die to the flesh always (and I use *"always"* advisedly) tries to do so by the flesh. To be sure, the flesh cannot subdue the flesh. All of this results in such a Christian being about one of the meanest Christians you've ever met in all your life.

The only way that one can *"die to the flesh"* is by simply looking to Christ and what Christ did at the Cross, understanding that we are now *"in Him"* (Jn. 14:20). This means that we are not trusting in ourselves but totally in what He has done for us.

This is something that we must actually do on a daily basis, hence, Jesus saying: *"If any man will come after Me, let him deny himself, and take up his cross daily, and follow Me"* (Lk. 9:23).

This is something we work at day-by-day, even as the Master said. We die to the flesh by being in what He has done, and only what He has done.

THE BLESSING

"And He (the Lord) said, Let Me go, for the day breaks. And he (Jacob) said, I will not let You go, except You bless me" (Gen. 32:26).

When sore broken by that mighty Hand, he ceased to wrestle and clung with weeping and supplication to the very God Who wounded him. Then it was that he got the victory and the glorious name of Israel.

Up to this point he had held fast by his own ways and means, but now, he is brought to say, *"I will not let You go."* Let the reader understand that Jacob did not express himself thus until *"the hollow of his thigh was touched."* May we learn to cling more simply to God Alone so that our history may be more character- ized by that holy elevation above the circumstances through which we are passing. It is not by any means an easy matter to get to the end of *"flesh,"* in every shape and form, so as to be able to say, *"I will not let You go except You bless me."*

EXCEPT YOU BLESS ME

To say this from the heart, and to abide in the power of it is the secret of all true strength. Jacob said it when the hollow of his thigh was touched, but not until then. He struggled long ere he gave way because his confidence in the flesh was strong. *"The Power of Christ"* can only *"rest on us"* in connection with the knowledge of our infirmities. Christ cannot put the seal of His Approval upon nature's strength, its wis- dom, or its glory: all these must sink that He may rise. Nature can never form, in any one way, a pedes- tal on which to display the Grace or Power of Christ. If it could, then might flesh glory in His Presence, but this we know can never be.

The *"Blessing"* which Jacob had schemed and planned to get for so many years, he now knows can only be given to him by God. Many presently, and possibly all of us at one time or the other, have tried to gain the Blessing in all the wrong ways. It can only be obtained through the Cross and our Faith in that Finished Work. There is no other way!

ISRAEL

"And He (the Lord) said unto him (Jacob), What is your name? And he said, Jacob.

"And He said, Your name shall be called no more Jacob, but Israel: for as a prince have you power with God and with men, and have prevailed" (Gen. 32:27-28).

It should be readily understandable that the Lord already knew Jacob's name. So, why did He insist on Jacob pronouncing his name?

He wanted Jacob to admit who and what he actually was. His name portrayed that. To be sure, that just might be the hardest task for the Lord to perform within our lives. We do not yield easily to the truth. We like to think of ourselves in glowing terms, and whatever our failures, we minimize them while at the same time, almost always, we magnify the failures of others. However, it was not until Jacob fully admitted what he actually was, which was a deceiver, a trickster, and a supplanter, that the Lord then blessed him.

Grace is a peculiar thing. We must be disqualified and admit that we don't deserve it before we are qualified to receive it. To say it another way: the qualification for Grace is to be disqualified.

Upon the admittance as to what he actually was, the Lord then instituted the change. It was symbolized by his name being changed from *"Jacob the deceiver"* to *"Israel the Prince with God."* What a change!

And yet, as we shall see, Jacob's change was instant but yet gradual. What do we mean by that?

PROGRESSIVE SANCTIFICATION

We are possibly witnessing here both *"positional Sanctification"* and *"conditional Sanctification."* As far as God was concerned, Jacob's new position regarding Sanctification had now been established and would be unmovable because it was established in Christ. However, his *"condition,"* as will be painfully obvious through the remainder of the Book of Genesis, will not always be up to his *"position."* So, during the times that the *"condition"* falls short, the Lord refers to the Patriarch as *"Jacob."* The times it reaches up to his *"position,"* he is referred to as *"Israel."* Consequently, we will find as Jacob's life goes forward that little by little through the years he is more and more referred to as *"Israel."* So it is prayerfully with us. We grow in Grace and the knowledge of the Lord, or at least that should be the idea (II Pet. 3:18).

PENIEL

"And Jacob asked Him, and said, Tell me, I pray You, Your Name. And He said, Wherefore is it that you do ask after My Name? and He blessed him there.

"And Jacob called the name of the place Peniel: for I have seen God face to face, and my life is preserved.

"And as he passed over Penuel the sun rose upon him, and he halted upon his thigh.

"Therefore the children of Israel eat not of the sinew which shrank, which is upon the hollow of the thigh, unto this day: because He touched the hollow of Jacob's thigh in the sinew that shrank" (Gen. 32:29-32).

As is obvious here, Jacob asked the name of the One with Whom he wrestled. The Lord's Answer is revealing. He responded with another question:

"Wherefore is it that you do ask after My Name?" The idea is, Jacob by now ought to know Who the One is with Whom he has been struggling. The next statements prove that he did.

When the Scripture says that the Lord *"blessed him there,"* He was, at that moment, in effect, giving Jacob *"power with God and with men."*

I HAVE SEEN GOD

Showing that Jacob now knew the One with Whom

he had struggled, he names the place, *"Peniel,"* which means, *"The Face of God,"* or *"I have seen God face to face, and my life is preserved."*

Man, whomever he might be and whatever he might be, must have a Revelation from God exactly as did Jacob. It may be somewhat different, and it may not be quite as dramatic as that which Jacob experienced; however, to the individual involved, it will definitely be dramatic and, therefore, life-changing.

Now, please understand, we're not speaking here of Manifestation nearly as much as we are speaking of Revelation.

I can say without fear of contradiction that every single person down through history who has truly been Born-Again has always come by this tremendous, life-changing experience by a Revelation from God. If there has been no Revelation, there has been no *"Born-Again"* experience. Please believe me, if there has truly been a Born-Again experience, the individual will know that of which I speak.

The church is too full of individuals who have mentally accepted the Lord, at least after a fashion. They have been somewhat intellectually moved, but they've never really had a Born-Again experience. In other words, there's never been a Revelation of God to their souls. Therefore, while they might be religious, they aren't truly Saved.

The means by which the Lord has chosen to make evident this Revelation is the Cross, always the Cross! Unless the Cross enters the picture, there can be no Revelation simply because the Cross is the means by which the Grace of God is extended to undeserving souls.

Whenever the unbelieving sinner sees the Cross, to be sure, he will see Christ, and the Revelation will be evident.

A NEW DAY

The sun is now rising, but upon a crippled Jacob. The crippling did not bring about instant Sanctification, at least as far as the conduct of Jacob was concerned. However, it brought about the possibility of such, which was ultimately made real in Jacob's life.

As Believers, we have to understand that all victory and all solutions, whatever the need might be, stem totally and completely from the Cross of Christ. Once we learn this Divine Truth, which is the Foundation of all Truth, then we will begin to properly see ourselves, i.e., *"the flesh."* Blessed be the day that the sun rose upon Jacob, for he has passed a milestone in the *"making of a man."*

THE SINEW WHICH SHRANK

This particular sinew is the proper name for the large tendon, which takes its origin from the spinal cord, and extends down the thigh unto the ankle. It was called by the Greeks the, *"Tendo Achilles,"* because it reaches to the heel. So, the *"heel-catcher"* became a *"prince with God."*

Whether Jacob remained crippled all of his life or was this way for a short period of time, we aren't told. Nevertheless, this was so prominent in Jewish thinking that it became a symbol of Jacob's tryst with God, or perhaps it could be better said, *"God's Tryst with Jacob."*

ESAU

"And Jacob lifted up his eyes, and looked, and, behold, Esau came, and with him four hundred men. And he (Jacob) divided the children unto Leah, and unto Rachel, and unto the two handmaids" (Gen. 33:1).

The action of Esau shows how groundless were Jacob's fears and how needless his plans. The straight path of Faith and obedience is free from the tormenting apprehensions which wear out the doubting heart.

It is obvious that Esau is a powerful chieftain. How so sad that this man did not see the great Spiritual Truths. In that case it would have been, *"The God of Abraham, Isaac, and Esau,"* but such was not to be!

The time has come that Jacob and Esau will now meet. Jacob sees him coming with his cortege of some 400 men.

At this particular time, Esau must have been a powerful chieftain, at least one of, if not the most, powerful in that part of the world.

However, while Esau had 400 men, armed, no doubt, Jacob had a host of Angels, while unseen, but yet, so powerful!

PERFECT FAITH?

Some have criticized Jacob as it regards the preparation concerning his family, especially considering that he has just had this great Visitation from the Lord with great Promises further extended to him. I think, however, we do wrong when we always judge Faith according to perfection. No man's Faith is perfect. Even the best of us, whomever that might be, are always in a growing process. If we demand perfection out of Jacob, why don't we demand perfection of ourselves, especially considering that we are now living under a better Covenant? While never condoning wrongdoing or even a lack of Faith, still, if in his shoes, would we have done any better or even as well? Armchair generals and Monday morning quarterbacks are a dime a dozen. Until you've been there, it is best to withhold judgment, and rather try to learn the lesson which the Holy Spirit desires to teach us from the Text.

Many, many years ago, one of the Pilgrim Fathers preached a message containing the following points, which we would do well to heed. They are:

• When we hear something bad about someone, we should realize that what we are hearing is gossip and treat it accordingly.

• Even if we actually know the facts of the case, the truth is, still, we little know the degree of spiritual warfare involved.

• If we were placed in their shoes, as stated, would we do any better, or even as well?

HIS BROTHER

"And he put the handmaids and their children fore-most, and Leah and her children after, and Rachel and Joseph hindermost.

"And he passed over before them, and bowed him-self to the ground seven times, until he came near to his brother.

"And Esau ran to meet him, and embraced him, and fell on his neck, and kissed him: and they wept" (Gen. 33:2-4).

If it is to be noticed, Jacob put the ones he thought the least important in the forefront, followed by Leah and her children, and then bringing up the very rear were Rachel and Joseph, whom Jacob looked at the most favorably. As it all proved out, all of this was unnecessary.

As Jacob was approaching Esau his brother, the Scripture says, *"Ran to meet him."* He embraced him and kissed him, with both of them weeping.

It was the Lord Who had mellowed Esau, and I think that is obvious. This should be a lesson to us as well.

The Holy Spirit gave to David the following formula, which he gave to us, and if followed, will lead to Spiritual prosperity. It is:

"Trust in the LORD, and do good; so shall you dwell in the land, and verily you shall be fed.

"Delight yourself also in the LORD: and He shall give you the desires of your heart.

"Commit your way unto the LORD; trust also in Him; and He shall bring it to pass.

"Rest in the LORD, and wait patiently for Him . . ." (Ps. 37:3-5, 7).

To abbreviate what is said here, we can reduce it to four words. They are:

1. Trust
2. Delight
3. Commit
4. Rest

A proper adherence to these Passages will solve any problem.

THE MEETING

"And he lifted up his eyes, and saw the women and the children; and said, Who are those with you? And he said, The children which God has graciously given your servant.

"Then the handmaidens came near, they and their children, and they bowed themselves.

"And Leah also with her children came near, and bowed themselves: and after came Joseph near and Rachel, and they bowed themselves" (Gen. 33:5-7).

All of this proclaims the fact that the entirety of the family of Jacob showed great respect to Esau, which they should have done. Little did the older brother know (older by a few moments) that this family was the seedbed of the great Nation of Israel, to whom would be given the great Promises of God. Here they stand by the brook Jabbok, and if the mighty men of the world had taken notice of this retinue, they would have scarcely given it a second glance.

From the time that God had called Abraham out of Ur of the Chaldees to this particular time of Jacob had been a little less than 200 years. The boys upon whom Esau looked would be the beginning of great Tribes, and from one of these, Judah, would come the Prince of Glory, of whom Esau had no knowledge. This, in effect, was the *"birthright"* of which he had no inter-est. In fact, he never did understand spiritual things, because he couldn't understand spiritual things.

THE GIFT

"And he said, What is the meaning of all these droves which I met? And he said, These are to find grace in the sight of my lord.

"And Esau said, I have enough, my brother; keep that you have unto yourself.

"And Jacob said, No, I pray you, if now I have found grace in your sight, then receive my present at my hand: for therefore I have seen your face, as though I had seen the Face of God, and you were pleased with me.

"Take, I pray you, my blessing that is brought to you; because God has dealt graciously with me, and because I have enough. And he urged him, and he took it" (Gen. 33:8-11).

In the eastern countries of that particular time, the thing which Jacob proposed, as it regarded the giving of this gracious gift to Esau, was very, very important.

In the first place, the gift was to be a token signify-ing that the difficulty had been settled.

Second, if the problem was serious, the one offering the gift was to make it commiserate with the problem itself. In other words, the largeness of Jacob's gift, and it was large, signified that he felt that he had greatly wronged Esau, which he had!

Last of all, if the recipient took the gift, it meant that the matter was dropped, forgiven, and would not cause further problems. So, concerning the gift, when the Scripture says that Esau *"took it,"* this signified that the differences between him and Jacob had now been settled.

SEIR

"And he said, Let us take our journey, and let us go, and I will go before you.

"And he said unto him, My lord knows that the children are tender, and the flocks and herds with young are with me: and if men should overdrive them one day, all the flock will die.

"Let my lord, I pray you, pass over before his servant: and I will lead on softly, according as the cattle that goes before me and the children be able to endure, until I come unto my lord unto Seir.

"And Esau said, Let me now leave with you some of the folk who are with me. And he said, There is no need! let me find grace in the sight of my lord" (Gen. 33:12-15).

Jacob, in a sense, mentioned the fact that he would eventually come to Esau in Seir; however, there is no record that Jacob ever went to this particular place.

Despite the fact that they had settled their differences between them, the two, although twins, had nothing in common.

Whenever a person comes to the Lord, everything changes. That's why the Scripture says, *"Old things pass away, and all things become new"* (II Cor. 5:17).

SUCCOTH

"So Esau returned that day on his way unto Seir.

"And Jacob journeyed to Succoth, and built him an house, and made booths for his cattle: therefore the name of the place is called Succoth.

"And Jacob came to Shalem, a city of Shechem, which is in the land of Canaan, when he came from Padan-aram; and pitched his tent before the city.

"And he bought a parcel of a field, where he had spread his tent, at the hand of the children of Hamor, Shechem's father, for an hundred pieces of money.

"And he erected there an Altar, and called it El-elohe-Israel" (Gen. 33:16-20).

Jacob went to Succoth, but the Lord had not said, *"I am the God of Succoth,"* but rather, *"I am the God of Beth-el."* Events will prove that he was not in the Will of God.

Jacob erects an Altar at Shechem, for the conscious is uneasy without religious forms, but the divinely chosen place for the Altar was Beth-el.

The Altar was a Type of the Cross. While the Cross is the place for wrongdoing, and, in fact, the only place, still, it is never to be used to condone wrongdoing. It cannot cover wrongdoing which the Believer has no intention of forsaking.

Several things are wrong as presented in these Passages:

• As stated, Jacob was not told by the Lord to go to Succoth.

• This is the first mention of a house being built by a Patriarch. He was to be a pilgrim instead.

• His *"buying a parcel of a field"* only made a bad matter worse.

• He built an Altar, but it was not in the right place.

• He called it, *"God, the God of Israel."* Its name given by him, however, couldn't atone for the Altar being built in the wrong place.

Some, if not all, these things may seem to be

innocent. In fact, they very well may be. However, the idea which we wish to present proclaims the fact that if one is out of the Will of God, everything one does lends toward the wrong direction.

> *"Hear the blessed Saviour calling the oppressed,*
> *"O ye heavy laden, come to Me and rest;*
> *"Come, no longer tarry, I your load will bear,*
> *"Bring Me every burden, bring Me every care."*

> *"Are you disappointed, wandering here and there,*
> *"Dragging chains of doubt and loaded down with care?*
> *"Do unholy feelings struggle in your breast?*
> *"Bring your case to Jesus, He will give you rest."*

> *"Stumbling on the mountains dark with sin and shame,*
> *"Stumbling toward the pit of Hell's consuming flame,*
> *"By the powers of sin deluded and oppressed,*
> *"Hear the tender Shepherd, Come to Me and rest."*

> *"Have you by temptation often conquered been,*
> *"Has a sense of weakness brought distress within?*
> *"Christ will sanctify you, if you'll claim His Best,*
> *"In the Holy Spirit, He will give you rest."*

JACOB

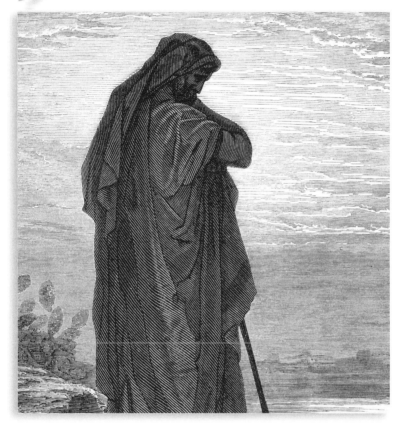

Chapter Nine

WRONG DIRECTION

WRONG DIRECTION

DINAH

"And Dinah the daughter of Leah, which she bore unto Jacob, went out to see the daughters of the land" (Gen. 34:1).

Jacob is here personally responsible for the conduct of his children. This principle operates today as well.

Dinah went out to see the daughters of the land. That seemed very innocent, but these daughters led to a companionship with shame. The Christian has to be very careful concerning the world and its ways. Consequently, we see in this Chapter the bitter fruit of the sojourn of Jacob at Shechem.

It is believed that Dinah was about 16 or 17 years of age at the time. The thing which took place with her did not happen immediately after Jacob came to Succoth but, more than likely, several years later.

The evidence is, a festive gathering was taking place, and Dinah desired to be a part of the social entertainment.

Her going out to *"see the daughters of the land"* is not meant to imply that she had not done this previously. This particular time is highlighted for the simple reason of what happened to her.

The Believer has to be very, very careful so far as the world is concerned. While we must not become legalistic, at the same time, we must understand that the world and its ways are not our friend. Satan has many temptations and snares in the world which have tripped up many Believers, Dinah not being the first or the last.

Understanding these things, we are foolish if we ignore the allurement of the world and its dangers. While we as Believers are in the world, we must never be of the world. We believe in separation but not isolation. To be factual, separation is very, very important! The moment separation breaks down is the moment the problem begins, as with Dinah.

SHECHEM

"And when Shechem the son of Hamor the Hivite, prince of the country, saw her, he took her, and lay with her, and defiled her.

"And his soul clave unto Dinah the daughter of Jacob, and he loved the damsel, and spoke kindly unto the damsel" (Gen. 34:2-3).

Pulpit Commentary says: *"Dinah paid the full penalty of her carelessness. She suffered the fate which Satan had planned for Sarah and Rebekah in the land of Pharaoh and Abimelech; she was seen and taken by the son of the prince, forcibly it seems, against her will, but yet with the claims of affection by her lover."*

It does seem that he actually loved her and *"spoke kindly unto her,"* which probably refers to proposed marriage.

WATCH AND PRAY

Whatever it seemed at the moment, all of this was an attempt by Satan to spoil the godly line with intermarriage, which both Abraham and Isaac sought so diligently to avoid.

The Believer must ever understand that Satan and his demon hosts are forever seeking to hinder and hurt in some way. That's the reason the Scripture plainly tells us to *"Watch and pray . . ."* (Mat. 26:41). When we speak of Christians doing certain things or not doing certain things, it's not a matter of legalism, but rather a matter of the possibility of Satan getting the advantage. Because of its great significance, let us say it again:

We as Believers must evaluate every single thing we do, every place we go, and all the things we propose. Can the Evil One use whatever it is we propose to do as an avenue to cause us problems? That's the basic reason that the Scripture also says that we are to *"Abstain from all appearance of evil"* (I Thess. 5:22).

THE PLAN OF SATAN

"And Shechem spoke unto his father Hamor, saying, Get me this damsel to wife.

"And Jacob heard that he had defiled Dinah his daughter: now his sons were with his cattle in the field: and Jacob held his peace until they were come.

"And Hamor the father of Shechem went out unto Jacob to commune with him.

"And the sons of Jacob came out of the field when they heard it: and the men were grieved, and they were very angry, because he had wrought folly in Israel in lying with Jacob's daughter: which thing ought not to be done" (Gen. 34:4-7).

The Scripture uses the phrase, *"Jacob's daughter,"* in order to proclaim the fact that this was as bad as it could be. It would have been bad enough if one of Jacob's handmaids had been raped, but his daughter. . . .

Marriages were arranged in those days, so Shechem asked his father Hamor to work out the arrangement with Jacob that Dinah could now be his wife.

The account of all of this tells us that Dinah's brothers were extremely angry when they heard this sordid news about their sister.

In those times, it was thought that a brother was more dishonored by the seduction of his sister than a man could be by the infidelity of his wife. A man could divorce his wife and then she was no longer his, they reasoned, while a sister and daughter remained always sister and daughter.

ISRAEL

In Verse 7, the word, *"Israel,"* is used for the first time to designate Jacob's descendants, who ultimately actually became the great Nation of Israel. The phrase, *"Folly in Israel,"* became a standing expression for acts done against the sacred character that belonged to Israel as a separated and covenanted community as the People of God. This expression was used more so for sins of the flesh than anything else (Deut. 22:21; Judg. 20:10; Jer. 29:33).

Pulpit Commentary says: *"The special wickedness of Shechem consisted in dishonoring a daughter of one who was the head of the theocratic line, and therefore under peculiar obligations to lead a holy life."*

Unfortunately, it becomes painfully obvious as to the sordid failure of almost all concerned, even as shortly we will read the account of Joseph's brothers seeking to kill him. Despite the fact that the Church is also a holy line in this world, even more so, one might say, than Israel of old, still, the problem is just as acute presently, if not more so, than then.

JACOB AND LEAH

Dinah was partly to blame here, but Jacob and Leah were far more to blame. They should not have allowed their daughter to frequent the festivities of the Canaanites.

It is understandable that young girls and young boys would want companionship of their own age, which, more than likely, Dinah lacked. As well, it is almost certain that the festivities of that particular time were very enticing, whatever they would have been.

Perhaps Dinah went to this entertainment without the knowledge of her mother and dad; however, that is not likely. Not wanting to say, *"No,"* to their daughter, the thought is probably correct that they allowed her to attend, but to their chagrin. As young girls would do, she, no doubt, pestered them for permission, wanting to go. In such a situation, it is much easier to say, *"Yes,"* than it is to say, *"No."* However, the results of saying, *"Yes,"* can be very painful, as the Holy Spirit here makes such very plain.

DWELL WITH US

"And Hamor communed with them, saying, The soul of my son Shechem longs for your daughter: I pray you give her him to wife.

"And you make marriages with us, and give your daughters unto us, and take our daughters unto you.

"And you shall dwell with us: and the land shall be before you; dwell and trade you therein, and get you possessions therein" (Gen. 34:8-10).

We shall see when we come to Chapter 35 that Jacob was led to take a higher and a wider view of God. However, at Shechem, he was manifestly on low ground, and he was made to smart for it, as is always the case when we stop short of God's Own Ground. So, we see in Chapter 34 the bitter fruits of his sojourn at Shechem.

Due to being out of the Will of God, which means he was in the wrong place, he walked in constant apprehension of danger to himself and his family. The manifestation of an anxious, cautious, timid, and calculating spirit is utterly incompatible with a life of genuine Faith in God.

The plan of Satan was to corrupt the sacred line by intermarriage with the Canaanites, who were a part of the curse originally placed on Canaan, the son of Ham, regarding the situation with Noah (Gen. 9:23-27).

PAYMENT

"And Shechem said unto her (Dinah's) father and unto her brethren, Let me find grace in your eyes, and what you shall say unto me I will give.

"Ask me never so much dowry and gift, and I will give according as you shall say unto me: but give me the damsel to wife" (Gen. 34:11-12).

The *"dowry"* represented the price paid for a wife and given to her parents (Ex. 22:16; I Sam. 18:25).

In essence, Shechem was saying that whatever they asked, as far as monetary value was concerned, he would pay it.

CIRCUMCISION

"And the sons of Jacob answered Shechem and Hamor his father deceitfully, and said, because he had defiled Dinah their sister:

"And they said unto them, We cannot do this thing, to give our sister to one who is uncircumcised; for that is a reproach unto us:

"But in this will we consent unto you: If you will be as we be, that every male of you be circumcised;

"Then will we give our daughters unto you, and we will take your daughters to us, and we will dwell with you, and we will become one people.

"But if you will not hearken unto us, to be circumcised; then will we take our daughter, and we will be gone" (Gen. 34:13-17).

The sons of Jacob practiced deceit in this situation, which Jacob personally had no part therein. They pledged an agreement with the Canaanites but demanded that all the males in that area be circumcised.

This proposal was sinful since they had no right to offer the sign of God's Covenant to a heathen people.

Verse 23 proclaims the fact that Hamor was practicing deceit as well. In this, Hamor said they would ultimately have all the cattle and substance which then belonged to Jacob.

The sons of Jacob are now beginning to show the traits which will lead to their desire to murder Joseph. They concoct a plan, an evil plan, incidentally, to avenge their sister Dinah. They will have vengeance not only on the boy who did this and his father, but on all the men and boys of the city, who, incidentally, had no part in this thing. The sad thing is, this was the Church of its day!

Their proposal to the Shechemites is if all of their men and boys will be circumcised, then all the people can be joined together. Of course, they had absolutely no intention of doing such a thing.

This thing which they would do would be so cruel and so ungodly that Jacob, on his deathbed, could offer no excuse or reason for the atrocious cruelty practiced there.

This proposal was sinful and wicked for three reasons:

1. As stated, they had no right to offer the sign of God's Covenant to a heathen people.

2. They had less right to employ it in ratification of a merely human agreement.

3. They had the least right of all to employ it in duplicity as a mask for their treachery.

THE PROPOSAL ACCEPTED

"And their words pleased Hamor, and Shechem Hamor's son.

"And the young man deferred not to do this thing, because he had delight in Jacob's daughter: and he was more honorable than all the house of his father.

"*And Hamor and Shechem his son came unto the gate of their city, and communed with the men of their city, saying,*

"*These men are peaceable with us; therefore let them dwell in the land, and trade therein; for the land, behold, it is large enough for them; let us take their daughters to us for wives, and let us give them our daughters.*

"*Only herein will the men consent unto us for to dwell with us, to be one people, if every male among us be circumcised, as they are circumcised.*

"*Shall not their cattle and their substance and every beast of theirs be ours? only let us consent unto them, and they will dwell with us.*

"*And unto Hamor and unto Shechem his son hearkened all who went out of the gate of his city; and every male was circumcised, all who went out of the gate of his city*" (Gen. 34:18-24).

In that Hamor agreed so readily, we must come to the conclusion that circumcision was something not unknown to them and, as well, something that they regarded as a small price to pay for what they believed they would receive.

It is obvious that the Hivites were few in number, and so the addition of Jacob's large family would make their tribe even stronger, or so they reasoned.

Jacob's sons were of the Semitic stock and, therefore, possessed of high physical and mental endowments. As they were rich in cattle and other wealth, their incorporation with the people of Shechem, or so they reasoned, would raise it to a high rank.

So they agreed to Hamor's proposal.

THE TERRIBLE DEED

"*And it came to pass on the third day, when they were sore, that two of the sons of Jacob, Simeon and*

Levi, Dinah's brothers, took each man his sword, and come upon the city boldly, and killed all the men.

"And they killed Hamor and Shechem his son with the edge of the sword, and took Dinah out of Shechem's house, and went out.

"The sons of Jacob came upon the slain, and spoiled the city, because they had defiled their sister.

"They took their sheep, and their oxen, and their asses, and that which was in the city, and that which was in the field.

"And all their wealth, and all their little ones, and their wives took they captive, and spoiled even all that was in the house.

"And Jacob said to Simeon and Levi, You have troubled me to make me to stink among the inhabitants of the land, among the Canaanites and the Perizzites: and I being few in number, they shall gather themselves together against me, and kill me; and I shall be destroyed, I and my house.

"And they said, Should he deal with our sister as with an harlot?" (Gen. 34:25-31).

There is nothing that could justify what these men did.

They murdered all the men and boys of the small town, and did so in cold blood, one might say. It was Simeon and Levi who committed this vile deed, but their brothers, it seems, helped them in the confiscating of the sheep and oxen, along with *"all their wealth."* Joseph didn't join in this debacle.

The Scripture says that they also made captives of all the women and the little children. What they did with these, we aren't told. It even appears that they stripped the dead. In fact, the annals of uncivilized warfare scarcely record a more atrocious crime.

The sin of Shechem was avenged, but it was avenged by the commission of an even greater sin by Simeon and Levi. To say the least, this is certainly not the way that the Kingdom of God was to be spread.

> *"One day when Heaven was filled with His*
>   *Praises,*
> *"One day when sin was as black as could be,*
> *"Jesus came forth to be born of a virgin,*
> *"Dwelt among men, my example is He!"*
>
> *"One day they led Him up Calvary's mountain,*
> *"One day they nailed Him to die on the tree;*
> *"Suffering anguish, despised and rejected:*
> *"Bearing our sins, my Redeemer is He!"*
>
> *"One day they left Him alone in the garden,*
> *"One day He rested, from suffering free;*
> *"Angels came down over His Tomb to keep vigil;*
> *"Hope of the hopeless, my Saviour is He!"*
>
> *"One day the grave could conceal Him no longer,*
> *"One day the stone rolled away from the door;*
> *"Then He arose, over death He had conquered;*
> *"Now is ascended, my Lord evermore!"*
>
> *"One day the trumpet will sound for His Coming,*
> *"One day the skies with His Glories will shine;*
> *"Wonderful day, my Beloved One, bringing:*
> *"Glorious Saviour, this Jesus is mine!"*

JACOB

<u>Chapter Ten</u>

THE ALTAR

THE ALTAR

"And God said unto Jacob, Arise, go up to Beth-el, and dwell there: and make there an Altar unto God, Who appeared unto you when you fled from the face of Esau your brother" (Gen. 35:1).

Jacob is called back to the Altar, the true Altar! He goes *"up"* to Beth-el. Physically and morally, it was indeed a going up.

When, therefore, he learns that he is to meet God publicly at Beth-el, he at once feels that idols cannot be brought into fellowship with that House. Accordingly, he commands the surrender of all the strange gods that were in the hands and ears of his clan, and he buried them beneath the oak at Shechem.

Nearly 10 years had passed since Jacob had come back to the Land of Promise. At that time, those 10 years ago, the Lord had said to Jacob, *"Return unto your land, I am the God of Beth-el."* The Lord did not say, *"I am the God of Succoth,"* but how slow was he to obey this command! Had he gone immediately to Beth-el, and had he *"dwelt"* there as commanded, what sin and sorrow would have been avoided!

The Lord tells the Patriarch to build an *"Altar"* at Beth-el. He had built one at Succoth, but being out of the Will of God, the Grace of God was hindered.

THE WILL OF GOD

The words of Paul, some 1,800 years before that great Apostle uttered them, come into play here. They are: *"Shall we continue in sin, that Grace may abound?"* The answer was instant: *"God forbid. How shall we, who are dead to sin, live any longer therein?"* (Rom. 6:1-2).

Jacob was out of the Will of God at Succoth, as I

think is overly obvious. All the altars in the world cannot rectify that. In fact, I think one can say without fear of contradiction that the altar at Succoth was not recognized by God.

It is amusing that the Lord would pinpoint the place by saying to Jacob, *"When you fled from the face of Esau your brother."*

It's like the Lord was saying to Jacob, *"I told you to go there 10 years ago, but you didn't obey Me; consequently, you've brought on yourself real trouble. Now I'm telling you the second time, 'Go up to Beth-el.'"*

This confirms the principle on which we have been dwelling. When there is failure or declension, the Lord calls the soul back to Himself. *"Remember therefore from where you have fallen; and repent, and do the first works . . ."* (Rev. 2:5).

This is the Divine principle of Restoration. The soul must be recalled to the very highest point; it must be brought back to the Divine Standard.

GOD'S STANDARD

It is when thus recalled to God's High and Holy Standard that one is really led to see the sad evil of one's fallen condition. What a fearful amount of moral evil had gathered around Jacob's family, unjudged by him until his soul was roused by the call to *"go up to Beth-el."* Shechem was not the place in which to detect all this evil. The atmosphere of that place was too much impregnated with impure elements to admit of the soul's discerning, with any degree of clearness and precision, the true character of evil. However, the moment the call to Beth-el fell on Jacob's ear, *"Then Jacob said unto his household, and to all who were with him, 'put away the strange gods that are among you. . . .'"*

STRANGE GODS

"Then Jacob said unto his household, and to all who were with him, Put away the strange gods that are among you, and be clean, and change your garments:

"And let us arise, and go up to Beth-el; and I will make there an Altar unto God, Who answered me in the day of my distress, and was with me in the way which I went.

"And they gave unto Jacob all the strange gods which were in their hand, and all their earrings which were in their ears; and Jacob hid them under the oak which was by Shechem" (Gen. 35:2-4).

As we've said some pages back, while the new cross might be in vogue, it is the old Cross that brings one to Repentance. Jacob and all with him were to do five things:

1. Put away the strange gods that were among them.
2. Be clean.
3. Change your garments.
4. Arise and go up to Beth-el.
5. Make there an Altar unto God.

Due to the manner in which this is written, the Hebrew scholars claim there were many strange gods among them. These were objects of idolatrous worship, even brought by Jacob's servants from Mesopotamia, or adopted in Canaan, or perhaps possessed by the women taken captive during the problem of the recent past.

Regrettably, the modern church is full of strange gods. We have with us the gods of humanistic psychology, the gods of so-called contemporary Christian music, the gods of false doctrine, which promise material riches, and many more we could name. As the command was given to Jacob so long ago, it is given now as well.

THE THREEFOLD DANGER

While preaching a Campmeeting many years ago with A.N. Trotter, he made a statement which I have never forgotten.

He brought out the fact that the church was running aground, as he put it, on three things. Those three things are:

1. Education: He was actually referring to the wrong kind of education. More and more, the colleges built by denominations are less and less Bible and more and more secular. Education is attained in the things of the world but woefully lacking as it regards the Word of God. This is a sure way to destroy the People of God! In other words, the church is too much depending on education and not the Spirit of God.

2. Money: The church is running aground on money. While, of course, money is needed, if we, however, compromise the Message for the sake of money, then we've sold out for the proverbial 30 pieces of silver.

3. People: If we sacrifice the Message in order to get people, then we have destroyed ourselves. Our primary purpose and goal are not people, but rather the Will of God.

He was right: the church is running aground today on education, money, and people.

MUSIC

Some paragraphs back I mentioned contemporary Christian music as being one of the *"strange gods."* To try to justify this type of music, which, incidentally, is not of God, which means that it's ultimately of the

Devil, the claim is made that this music reaches the young people, etc.

There are two answers to that:

1. It is only the Holy Spirit Who can reach anybody for God. Our problem is, we're reaching too many without the Holy Spirit, thereby, filling our churches with people who aren't even saved.

2. Our purpose in music, which is an integral part of worship, must never be to reach people, but rather to please God. I have little interest in what the young people want or what the older people want, but only what the Holy Spirit wants.

Now you know why most of the church world doesn't too very much like Jimmy Swaggart. Irrespective of that, I must one day stand before God. The bottom line then will not be whether people like me or not, but whether I obeyed the Lord as it regards this Ministry. That's the only thing that counts.

The Scripture mentions *"their earrings which were in their ears."* These were employed for purposes of idolatrous worship, which were often covered with allegorical figures and mysterious sentences, and supposed to be endowed with a talismanic virtue (Judg. 8:24; Isa. 3:20; Hos. 2:13).

The Scripture says that Jacob buried all of these *"strange gods under the oak which was by Shechem."*

The cleansing and changing of garments were meant to symbolize moral and spiritual purification of the mind and heart.

EL-BETH-EL

"And they journeyed: and the Terror of God was upon the cities that were round about them, and they did not pursue after the sons of Jacob.

"So Jacob came to Luz, which is in the land of

Canaan, that is, Beth-el, he and all the people who were with him.

"And he built there an Altar, and called the place El-beth-el: because there God appeared unto him, when he fled from the face of his brother.

"But Deborah Rebekah's nurse died, and she was buried beneath Beth-el under an oak: and the name of it was called Allon-bachuth" (Gen. 35:5-8).

The Scripture says, *"And they journeyed."* This is a journey that they should have taken when Jacob came back into the Land of Promise some years before.

No doubt, the news got out among the various different tribes in that part of the world concerning what had happened at Shechem. However, the Scripture says that no one touched Jacob as he and his retinue journeyed toward Beth-el because *"the terror of God was upon the cities that were round about them."*

What exactly the Lord did, we aren't told, but one thing is certain: had the Lord not done this thing to protect Jacob and his family, they would, no doubt, have been slaughtered.

THE ALTAR

When Jacob arrived at Beth-el, in accordance with the Command of the Lord, *"He built there an Altar."* He called the place, *"El-beth-el."* The name means, *"God of the House of God."* At Shechem, he kept his Saviour and his Salvation to himself and permitted his family and household to retain their idols. However, this cannot be suffered if God is to be recognized and publicly confessed as the God of Beth-el, that is, *"The God of the House of God;"* for the elect are His House, and *"judgment must begin at the House of God."* Then we can say, *"Holiness becomes Your House, O Lord, forever!"* When, therefore, he learns that he is to meet

God publicly at Beth-el, he at once feels that idols cannot be brought into fellowship with that House, and accordingly, he commands, as stated, the surrender of all the strange gods that were in their hands and in their ears.

The Divine Command to Jacob some 10 years back, and now renewed, was, *"Go up to Beth-el and dwell there."* Disobedience preceded this command and followed it. In Beth-el itself, there was victory, but before Beth-el was Shechem, and after Beth-el, Edar. The one was the scene of Dinah's dishonor; the other, as we shall see, was of Reuben's incest.

FAITHFULNESS

We're told here that Deborah, Rebekah's nurse, died. The introduction of this aged servant is very affecting, and Jacob's excessive grief reveals an affectionate nature.

What, no doubt, sharpened his grief was that though he might close the eyes of his mother's servant, who was well over 150 years old when she died, he, by his own misconduct, was not to see that mother herself!

That she was now with Jacob may be accounted for by supposing that Jacob had paid a visit to his father at Hebron and brought her back with him to Shechem.

She, along with Rebekah, had left Padan-aram for Canaan upwards of 150 years ago. That the Holy Spirit would mention her passing proclaims to us the fact that she was faithful all of those years, and that she is now with Christ. As Abraham, Isaac, and Jacob kept account of these happenings, and years later, Moses, under the Inspiration of the Holy Spirit, would place these accounts in the Holy Writ, little did she realize that thousands of years later untold millions would read these Verses. However, let those who live for God, no matter how menial their task may seem to be, know and understand that what they do is eternal.

THE APPEARANCE OF GOD

"And God appeared unto Jacob again, when he came out of Padan-aram, and blessed him" (Gen. 35:9).

The renewal of the name given to Jacob some 10 years earlier at Peniel was possibly done because the Patriarch feared that he had forfeited the Blessing. However, the Calling of the Gifts is without Repentance.

Along with this renewal is revealed to Jacob the glorious title of, *"El-Shaddai,"* i.e., *"God Almighty,"* the God Who is able to fulfill to him the Promises made here.

Incidentally, in Verse 14 is found the first mention of a Drink-Offering.

The Lord appearing to Jacob was a visible Manifestation. The appearance was similar to what had taken place with Jacob when he had wrestled with the Lord, which took place some 10 years earlier.

The Lord blessed the Patriarch, and we find the account of the Blessing which follows.

The phrase, *"When he came out of Padan-aram,"* should have been translated, *"When he came from Padan-aram."* The word, *"Out,"* is not in the Hebrew.

ISRAEL

"And God said unto him, Your name is Jacob: your name shall not be called any more Jacob, but Israel shall be your name: and He called his name Israel" (Gen. 35:10).

I personally feel that the Lord reaffirmed this great Promise and action which He had taken with Jacob some years earlier. I have no doubt that the Patriarch was fearful that he had forfeited this great Blessing because of not going to Beth-el when commanded to do so by the Lord, but rather going to Succoth where had been the occasion of much failure.

The path of Faith is not one that we trod without mishap. I can remember a day way back in the early 1990s when I felt the same as Jacob must have felt. Had I forfeited the great Call of God upon my life? Then, in a prayer meeting that October night, the Lord wondrously and graciously spoke to my heart, saying: *"I'm not a Man that I should lie, neither the Son of Man that I should repent. What I have blessed, nothing can curse."* The statement was taken from Numbers 23:19-20. There was no doubt in my mind then as to what I must do. As well, there is no way that I have words to properly express the joy that filled my heart, that the Lord had spoken to me, reaffirming all that He had called me to do. Jacob must have felt the same way when the Lord spoke to him.

GOD ALMIGHTY

"And God said unto him, I am God Almighty: be fruitful and multiply; a Nation and a company of nations shall be of you, and kings shall come out of your loins" (Gen. 35:11).

The Lord repeated to Jacob substantially the Promises made to Abraham.

Perhaps Jacob had many questions in his mind concerning his own conduct in that many problems, no doubt, had arisen because of that. These tribes were bitterly opposed to him because of the action at Succoth. So, the Lord not only reaffirmed His Promise in action as it regarded Jacob becoming *"Israel,"* but further told him that whatever needed to be done, God was able to do it, for He is *"Almighty."*

Jacob's purpose, the very reason for his being, was to raise up a Nation for the elect purpose of bringing the Redeemer into the world.

The *"kings"* of which the Lord spoke at this time began with Saul but actually should have begun with David. However, the ultimate King will be, and is, the Lord Jesus Christ.

Could Jacob's Faith reach out and claim all of this? It not only could, but it did!

THE LAND

"And the land which I gave Abraham and Isaac, to you I will give it, and to your seed after you will I give the land" (Gen. 35:12).

While Jacob had purchased a piece of land close to Shechem (Gen. 33:19), due to the action of his sons, he had been forced to leave it. So, in reality, he owned nothing of this land of which the Lord promised to give him. In effect, it would be his seed which would inherit the land, and would do so about 275 years later.

For the people of whom the Lord spoke here, who would be raised up out of Jacob's loins, they would have to have a domicile, a place that would be specifically for them. Canaan was that land, hence, the Lord calling Abraham to this place at the very beginning. As we've said, all of this was for the purpose of bringing the Redeemer into the world, Who would be the *"Seed of the woman,"* and Who would bruise Satan's head (Gen. 3:15).

THE PILLAR OF STONE AND THE DRINK-OFFERING

"And God went up from him in the place where He talked with him.

"And Jacob set up a pillar in the place where He talked with him, even a pillar of stone: and he poured a Drink-Offering thereon, and he poured oil thereon.

*"And Jacob called the name of the place where God
spoke with him, Beth-el"* (Gen. 35:13-15).

Williams says: *"In Verse Fourteen is found the first
mention of a Drink-Offering. When God first revealed
Himself to Jacob at this spot, which was some thirty
years earlier, Jacob poured oil upon the pillar; now he
pours both oil and wine. Then, there was Godly fear,
now, there is joy as well as fear.*

*"This Stone figures Christ the Rock of Ages, anointed
with the Holy Spirit, typified by the oil, and filled with
the joy of God, typified by the 'Drink-Offering.'"*

All of this which happened to Jacob at this particular time, this great manifestation of God's Presence,
was more solemn than any of the previous occasions
upon which the Deity had revealed Himself to Jacob.
It was, in fact, the acknowledgment of the Patriarch as
the heir of the Abrahamic Covenant.

DRINK-OFFERING

The *"Drink-Offering"* used here was probably grape
juice. It would then have been called, *"Wine"*; however, the word, *"Wine,"* could mean either grape juice
or the fermented variety. Considering that this represented Christ, it is highly unlikely that the fermented
variety would have been used.

The *"Drink-Offering"* symbolized joy, but, as well,
it symbolized helplessness on the part of both the
Redeemer and the Believer. It symbolized the Redeemer
in His Incarnation, God becoming Man, which meant
that He would be helpless within Himself, but yet, would
do great and mighty things because of the Empower-
ment of the Holy Spirit (Lk. 4:18-19).

As it regards the symbolization of the Believer, the
pouring out of a *"Drink-Offering,"* which was done before
the Lord, or, in essence, *"before His Face,"* pointed to

the helplessness of the one doing the pouring, and that he recognized his helplessness. Consequently, Jacob pouring out the *"Drink-Offering"* here symbolized far more than meets the eye. At long last, he is, in essence, saying, *"Lord, I cannot do this thing without You. Within myself I am helpless, so I must have Your Leading, Grace, and Power."*

THE CROSS

". . . If any man will come after Me, let him deny himself, and take up his cross daily, and follow Me.

"For whosoever will save his life shall lose it: but whosoever will lose his life for My Sake, the same shall save it" (Lk. 9:23-24).

In essence, as the Believer takes up his cross, and does so daily, which means that he renews his Faith each and every day, this specifies that he is looking to the benefits of what Jesus did there in the giving of Himself in Sacrifice. In looking to the Cross, and doing so on a daily basis, in essence, the Believer is saying that he cannot do this thing himself, cannot live this life by his own strength and power, and must have the Power of the Holy Spirit, which is obtained by exhibiting Faith in the Finished Work of Christ. In the doing of this, as stated, even on a daily basis, the Believer is, in essence, pouring out a *"Drink-Offering"* each and every day.

The doing of this, which loses one's life in Christ, in effect, *"saves it."* This brings a joy unspeakable and full of glory, which, as well, and, as stated, the *"Drink-Offering"* symbolized.

PERSONAL WEAKNESS

One cannot have the strength of the Lord until one recognizes one's own weakness. As long as one is relying upon his personal strength, acumen, ability, education, motivation, power, etc., he frustrates the Grace of God simply because the *"Strength of the Lord is made perfect only in weakness"* (II Cor. 12:9). This means that the Believer recognizes that within his own strength and power, he cannot do what ought to be done or be what he ought to be. He must understand this. If we understand such, then the Holy Spirit can do for us what we cannot do for ourselves.

In fact, this is the greatest struggle of the Christian, even as it was the greatest struggle for Jacob. The Patriarch depended long upon his own strength and cunning. It took much time, test, and trial before he realized that he couldn't do this thing as it should be done, and that he must rely totally and wholly on the Lord.

Even in this Age of Grace, and as one might say, the Age of the Holy Spirit, this remains the biggest problem for the Believer. We talk about leaning totally on Christ and solely trusting Christ, but the truth is, if the Believer is not looking exclusively to the Cross, then in some way, the Believer, whether he realizes it or not, is looking to himself. *"Self,"* to be sure, is so very, very subtle. We know how to dress up self until it looks like the Lord, but, in reality, it isn't. In this problem which plagues all Believers and, in effect, is the cause of every difficulty, the Cross of Christ becomes the bone of contention, so to speak.

THE CROSS AND UNBELIEF

Faith is judged by the Lord as it relates to the Cross (Rom. 6:3-5, 11; I Cor. 1:17-18, 23; 2:2, 5). Faith is either registered in the Cross, or it's registered in self. God will not honor the type registered in self. It is only Faith in the Cross that He honors and recognizes, which says that Jesus paid it all, and, in fact, accomplished a Finished Work (Rom. 6:1-14; 8:1-11; I Cor. 1:17, 18, 23; 2:2).

Let the reader understand, while we may speak of having Faith in Christ or in the Word of God, if it's not Faith in the Cross, in essence, what Jesus there did, then it's not really Faith in Christ. That's why Paul spoke of *"another Jesus,"* *"another spirit,"* and *"another gospel"* (II Cor. 11:4). If Christ is at all divorced from the Cross, then He becomes *"another Jesus,"* meaning it's not the Jesus of the Bible. Regrettably, that's where the majority of the modern church actually is. It talks about Jesus constantly but not about the Cross. In fact, the Cross is ignored in most circles, if not downright rejected. That is the blueprint for spiritual disaster.

So, Jacob now poured out a *"Drink-Offering"* before the Lord, which represented something wonderful and glorious in his life. Of course, he did this at the behest of the Holy Spirit. However, the Spirit had him to do such simply because Jacob had now come to a place to where he was beginning to let the Lord plan for him instead of him trying to do the planning himself. In other words, he was admitting that he was as weak as water; therefore, he needed the Leading and Guidance of the Lord in every aspect of his life, and so do we!

BENJAMIN

"And they journeyed from Beth-el; and there was but a little way to come to Ephrath: and Rachel travailed, and she had hard labour.

"And it came to pass, when she was in hard labour, that the midwife said unto her, Fear not; you shall have this son also.

"And it came to pass, as her soul was in departing, (for she died) that she called his name Ben-oni: but his father called him Benjamin.

"And Rachel died, and was buried in the way to Ephrath, which is Beth-lehem.

"And Jacob set a pillar upon her grave: that is the pillar of Rachel's grave unto this day" (Gen. 35:16-20).

The journey that Jacob was taking was probably to Mamre to visit Isaac. From the last Verses of this Chapter, it seems that Jacob made it there before the great Patriarch died.

In the journey to Mamre, they were close to Beth-lehem when Rachel began to go into labour. Twice the Scripture says that she had *"hard labour."*

The baby was born, which occasioned the death of Rachel. However, before she died, *"She called his name Ben-oni,"* which means, *"Son of my sorrow."* She had asked the Lord for another son when Joseph was born, and the Lord had answered her prayer, but it occasioned her death.

In the culture of that day, the mother usually named the child, as here. If the father stepped in, it would be an unusual situation, even as it was here. Jacob felt that the name she had chosen was not appropriate, so the Patriarch countermanded her request and *"called him Benjamin,"* which means, *"Son of my right hand."* Rachel was buried near Beth-lehem.

ISRAEL

"And Israel journeyed, and spread his tent beyond the tower of Edar" (Gen. 35:21).

It had possibly been some 10 years since the Lord had spoken to Jacob about his name change, which took place at the great wrestling (Gen. 32:24-28). Even though the Lord had said to him at that time, *"Your name shall be called no more Jacob, but Israel: for as a prince you have power with God and with men, and have prevailed,"* in the intervening 10 years, Jacob had not been referred to by that name at all. However, now, for the first time, the Holy Spirit refers to the Patriarch as *"Israel."*

It is strange that this would be done at a time of great sorrow on Jacob's part when he had lost his most wonderful possession, his Rachel. As we have stated, Jacob was his name of weakness, Israel, of strength, and yet, he was only named Israel in connection with suffering, wandering, and dishonor. But yet, this illustrates exactly what happened to Paul when the Lord said to him: *". . . My Grace is sufficient for you: for My Strength is made perfect in weakness . . ."* (II Cor. 12:9).

The point I wish to make is, if the modern church would analyze Jacob at this point, they would see his failure at Succoth, which came about because he was out of the Will of God, and now the loss of Rachel, and would hardly think of him as *"Israel."* In fact, at this stage, he would be greatly depreciated in the eyes of the church. His outward circumstances certainly don't look favorable. He seems to be in a state of disarray. He is brokenhearted, disconcerted, and in just a few days, will lose his father as well. But yet, the Holy Spirit refers to him now as *"Israel."*

This means that we must be very careful as to how we judge people. In fact, we should not judge them at all! Through many dangers, toils, and snares, Jacob was learning to lean totally on the Lord and to trust Him completely. As stated several times, this position doesn't come quickly, easily, or without difficulty.

ISRAEL AND SINFUL FAILURE

"And it came to pass, when Israel dwelt in that land, that Reuben went and lay with Bilhah his father's concubine: and Israel heard it. Now the sons of Jacob were twelve" (Gen. 35:22).

Understanding that Jacob is referred to as *"Israel"* two times in this one Verse, considering the circumstances, again it is incumbent upon us to see what the Holy Spirit is doing.

Why would the Holy Spirit at this time refer to Jacob twice as *"Israel,"* considering the circumstances in which it is given? Reuben, his first born, commits incest with Bilhah, which is an abomination, to say the least. And yet, in this setting the Holy Spirit will refer to Jacob in a very positive manner.

The only answer that one could give is that during this very trying time, Jacob leaned on the Lord totally and completely, looking to Him for Leading and Guidance.

The old Jacob would, no doubt, have taken matters into his own hands upon hearing what Reuben had done, with very negative results. The new *"Israel"* does what should be done and no more, and then puts everything into the Hands of the Lord.

For this sin, Reuben was afterwards disinherited (Gen. 49:4; I Chron. 5:1).

THE SONS OF JACOB

"The sons of Leah; Reuben, Jacob's firstborn, and Simeon, and Levi, and Judah, and Issachar, and Zebulun:

"The sons of Rachel; Joseph, and Benjamin:

"And the sons of Bilhah, Rachel's handmaid; Dan, and Naphtali:

"And the sons of Zilpah, Leah's handmaid: Gad, and Asher: these are the sons of Jacob, which were born to him in Padan-aram" (Gen. 25:23-26).

All except Benjamin were born in Padan-aram.

For all of its problems, this family consisted of the Church of that day, one might say.

These men, with the exception of Joseph and Benjamin, were anything but examples of Righteousness. In fact, they were examples of unrighteousness. However, gradually over time, they would change, which we will witness before the end of this account in the great Book of Genesis.

ISAAC

"And Jacob came unto Isaac his father unto Mamre, unto the city of Arbah, which is Hebron, where Abraham and Isaac sojourned.

"And the days of Isaac were an hundred and fourscore years.

"And Isaac gave up the ghost, and died, and was gathered unto his people, being old and full of days: and his sons Esau and Jacob buried him" (Gen. 35:27-29).

This account is not given in chronological order. The death of Isaac took place some 10 to 12 years after Joseph had been sold into Egypt.

Isaac was 60 when his sons were born; Jacob was 120 years of age at his father's death, and 130 when he appeared before Pharaoh (Gen. 47:9). As Joseph was 17 when sold into Egypt (Gen. 37:2), and 30 when raised to power in Egypt (Gen. 41:46), and as the seven years of plenty and two of the years of famine had passed before Jacob went down into Egypt, it follows that the cruel deed whereby he was robbed of Joseph was committed about 10 to 12 years before the death of Isaac.

Esau came from Mount Seir to pay the last service due to his deceased parent. Jacob accords him that precedence, which had once belonged to him as Isaac's firstborn, by placing his name first.

They laid Isaac beside his ancestral greats in the family burying-place of Machpelah, where already slept the lifeless bodies of Abraham and Sarah, awaiting the Resurrection, while his spirit and soul went to company with theirs in the better country, even an Heavenly.

Jacob was with Isaac when he died, and Esau came to the grave.

"My Faith looks up to Thee, Thou Lamb of Calvary,
"Saviour Divine! Now hear me while I pray,
"Take all my guilt away,
"O let me from this day be wholly Thine!"

"May the rich Grace impart strength to my faint-
    ing heart,
"My zeal inspire; as You have died for me,
"O may my love to Thee,
"Pure, warm, and changeless be a living fire!"

"While life's dark maze I tread,
"And griefs around me spread,
"Be Thou my guide; bid darkness turn to day,
"Wipe sorrow's tears away,
"Nor let me ever stray from You aside."

"When ends life's transient dream,
"When death's cold, sullen stream shall over me
    roll,
"Blest Saviour, then in love,
"Fear and distrust remove,
"O bear me safe above, a ransomed soul!"

JACOB

<u>Chapter Eleven</u>

JOSEPH

JOSEPH

THE LAND OF CANAAN

"And Jacob dwelt in the land wherein his father was a stranger, in the land of Canaan" (Gen. 37:1).

Jacob had spent some 20 years in Syria and, as well, approximately 10 years in Shechem where he was out of the Will of God. However, he has now settled himself in Mamre in the vale of Hebron beside his aged and bedridden father Isaac.

We must realize that the families of Abraham, Isaac, and Jacob were, in essence, the Church of that day. Regrettably, it does not present a very pretty picture. The increase in numbers does not bring about an increase in Holiness, but rather the very opposite. However, ultimately, the Grace of God would gain the upper hand, but the change would not come quickly or easily.

JOSEPH

"These are the generations of Jacob. Joseph, being seventeen years old, was feeding the flock with his brethren; and the lad was with the sons of Bilhah, and with the sons of Zilpah, his father's wives: and Joseph brought unto his father their evil report" (Gen. 37:2).

The Second Verse in this Chapter sets Joseph forward as a shepherd, 17 years of age. It is believed that his mother Rachel was still living at this time but died within the year. It must be remembered that these accounts are not necessarily given in chronological order.

The story which is about to unfold before us, of which we will only partly relay, presents itself as one of the most powerful and remarkable stories in the entirety of the Word of God. It is a powerful Testimony to the Inspiration of the Word of God; for no man, either before or after the writing of the New Testament, could have composed such a story as that of Joseph. As stated, it is one of the most remarkable in history.

Evidently, Jacob's vast herds were divided into at least two flocks, and perhaps even more. Joseph was with the sons of Bilhah and the sons of Zilpah, while the sons of Leah were evidently shepherding the other flock.

We aren't told exactly what the evil report was, which Joseph related to his father. However, it probably had to do with the immoral Canaanite practices, which his brothers evidently were participating. There is some indication that he had spoken first to them about these practices, but that only aroused resentment against him in their hearts. While these men were in the Covenant, so to speak, they were actually not a part of the Covenant, at least at this time. In other words, they knew about God, but they really didn't know God.

THE MODERN CHURCH

As one looks at this scenario, one is, as well, looking at the modern church. Out of this family of brothers, the only one presently who knew the Lord was Joseph although, as stated, all were part of the Covenant. One must remember, merely being a part of the Covenant did not mean that one necessarily knew the Lord. They gained this position by natural birth. They could only gain the latter position of knowing the Lord by a New Birth, which is evident they had not yet experienced.

So, we find here that only about one out of 11 truly knew the Lord. Benjamin had not yet been born, that is, if our chronology is correct.

Out of the 11 brothers, the Church of that day, only Joseph knew the Lord. Considering all the various denominations of the modern church, I'm not sure if the percentage is presently that high.

Out of the approximate one billion Catholics in the world, that is, if we would conclude Catholicism to be Christian, which it really isn't, the number who are truly Saved in that particular religion, and a religion it is, is abysmally small. In fact, any Catholic who truly comes to Christ, and some few do, is going to have to leave out of Catholicism. It is not possible for a true Believer to remain in that ungodly, unscriptural system.

ANOTHER GOSPEL

It grieved me to read sometime back where a group of well-known, so-called protestant preachers signed a concordant that they wouldn't try to evangelize Catholics. Their conclusion was, *"Catholics are already Saved, and so our efforts must be spent on the unsaved."*

Catholics aren't saved. If they are, the Bible means nothing. As well, these preachers, whomever they may be, aren't going to get anyone Saved, Catholics or otherwise, because the Gospel they preach is, pure and simple, *"another gospel"* (II Cor. 11:4).

When we come to the denominational world, while there are some people who are truly Saved in these ranks, that number is, as well, abysmally small. When I speak of the denominational world, I speak of those who have rejected and even denounced the Baptism with the Holy Spirit with the evidence of speaking with other Tongues. The reasons the number is small would be obvious. Having rejected the Light given on the Holy Spirit, which has taken place beginning approximately with the Twentieth Century, they have, for all practical purposes, shut the door to Christ. Understanding that every single thing done in this world, as it regards the Godhead, is done by the

Holy Spirit, the denominational world is left with little more than a philosophy of Christ.

These people, of course, claim that they haven't rejected the Holy Spirit; however, if we reject the *"Work"* of the Spirit, and I speak of the Holy Spirit Baptism, we have, in effect, rejected the Holy Spirit (Acts 2:4; 10:44-47; 19:1-7).

Sadder still, most of the modern pentecostal denominations, at least in America and Canada, are pentecostal in name only. In fact, I am told that only about one-third of the people in Assemblies of God churches and Church of God churches, the two largest pentecostal denominations, even claim to be baptized with the Holy Spirit. If that is, in fact, true, then these denominations cannot even rightly and honestly claim to be pentecostal. Sadly, many in the pentecostal world have attempted to preach the Holy Spirit without the Cross, and they are left now with neither. Likewise, but in the opposite direction, the denominational world has tried to preach the Cross without the Holy Spirit, and they are left with neither. To preach the Cross without the Holy Spirit leads to nothing but Spiritual deadness, while to preach the Holy Spirit without the Cross leads to fanaticism. That's exactly where the majority in the pentecostal world actually is.

THE SPIRIT OF THE LAODICEANS

The Charismatic world, for all practical purposes, has been rendered totally ineffective because it is shot through with false doctrine, especially the *"Jesus Died Spiritually doctrine."* This doctrine is, pure and simple, a repudiation of the Cross, which is a direct attack on the Atonement, and there could be no more serious offense than that.

Regrettably, the modern church finds itself with the spirit of the Laodiceans. Jesus said of that church:

"I know your works, that you are neither cold nor hot: I wish that you were cold or hot.

"So then because you are lukewarm, and neither cold nor hot, I will spew you out of My Mouth.

"Because you say, I am rich, and increased with goods, and have need of nothing; and know not that you are wretched, and miserable, and poor, and blind, and naked" (Rev. 3:15-17).

Coming from none other than the Lord of Glory, that is a powerful indictment! However, that characterizes the modern church to the proverbial T.

THE MESSAGE OF THE CROSS

Considering that the Holy Spirit works exclusively through the Finished Work of Christ, which, in effect, makes His Work possible, He is raising up the Message of the Cross presently, equal, I believe, to the days of the Apostle Paul. The Story of the New Covenant is the Story of the Cross, i.e., *"Jesus Christ and Him Crucified."* One might say, the Story of the Cross is the explanation of the New Covenant. Actually, the Lord Jesus Christ is the New Covenant.

The Lord gave this explanation to Paul, which he gave to us in all of his Epistles, but especially in his Epistle to the Romans.

I believe that the Lord is raising up the Message of the Cross, which, at the same time, is the Message of the Holy Spirit, as a dividing line between the true Church and the apostate church. In other words, as one looks at the Cross, so will one be either in the true Church or the apostate church. That's how important all of this is.

In fact, the Cross has always been the dividing line. However, I personally believe the Holy Spirit is going to make it an even greater Testimony today than ever before because we're coming down to the end of the Church Age.

JESUS CHRIST AND HIM CRUCIFIED

One can read the Book of Acts and see how the Church was brought in. I believe it's going to be taken out in the same manner. The facts are, most will be apostate. However, for those who embrace the Message of *"Jesus Christ and Him Crucified,"* they are going to portray the Book of Acts all over again. This means that the true Church will not be wretched, miserable, poor, blind, and naked, and we speak of the spiritual sense, but rather will have done what Christ said to do. We will *"buy of Him gold tried in the fire, that we may be (truly) rich; and white raiment (true Righteousness), that we may be clothed, and that the shame of our nakedness does not appear; and (we will) anoint our eyes with eyesalve, that we may see"* (Rev. 3:18).

The *"gold"* typifies Deity, in other words, that which is of God and not of man. The *"white raiment"* typifies the Righteousness of Christ and not the righteousness of man. The *"eyesalve"* typifies the Anointing of the Holy Spirit, which can only come upon that which is of Christ.

Because it's so very important, please allow me to say it again:

The Message of the Cross has always been the Message, is the Message now, and will ever be the Message. To reject that Message is to reject the entirety of the Word of God. One cannot have it both ways. Either what Christ did for us at the Cross suffices, or else, it doesn't, and we must turn to other things.

However, I know that it does suffice. Paul said:

"For Christ sent me not to baptize, but to preach the Gospel: not with wisdom of words, lest the Cross of Christ should be made of none effect.

"For the preaching of the Cross is to them who perish foolishness; but unto us who are Saved it is the Power of God" (I Cor. 1:17-18).

THE COAT OF COLORS

"Now Israel loved Joseph more than all his children, because he was the son of his old age: and he made him a coat of many colors" (Gen. 37:3).

If it is to be noticed, the Holy Spirit uses here the name, *"Israel,"* signifying that what was done here regarding Joseph was totally of the Lord. Many have claimed that Jacob caused this problem among his sons by favoring Joseph, etc. Not true!

The *"love"* expressed here had to do with the Lord laying His Hand on Joseph, while Jacob's other sons had rejected the Lord. Even though Jacob loved all his sons, his love for Joseph had to do with the Will of God. While he was his youngest, Benjamin not yet having been born, still, that was not the primary reason.

Because of sin on the part of his other sons, there was no fellowship between Jacob and these sons. In fact, there couldn't be any fellowship, as would be obvious. There was fellowship with Joseph because of the Touch of God on his life, and above all, his love for God.

A SPECIAL MEANING

The *"coat of many colors"* holds a special meaning. It was to be worn by the one who was to have the birthright, normally the firstborn. However, as it had been with Jacob and Esau, the firstborn, who was Reuben, would not have this position of leadership. The Holy

Spirit proclaimed that it should go to Joseph. When Jacob left this mortal coil, Joseph, in essence, was to be the High Priest of the family, which the following years graphically proved to be the case!

Jacob didn't want to make the mistake his father Isaac had made. Isaac didn't want to give the birthright to Jacob even though the Lord had made it very plain, even at the birth of the two boys, that this was to be the case. Jacob, coming by that position as a result of Isaac's procrastination, was fraught with difficulties and problems. Jacob was determined that this would not be the case with his actions. The moment the Lord told him that Joseph was to be the one, however that happened, Jacob immediately proclaimed his position by making Joseph the many-colored coat, which he would wear at certain times. As we shall see, this didn't sit well at all with his brothers.

HATRED

"And when his brethren saw that their father loved him more than all his brethren, they hated him, and could not speak peaceably unto him" (Gen. 37:4).

This perfectly epitomizes Christ, of Whom Joseph was one of the most remarkable Types found in the Word of God. God loved His Son and showed it greatly by lavishing upon Him all the Power of the Holy Spirit. As a result, the Jews, who were His Brethren, so to speak, hated Him.

So, what we see here regarding this scenario is a perfect picture of Christ.

This *"hatred,"* and hatred it is, follows down in the church regarding the same principles. What do I mean by that?

Those on whom the Lord has laid His Hand will ultimately be hated by the church. As we have previously stated, this small family, which constituted the Church of its day, had little trouble with surrounding neighbors, although they were heathen. The greatest problems came from within, even as we are studying here. It is the same with the Church. The hatred and animosity little come from without, but rather from within.

A PERSONAL EXPERIENCE

In 1982, if I remember the year correctly, the Lord spoke something to my heart that was to come to pass in totality.

It was a Saturday morning. I had gone to a place close to the Mississippi River, which is not far from our home, in order to seek the Face of the Lord, even as I often did. That morning was not to be uneventful.

As my custom then was, I would pray approximately 30 minutes, and then sit in the car and study the Word for approximately the same period of time. I would alternate doing this for most of the day.

It was sometime before noon when the Spirit of God came over me greatly, actually telling me what the core of my Message was to be as it regarded our Ministry.

At that time, we were on television over much of the free world. In fact, the telecast was translated into several languages. As a result of all this, and above all, the Anointing of the Holy Spirit, we had the largest audience in the world by far as it regarded Gospel. Many people were being Saved, even hundreds of thousands, with many lives being changed. At that time, we were in the process of constructing Family Worship Center as well as building the Bible College. That morning the Lord said this to me:

• You must use the platform of television, which I have given you, to preach Justification by Faith to the Catholics. Tell them that their church cannot save them.

- As well, you must tell the denominational world that it must come to the Holy Spirit.
- And, the Pentecostal world must come back to the Holy Spirit.

I am not quoting verbatim that which the Lord gave to me, but what I have given is the gist of what was said.

YOUR OWN WILL TURN AGAINST YOU

And then the Lord spoke again to my heart, saying, *"If you preach what I tell you to preach, you will see many Saved, but your own will turn against you."*

Then: *"Are you willing to do what I want you to do, even though the price will be high?"*

Once again, I emphasize that these are not the exact words, but basically the gist of what was said.

I knew what I was hearing was from the Lord, but I wondered as to what He meant by *"your own will turn against you."*

After a short time of deliberation, I told the Lord that I would do my very best to preach what He gave me, not adding to or taking away from the Message.

THE FULFILLMENT

I'm so very glad that I didn't know at the time the extent to what the Lord was speaking to my heart regarding my own turning against me. I'm not sure I could've stood it.

It all happened exactly as the Lord said it would. I began to preach what I felt God gave me to preach, which resulted in literally hundreds of thousands all over the world being brought to a Saving Knowledge of Jesus Christ. As well, we saw tens of thousands baptized with the Holy Spirit and untold numbers of lives gloriously and wondrously changed by the Power of God, and I exaggerate not!

However, at that time, while I understood the Cross of Christ graphically so as it regarded the initial Salvation experience, and preached it powerfully and strongly, I didn't understand the Cross as it regards Sanctification. I didn't know that the Cross plays a role just as important in our Sanctification, in other words, how we live for God even on a daily basis, as it does in the initial Salvation experience. Not knowing that, I found myself in the same situation as the Apostle Paul, which he reiterated in Romans, Chapter 7. Let me address that for a moment:

THE CROSS

I don't care who the person is or how much God is using him; if he does not understand the Cross according to Romans, Chapter 6, and the part it plays in our everyday living for God, it is absolutely impossible for that person to live a victorious life. In some way, the works of the flesh will be made evident in that person's life (Gal. 5:19-21).

SATAN

The Evil One, taking advantage of this Scriptural ignorance, which, no doubt, was also accompanied by much self-will on my part, succeeded in bringing about a terrible rupture in my life. It would cause untold heartache.

Because of my strong stand on many issues as it regarded the Word of God, I found to my dismay that many in the Church, and especially the leadership of the denomination with which I was then associated, had developed a strong animosity against me. They took full advantage to express their animosity. Not at all attempting to be melodramatic, I can describe it as nothing but *"hatred."* To boil it all down, their hatred for me was because of the Anointing of the Holy Spirit within my heart and life. They would use other things as an excuse, but what I've said is actually the truth of the matter. Sadly and regrettably, that hatred is no less today than it was then.

Now that the Lord has given me the Revelation of the Cross, which is actually the same Revelation that He gave to Paul, they are faced with a dilemma. It makes it very hard for them to accept the Message when they so very much dislike the messenger. Unfortunately, the Church doesn't have any say as it regards who the messenger is, and that's one of the great problems!

The Lord has His Messengers, and the church, through carnal activity, has its messengers. So, between these two sets of messengers, the *"hatred"* continues. How sad!

THE DREAMS

"And Joseph dreamed a dream, and he told it to his brethren: and they hated him yet the more.

"And he said unto them, Hear, I pray you, this dream which I have dreamed:

"For, behold, we were binding sheaves in the field, and, lo, my sheaf arose, and also stood upright: and, behold, your sheaves stood round about, and made obeisance to my sheaf.

"And his brethren said to him, Shall you indeed reign over us? or shall you indeed have dominion over us? And they hated him yet the more for his dreams, and for his words" (Gen. 37:5-8).

The Lord revealed the future to Joseph in a Dream. While the Dream definitely referred to him, it more so referred to Christ and Israel. He told his brothers the truth, and they hated him even more. Thus was it with Joseph's great Antitype. He bore witness to the

Truth, and his Testimony to the Truth was answered on man's part by the Cross.

The mention of Joseph's mother in Verse 10 is thought by some to be a mistake in the Sacred Text, Rachel being already dead. However, she was still living at the time and died shortly afterwards. As stated, these accounts are not necessarily given in chronological order.

Looking at these Dreams from the natural viewpoint, many have suggested that it was prideful arrogance which had Joseph to relate these dreams to his brothers. However, it was not done in pride since there is no reason to suppose that Joseph, as yet, understood the celestial origin of his dreams, much less what they meant.

JOSEPH, A TYPE OF CHRIST

Pulpit Commentary says, *"He related this in the simplicity of his heart, and in doing so he was also guided, unconsciously it may be, but still really, by an overruling providence, Who made use of this very telling of the dream as a step toward its fulfillment."*

Pulpit Commentary continues, *"In the absence of information to the contrary, we are warranted in believing that there was nothing either sinful or offensive in Joseph's spirit or manner in making known his dreams. That which appears to have excited the hostility of his brothers was not the mode of their communication, but the character of their contents."*

In fact, due to the principle of Joseph being a Type of Christ and, without a doubt, the most powerful Type in the Old Testament, no sin whatsoever is recorded as it regards this man. While he very definitely did commit sins at times simply because the Scripture says that *"all have sinned and come short of the Glory of God,"* still, these sins were not recorded because of his place and position. To be sure, if what Joseph did in relating these Dreams was wrong, the Holy Spirit would have said so, or else, ignored the incident.

While the Dream definitely had to do with Joseph, as we shall see, Joseph's life and experiences far more portray Christ. Concerning the Dream, while his brothers would definitely bow down to him, the greater meaning has to do with the time that is coming when Israel will bow down to Christ, which will take place at the Second Coming. That is by far the greater meaning, and that which the Holy Spirit intends to present.

THE TRUTH

The hatred that Joseph's brethren exhibited toward him represents the Jews in Christ's day. *"He came to His Own, and His Own received Him not."* He had *"no form nor comeliness"* in their eyes. They would not own Him as the Son of God or as the King of Israel. Their eyes were not open to behold *"His Glory, the Glory of the Only Begotten of the Father, full of Grace and Truth."* They would not have Him; they hated Him.

REVELATION

"And he dreamed yet another dream, and told it his brethren, and said, Behold, I have dreamed a dream more; and behold, the sun and the moon and the eleven stars made obeisance to me.

"And he told it to his father, and to his brethren: and his father rebuked him, and said unto him, What is this dream that you have dreamed? Shall I and your mother and your brethren indeed come to bow down ourselves to you to the earth?

"And his brethren envied him; but his father observed the saying" (Gen. 37:9-11).

As it regards Joseph, we see that in no wise did he relax his Testimony in consequence of his brothers' refusal of his first Dream. He dreams another Dream and tells it, as well, to his brethren and his father.

This was simple Testimony founded upon Divine Revelation, but it was Testimony which brought Joseph down to the pit. Had he kept back his Testimony or taken off part of its edge and power, he might have spared himself. But no, he told them the truth and, therefore, they hated him even more.

GRACE AND TRUTH

Concerning this, Mackintosh said: *"Thus was it with Joseph's great Antitype. He bore witness to the Truth — he witnessed a good confession — he kept back nothing — he could only speak the Truth because he was Truth, and his testimony to the Truth was answered, on man's part, by the Cross, the vinegar, the soldier's spear.*

"The Testimony of Christ, too was connected with the deepest, fullest, richest Grace. He not only came as 'the Truth,' but also as the perfect expression of all the love of the Father's heart: 'Grace and Truth came by Jesus Christ.' He was the full disclosure to man of what God was, and was the full disclosure to God of what man ought to have been, but was not; hence man was left entirely without excuse. He came and showed God to man, and man hated God with a perfect hatred. The fullest exhibition of Divine Love was answered by the fullest exhibition of human hatred. This is seen in the Cross; and we have it touchingly foreshadowed at the pit into which Joseph was cast by his brethren."

THE SENDING OF JOSEPH

"And his brethren went to feed their father's flock in Shechem.

"And Israel said unto Joseph, Do not your brethren feed the flock in Shechem? come, and I will send you unto them. And he said to him, Here am I.

"And he said to him, Go, I pray you, see whether it is well with your brethren, and well with the flocks; and bring me word again. So he sent him out of the vale of Hebron, and he came to Shechem" (Gen. 37:12-14).

Joseph, as we have seen, is given more Revelation through another Dream. Little did all of these men know, even Joseph or his father, as to exactly how important this Revelation actually was. In these Dreams, the Holy Spirit portrays Israel's acceptance of Christ when, in fact, at the time the Dream was given, there was no Israel, at least as far as a Nation was concerned.

The conspiracy against Joseph to murder him foreshadowed the conspiracy of the religious leaders of Israel to murder Christ.

Jacob sending Joseph to his brethren in order to find out how they were doing proves that he did not understand at all the depths of their hatred for Joseph. All of this foreshadows God sending His Son, the Lord Jesus Christ, to the Nation of Israel, even as Israel was raised up for this very purpose. However, the difference is, whereas Jacob was ignorant of the degree of hatred evidenced against Joseph, God was not ignorant at all, but knew totally of the hatred on the part of Israel, which would be evidenced toward Christ. Nevertheless, this did not deter Him at all!

THE CONSPIRACY

"And a certain man found him, and, behold, he was wandering in the field: and the man asked him, saying, What do you seek?

"And he said, I seek my brethren: tell me, I pray you, where they feed their flocks.

"And the man said, They are departed from here;

for I heard them say, Let us go to Dothan. And Joseph went after his brethren, and found them in Dothan.

"And when they saw him afar off, even before he came near unto them, they conspired against him to kill him" (Gen. 37:15-18).

Little does Jacob realize that his sending Joseph to his brothers will instigate a time of sorrow of unparalleled proportions. It will break his heart to such an extent that, in fact, there are no words that could describe, at least properly so, what Joseph's brothers did to him and, thereby, to their aged father, Jacob.

Such is sin. It has no heart. It truly steals, kills, and destroys.

The sons of Jacob were guilty of murder, for their hatred fostered such. The Scripture plainly says that *"Whosoever hates his brother is a murderer . . ."* (I Jn. 3:15), and this is so even though the deed itself may not be carried out.

A TYPE OF CHRIST

The sons of Jacob hated their brother because their father loved him. Joseph was a Type of Christ, for though He was the Beloved Son of His Father and hated by a wicked world, yet the Father sent Him out of His Bosom to visit us in great humility and love. He came from Heaven to Earth to seek and save us, and that, despite our hatred toward Him.

He came to His Own, and His Own not only received Him not but consulted, saying, *"This is the Heir, Come, let us kill Him; crucify Him, crucify Him!"* This He submitted to in pursuance of His Design to redeem and save us.

As we go forward in this narrative, we will see Christ in the actions of Joseph set out perfectly before us. As such, we must learn what the Holy Spirit is telling us through the life of this man.

Dothan was about 12 miles north of Shechem, with Shechem being about 50 miles north of Hebron. So, Joseph would have to walk about 62 miles to find his brothers.

Even before he arrived there, that is, when they saw him coming, they conspired to kill him. It was thus so with Christ, as well. When He was born, Herod sought to kill Him (Mat., Chpt. 2).

If it is to be remembered, Shechem is the place where Simeon and Levi killed all the men of that small town because their sister Dinah had been raped.

Some period of time had now passed, but the greater reason that the brothers were not fearful of reprisal is probably due to their great strength.

That Jacob would have to send a part of his herds so far away as to Shechem, a distance of some 50 miles, tells us how large these herds were and, therefore, the power of Jacob. There is a possibility that there were quite a number of other men with the brothers at this time, actually serving in their employ, which would have made this group powerful indeed.

REUBEN

"And they said one to another, Behold, this dreamer comes.

"Come now therefore, and let us kill him, and cast him into some pit, and we will say, Some evil beast has devoured him: and we shall see what will become of his dreams.

"And Reuben heard it, and he delivered him out of their hands; and said, Let us not kill him.

"And Reuben said unto them, Shed no blood, but cast him into this pit that is in the wilderness, and lay no hand upon him; that he might rid him out of their hands, to deliver him to his father again" (Gen. 37:19-22).

Partly through the personal character of Joseph,

partly through the evil passions of his brethren, partly through the apparently casual incidents of the neighborhood, partly through the Spirit of Righteousness working in the heart of Reuben, and partly through the weakness and fondness of Jacob, we see *"all things working together"* in God's Hands! He weaves the web composed of many single threads into one united, orderly pattern as a whole in which we are able to trace His Own Thought and Purpose.

When we look at Joseph in the pit and in the prison, and look at him afterwards as ruler over all the land of Egypt, we see the difference between the Thoughts of God and the thoughts of men. So, when we look at the Cross and at *"the Throne of the Majesty in the Heavens,"* we see the same thing.

Nothing ever brought out the real state of man's heart toward God but the Coming of Christ.

JUDAH

Reuben was actually the firstborn. Consequently, it was to him that the birthright should have come, which would have guaranteed him a double portion of Jacob's riches when the Patriarch came down to die. So, he would have had the most to gain from Joseph's death, who, by now, had been given the birthright instead. However, Reuben seemed to have some conscious left where his brethren did not. As such, the Scripture says, *"He delivered him out of their hands; and said, Let us not kill him."*

Several things greatly rankled these men.

The Dreams angered them greatly as did the coat of many colors. So, they would kill the one who dreamed the Dreams and strip the coat from him, thinking to silence his voice. Little did they know what the future held!

Reuben suggested that they put Joseph in a pit, which they did, with him thinking that he would come back later and rescue the boy. Evidently he had to go some place. When he returned, he found that Joseph was gone. They had sold him to the Ishmaelites.

Along with Reuben, Judah is the one who saved the life of Joseph, suggesting that they sell him as a slave. However, this was little an act of Mercy on the part of Judah inasmuch as under normal circumstances, they were consigning him to a life worse than death.

TWENTY PIECES OF SILVER

"And it came to pass, when Joseph was come unto his brethren, that they stripped Joseph out of his coat, his coat of many colors that was on him;

"And they took him, and cast him into a pit: and the pit was empty, there was no water in it.

"And they sat down to eat bread: and they lifted up their eyes and looked, and, behold, a company of Ishmaelites came from Gilead with their camels bearing spicery and balm and myrrh, going to carry it down to Egypt.

"And Judah said unto his brethren, What profit is it if we kill our brother, and conceal his blood?

"Come, and let us sell him to the Ishmaelites, and let not our hand be upon him; for he is our brother and our flesh. And his brethren were content.

"Then there passed by Midianites merchantmen; and they drew and lifted up Joseph out of the pit, and sold Joseph to the Ishmaelites for twenty pieces of silver: and they brought Joseph into Egypt" (Gen. 37:23-28).

THE BROTHERS

These brothers sitting down to eat bread, even after they had thrown Joseph into the pit, shows how hard their hearts were, indicating deplorable brutality on their part. In their minds, they had satisfactorily disposed of the young man and his Dreams. This *"coat of colors,"* which signified that he had now been chosen for the birthright instead of Reuben, would be used to deceive his father.

Evidently, their idea when they put him in the pit was to let him starve to death. But now, a change of events comes about in that they spotted a camel train coming near them and going down to Egypt. They would sell Joseph as a slave to these Ishmaelites and make some profit from the transaction. Judah was the one who suggested this. They would get 20 pieces of silver. This is a Type of Christ being sold for 30 pieces of silver.

As they stripped the coat from Joseph, likewise, they cast lots for Jesus' Robe.

Verse 25 says they *"sat down to eat bread: And they lifted up their eyes and looked,"* likewise, Matthew said concerning the Crucifixion of Christ, *"And sitting down they watched Him there"* (Mat. 27:36).

Verse 27 speaks of Joseph being sold *"to the Ishmaelites"* (Gentiles). Likewise, Matthew said, *"When they had bound Him, they led Him away, and delivered Him to Pontius Pilate the governor"* (Mat. 27:2).

THE DECEPTION

"And Reuben returned unto the pit; and, behold, Joseph was not in the pit; and he rent his clothes.

"And he returned unto his brethren, and said, The child is not; and I, where shall I go?

"And they took Joseph's coat, and killed a kid of the goats, and dipped the coat into the blood;

"And they sent the coat of many colors, and they brought it to their father; and said, This have we found: know now whether it be your son's coat or no.

"And he knew it, and said, It is my son's coat; an evil beast has devoured him; Joseph is without doubt rent in pieces" (Gen. 37:29-33).

It seems that Reuben is genuinely sorry about the turn of events; however, they explained to him what they had done, and the record proclaims the fact that he did nothing further.

A WILD ANIMAL?

To be frank, Reuben could easily have overtaken the Ishmaelites and Midianites and bought Joseph back, but he made no effort to do so.

In order to deceive their father, they evidently got an employee or slave to take the bloody coat to Jacob and to give him the story they had concocted. More than likely the slave didn't know the truth of the matter either. He would in all good conscious have related to Jacob what they told him to say.

This being the case, he would not have had any knowledge of this coat of many colors, or that it had been given to Joseph by his father. The slave only knew what he had been told to say, so he handed Jacob the coat, with others probably with him, and asked Jacob if this coat actually belonged to Joseph.

Jacob recognized it immediately and then surmised what his evil sons wanted him to surmise, that a wild animal had killed Joseph.

Knowing how much Jacob loved Joseph, it seems that the brothers took some glee in the suffering they caused the Patriarch at this time. However, even as the next two Verses portray, his grief, it seems, was even greater than they had anticipated it would be. It almost killed the old man!

WHY WOULD GOD ALLOW THIS
TO HAPPEN TO JACOB?

"And Jacob rent his clothes, and put sackcloth upon

his loins, and mourned for his son many days.

"And all his sons and all his daughters rose up to comfort him; but he refused to be comforted; and he said, For I will go down into the grave unto my son mourning. Thus his father wept for him" (Gen. 37:34-35).

As the test regarding Abraham concerning the offering of Isaac in sacrifice, even as the Lord commanded him, was, no doubt, the most difficult test that God ever required of any man, to be sure, that which was demanded of Jacob wasn't far behind. In some ways, it was even worse.

As difficult as was the test with Abraham, it was over in three days. Jacob's would last about 20 years. Isaac was alive during this three days and nights, but in the mind of Jacob, he thought that Joseph was dead.

He knew that the Lord had told him to give Joseph the birthright. That being the case, why would the Lord then allow his life to be taken by a wild animal, or so Jacob thought?

In fact, there was no answer to this question, plus a thousand others, at least as far as Jacob was concerned. However, to his credit, despite the sorrow and heartache, the aged Patriarch didn't give up, at least as far as his Faith in God was concerned. Despite questions which seemed to have no answers, he continued to believe. In fact, circumstances seemed to prove God wrong.

A LESSON!

What a lesson for all of us. It is one thing to wait, but it is something else altogether to not even know that for which one is waiting.

There are questions in life for which we do not have any answers. And yet, we know that the great Planner of all the ages, the Creator of all things, has everything under control. Not one single piece is out of place as it regards His Plan or His Way.

EGYPT

"And the Midianites sold him into Egypt unto Potiphar, an officer of Pharaoh's, and captain of the guard" (Gen. 37:36).

It is said that in those days the method for transporting slaves was to put each one in a wicker basket where they would be placed in a cart or strapped to the side of a camel. This would keep them from escaping.

So Joseph, on his way to Egypt, would have passed very close to his home in Hebron, but he was powerless to say or do anything. Bottled up in this awkward setting, and unable to stretch his legs, after awhile, the pain would have become excruciating, but to be sure, those who had bought him little cared for his comfort, as would be obvious.

It is also obvious that the Lord was watching over him every mile of the way. Joseph being sold to Potiphar, the captain of Pharaoh's guard, was no accident. It was planned by the Lord.

A TYPE OF CHRIST

Regarding Joseph, one may wonder, especially considering that he was a Type of Christ and, as well, considering his righteous life, as to why the Lord would submit him to such difficulties. Well, the same could be said for Jacob and untold millions of other Believers down through the many centuries.

Faith must be tested, and great Faith must be tested greatly. As it regards the Child of God, every single thing with the Believer, even as we have stated some Chapters back, is a test.

As should be obvious, this hardly matches up to the modern gospel being preached, claiming that proper

Faith will exempt one from all difficulties. No, it doesn't match up because the modern gospel is wrong.

FAITH

It is pathetic when one's Faith is measured against the price of the suit he wears or the model of car he drives. How would such foolishness have stacked up with Joseph, or Jacob, for that matter?

The Christian life, at least according to the Bible, doesn't claim a life exempt from all problems and difficulties. In fact, the Lord definitely allows certain adverse things to come our way in order that our Faith be tested.

When God blesses us, we learn about God and how wonderful and glorious that He is; however, we learn nothing about ourselves. It takes adversity, trouble, and difficulties for us to learn about ourselves, and most of the time, what we find is not very pleasant. So, the Blessings teach us about God while adversity teaches us about ourselves.

These last Verses of Chapter 37 say that Joseph was *"sold into Egypt."* As the story will tell, Joseph will become the second most powerful man in Egypt. As well, Jesus Christ would rise from the dead and become the Head of the Church, which is, by and large, made up of Gentiles.

CORN

"Now when Jacob saw that there was corn in Egypt, Jacob said unto his sons, Why do you look one upon another?

"And he said, Behold, I have heard that there is corn in Egypt: get you down thither, and buy for us from thence; that we may live, and not die" (Gen. 42:1-2).

Years have now passed, with Jacob thinking all the time that Joseph is dead. He has no knowledge of the Dreams that the Lord gave to Pharaoh, which were interpreted by Joseph, with Pharaoh then making Joseph the viceroy of Egypt, which, in essence, made Joseph the second most powerful man in Egypt and possibly the world. Of course, Jacob knew nothing of any of this.

Seven years of great harvest passed in Egypt with Joseph in charge, and now the famine, exactly as the Dreams of Pharaoh had portrayed, begins to grip the land plus all the surrounding countries.

Now it begins. Joseph's skill — that skill which only love can give — in leading his brothers step-by-step to a confession of their sin against him, and to a sense of its blackness in the Sight of God, is a picture of the future Action of the Lord Jesus Christ in bringing Israel to recognize her sin in rejecting Him, and the consequent enormity of that sin against God.

Now we find the real reason for the famine. Oftentimes, the Lord uses the elements, even in a negative way, to bring about His Will.

As stated, the seven years of great harvest have now ended in Egypt and, no doubt, the surrounding nations as well. The famine has set in and is so severe that whatever surplus these other nations had, including Jacob's family, had been quickly used up.

Somehow Jacob and his sons hear that Egypt has plenty of grain and other food stuff and is selling it to all who would desire to buy. Consequently, plans are made for the sons of Jacob, minus Benjamin, to travel to Egypt in order to purchase a supply, which was, no doubt, desperately needed.

ALL FOR ONE PURPOSE

Jacob had no way of knowing that all of these things which were happening, the seven years of excellent harvests and now the famine, were all being brought about by the Hand of God for a particular purpose, which centered upon this special family. Now, think of what we're saying:

All of these great happenings, which affected the entirety of the Middle East and involved quite a number of nations and untold thousands of people, were all for one purpose, and that was to bring about the Will of God as it regarded Jacob and his sons. From this, we must take a lesson.

With every happening in the world at the present time, in fact, as it always has been, the major purpose is to bring about the Will of God as it regards the Work of God and the People of God on Earth. It doesn't matter what those happenings might be or that they will involve many things. Let's look for a moment at the greatest happening of all, at least in the last 100 years. I speak of World War II.

THE FULFILLMENT OF BIBLE PROPHECY

As is obvious, in one way or the other, this great war involved the entirety of the world, but whatever happened militarily or economically, what were the spiritual reasons?

No doubt, there were many reasons as it concerns the Lord, Who overrules all things. The first reason pertained to Israel.

The time was drawing close for the fulfillment of Bible Prophecy as it regarded Israel once again, even after some 1,900 years, becoming a Nation. Satan knew this as well. Consequently, he moved upon Adolf Hitler and his thugs to exterminate the Jews, at least, all over whom they had control in Germany and the occupied countries, the number of whom was substantial, to say the least. According to the thinking of the

Evil One, if enough Jews could be slaughtered, Israel simply wouldn't have the strength to form a Nation. Of course, Satan very well knew if the Prophecies concerning Israel were stopped, then, in effect, God was defeated, and Satan had won. In fact, if any promise or prediction in the Word of God falls down, Satan has then won the age-long conflict. As well, in this great war, the United States would rise to world prominence in every capacity, and would be greatly instrumental in helping Israel to be formed once again as a Nation. In 1948, this was carried out by the unanimous vote regarding the United Nations.

Due to America's prominence, a great Move of God was brought about in this country. This also resulted in the greatest missionary efforts the world had ever known, with the Gospel being taken in one way or the other to every nation on the face of the Earth. In fact, our own Ministry (Jimmy Swaggart Ministries) had a part to play in all of this, for which we are so grateful to the Lord for allowing us this privilege.

SPIRITUAL SIGHT

As well, the Child of God should realize that whatever happenings may be taking place in the world and however they affect him personally, even though some may be very negative, all of this is the Plan of God designed to fall out to our good. Thus it was with Jacob.

The Patriarch never dreamed that all of these things, as negative as some of them were, were designed by the Lord for the express purpose of bringing about the Will of God regarding his particular family. It would all ultimately fall out to Jacob's good.

This is where Faith comes in. The Holy Spirit through Paul said: *"And we know that all things work together for good to them who love God, to them who are the called according to His Purpose"* (Rom. 8:28).

To be sure, God, in His Omnipotence, can bring all things out to the furtherance of His Will, even as it regards the entirety of the Church all over the world, and at the same time, deal with each particular individual accordingly. Man is limited, but God isn't limited.

Man has too many things for the overall welfare of all concerned, which sometimes affects certain people in a negative way. Man reasons that the overall good is more important, which, of course, is correct. However, God is able to deal not only with the corporate body but also each individual and make everything come out to our good, that is, if we truly love the Lord and are striving to bring about *"His Purpose."* Striving to bring about our own purposes, as should be obvious, cannot fall into the category of the Blessings of God.

BENJAMIN

"And Joseph's ten brethren went down to buy corn in Egypt.

"But Benjamin, Joseph's brother, Jacob sent not with his brethren; for he said, Lest peradventure mischief befall him.

"And the sons of Israel came to buy corn among those who came: for the famine was in the land of Canaan" (Gen. 42:3-5).

Both Joseph and Benjamin were the sons of Rachel and, thereby, special to Jacob. Even though he loved all his sons, it seems that these were the only two who, at least at this particular time, truly served the Lord.

Quite possibly, Jacob mused in his heart that with Joseph now being dead, or so he thought, the Lord would place the mantle on Benjamin. Therefore, he would specifically watch over the young man, who was now about 20 years of age.

The Lord had not revealed to Jacob that these were His Plans, but Jacob, not knowing what had actually happened, at least as it regarded Joseph, could only see Benjamin taking Joseph's place. So, he would not allow him to go into Egypt with his brothers.

JACOB

"And they came unto Jacob their father unto the land of Canaan, and told him all that befell unto them; saying,

"The man, who is the lord of the land, spoke roughly to us, and took us for spies of the country.

"And we said unto him, We are true men; we are no spies:

"We be twelve brethren, sons of our father; one is not, and the youngest is this day with our father in the land of Canaan.

"And the man, the lord of the country, said unto us, Hereby shall I know that you are true men; leave one of your brethren here with me, and take food for the famine of your households, and be gone:

"And bring your youngest brother unto me: then shall I know that you are no spies, but that you are true men; so will I deliver you your brother, and you shall traffick in the land" (Gen. 42:29-34).

From the terminology used by these men at this present time, it is obvious that a change has taken place in their lives; however, it is a change that is not quite yet complete.

For instance, even though their terminology is as it ought to be, in other words, they speak now with an entirely different spirit than they did those 20 odd years before when they sold Joseph, still, they haven't yet completely come clean with God and their father Jacob concerning what they had done. As far as Jacob knew, Joseph was dead, killed by a wild animal. That's what his sons had told him, and they had never rectified this thing as of yet.

REPENTANCE

However, as we shall see, the Holy Spirit will force them into a position to where they have to *"come clean."* He will do the same with every single Believer, even presently, because sin can only be handled in one way, and that is by proper confession. What does that mean?

It means that we confess our sin to God and do so unequivocally (I Jn. 1:9). If we have sinned against others, we must confess to them our wrong and seek their forgiveness, even as Joseph's brothers had to confess to their father Jacob what they had done and, thereby, seek his forgiveness. Ultimately, this they would do. No doubt, they thought that their confessing such to him under these circumstances would have made a bad matter worse. But still, they had wronged their father, and deeply so, in fact, almost enough to kill him, and so it had to be made right. As stated, ultimately, it would.

Unfortunately, millions of Christians, and I think in the present tense, do not properly follow this Scriptural admonition. They try to justify their actions, whatever those actions may have been. Proper Justification, however, can only be brought about by proper confession to the Lord and to those we have wronged, if, in fact, we have wronged them.

FEAR

"And it came to pass as they emptied their sacks, that, behold, every man's bundle of money was in his

sack: and when both they and their father saw the bundles of money, they were afraid" (Gen. 42:35).

The brothers of Joseph now fear, and for many things. What does it mean that their money has been restored unto them in the sacks of grain?

Actually, there was no way they could do this themselves. *"Why would the Lord of Egypt have this done?"* or so they reasoned in their minds. Actually, why did Joseph give them back their money, charging them nothing for the grain?

While Joseph was definitely taking stern measure to ensure himself of the change in his brothers, at the same time, he held in his heart nothing but good for them.

Even when the Lord is forced to chastise us, as He does all Believers, during the chastisement, He always does good things for us at different intervals. That's the reason, or at least one of the reasons, that it is such a joy to live for the Lord. Even when He is Stern, as He sometimes must be, He is at the same time Tender.

JACOB

"And Jacob their father said unto them, Me have you bereaved of my children: Joseph is not, and Simeon is not, and you will take Benjamin away: all these things are against me.

"And Reuben spoke unto his father, saying, Kill my two sons, if I bring him not to you: deliver him into my hand, and I will bring him to you again.

"And he said, My son shall not go down with you; for his brother is dead, and he is left alone: if mischief befall him by the way in which you go, then shall you bring down my gray hairs with sorrow to the grave" (Gen. 42:36-38).

We should study carefully the actions of Joseph as it regards the entirety of this scenario. Remembering that he is a Type of Christ, we can learn from this exactly how Christ loves us, teaches us, instructs us, leads us, and guides us. Joseph wanted only one thing from his brothers, and that was that they would *"do right."* That is all the Lord wants from us as well! He wants us to *"do right,"* which is *"right"* according to His Word.

While Jacob grieves over the situation, little does he realize just how close he is to the greatest and most wonderful happening of his life.

How often do we, as well, sorrow when at the moment of our sorrowing, God in His Heaven and on His Throne is at that very moment planning great, wonderful, and beautiful things for us.

What a mighty God we serve!

THE FAMINE

"And the famine was sore in the land" (Gen. 43:1).

Considering the severity of this famine and how that it affected several nations and untold numbers of people, we may very well ask the questions, *"Why would the Lord do all of this in order to bring one family to a desired position? Could He have not done so in various other ways much less severe?"*

God can do anything, but there are several things which must be taken into account.

Famines during Old Testament times, and, in fact, which probably continues unto this hour, are allowed by God because of the terrible wickedness and evil of the people.

For instance, in watching a newscast the other day, the newscaster remonstrated that war was not the only problem in Afghanistan. Drought, which had now lasted for several years, was bringing famine on the land, causing tremendous hardship.

As I looked at the dry riverbeds, the barren landscape, and the vineyards which had died or were dying, I knew the cause of this malady even though it would only be chalked up by the political pundits as the variances of the weather. However, there is a reason behind it all.

The religion of Islam is evil. Fostered and nurtured by Satan, it is more evil in Afghanistan than most. The drought causing the famine is the result. As well, we can look at the same in America. Our nation is slapping the Face of God. For instance, the so-called gay marriage situation is an insult to God of the highest order. The facts are, gay marriage is definitely not a civil rights problem; it is a moral problem. The Word of God alone serves as the foundation of all morals. When men ignore the Word of God, flaunting their evil in His Face, this is the cause of so much sorrow and heartache. For the terrible sin of abortion and the terrible sin of homosexuality, and above all, the church which has lost its way, this is the reason for so many problems in this nation. Unless there is revival, there won't be much change for the good, but rather for the worse.

THE PREACHING OF THE CROSS

The Cross of Christ alone stands as the avenue of Mercy and Grace. It alone holds back Judgment, and, of course, we speak of what Jesus there did. However, I would ask this question: *"How many churches presently are preaching the Cross?"* Not many I'm afraid!

Paul said:

"But God forbid that I should glory *(boast)***, save in the Cross of our Lord Jesus Christ** *(what the opponents of Paul sought to escape at the price of insincerity is the Apostle's only basis of exultation)***, by Whom the world is crucified unto me, and I unto the world.** *(The only way* *we can overcome the world, and I mean the only way, is by placing our Faith exclusively in the Cross of Christ and keeping it there)* **(Gal. 6:14).**

As it regards the famine in Jacob's time and the thought that such was too severe as it regards the manipulation of one family, we must remember the following:

There was nothing in the world more important than this one family, which means that the Work of God and the People of God are far, far more important than anything else. In other words, the little church on the corner with only a few people attending, that is, if the True Gospel is being preached from behind its pulpit, is far more important in the Eyes of God than even the mighty Microsoft, Apple, etc. While that certainly wouldn't be the case as is overly obvious with the world, it definitely is the case with God. Those other things will perish with the using, but the Word of God abides forever.

THE FOOD

"And it came to pass, when they had eaten up the corn which they had brought out of Egypt, their father said unto them, Go again, buy us a little food" (Gen. 43:2).

It seems that the grain which they obtained in Egypt was used solely as their own personal food, with the flocks and herds evidently eating other things. So, Jacob now admonishes his sons to go back to Egypt in order that they might secure more grain because what they bought on the first trip is now gone.

It may be thought peculiar that all of these men would go to Egypt as it regards such a transaction; however, travel was dangerous in those days, hence, all going. There was greater safety in numbers.

JUDAH

"And Judah spoke unto him, saying, The man did solemnly protest unto us, saying, You shall not see my face, except your brother be with you.

"If you will send our brother with us, we will go down and buy you food:

"But if you will not send him, we will not go down: for the man said unto us, You shall not see my face, except your brother be with you" (Gen. 43:3-5).

Reuben is the firstborn and should have taken the lead in all of these matters, but it is Judah who, in fact, stands in the position of leadership. Quite possibly the other brothers may have joined in, as well, as it regards what they had to say; however, it is Judah alone whom the Holy Spirit records.

Why?

Whatever happened that day which caused Judah to take the lead and, as well, with Joseph during the second trip to Egypt, which is portrayed in Chapter 44 of this Book of Genesis, had to be the Moving and Operation of the Holy Spirit on the heart. Judah would head up the Tribe from which the Messiah would come; therefore, we see traits of leadership beginning to show themselves.

Judah explains to Jacob that despite their long trip to Egypt, they will not be able to buy food unless Benjamin is with them.

"I know not why God's Wondrous Grace to me
"He has made known,
"Nor why, unworthy, Christ in love
"Redeemed me for His Own."

"I know not how this Saving Faith
"To me He did impart,

"Or how believing in His Word
"Wrought peace within my heart."

"I know not how the Spirit moves,
"Convincing men of sin,
"Revealing Jesus through the Word,
"Creating Faith in Him."

"I know not what of good or ill
"May be reserved for me,
"Of weary ways or golden days,
"Before His Face I see."

"I know not when my Lord may come,
"At night or noon-day fair,
"Nor if I'll walk the vale with Him,
"Or meet Him in the air."

JACOB

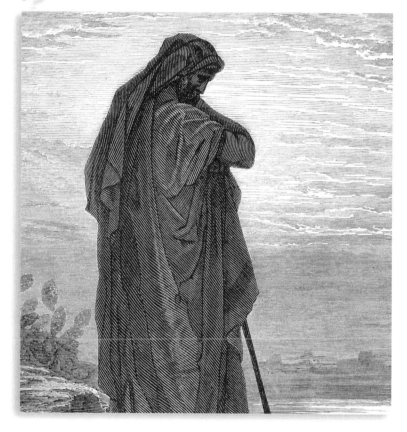

Chapter Twelve

ISRAEL

ISRAEL

"And Israel said, Wherefore dealt you so ill with me, as to tell the man whether you had yet a brother?

"And they said, The man asked us straitly of our state, and of our kindred, saying, Is your father yet alive? have you another brother? and we told him according to the tenor of these words: could we certainly know that he would say, Bring your brother down?

"And Judah said unto Israel his father, Send the lad with me, and we will arise and go; that we may live, and not die, both we, and you, and also our little ones.

"I will be surety for him; of my hand shall you require him: if I bring him not unto you, and set him before you, then let me bear the blame forever:

"For except we had lingered, surely now we had returned the second time" (Gen. 43:6-10).

If it is to be noticed, in Verses 6 and 8, the Holy Spirit refers to Jacob as *"Israel."* As remembered, the name means, *"Prince with God."* Whenever this name is used, it is always for purpose and reason. It shows an approval by God of Jacob. So, the question we must ask is, *"What is Jacob doing now that would cause the Lord to think so highly of him?"*

I think the answer would be in several parts.

Jacob is obeying as it regards the sending of Benjamin, which, of course, is what the Lord wants and desires. As well, for Jacob to do this, he has to exhibit Faith in God. It is Faith that is rightly placed, and that is always the criteria.

THE CROSS

All of this will ultimately play out to the Redeemer coming into this world, Who would die on a Cross, thereby, paying the terrible sin debt which man owed to God. Ultimately, it's the Cross, and ultimately, the Cross must always, in some way, be the Object of our Faith, or else, it's faith that God will not recognize!

The problem or the question is never faith as such. Everyone has faith, but with few exceptions, it is faith in something else other than Christ and the Cross. Remember, we must never divorce Christ from the Cross, which refers to His Redeeming Work. Of course, Christ is not still on the Cross, actually being seated with the Father in Heavenly Places, Victorious in every capacity. So, when we speak of Faith in the Cross, we are speaking of what Jesus there did. If it's not that kind of Faith, its faith that God will not recognize. The Faith that God honors and what caused Him to refer to Jacob as *"Israel"* is Faith in the Cross, at least that which pointed to the Cross. Every action of the Old Testament Greats did point to the Cross.

While, of course, Jacob would have known nothing about a Cross, all the things being done, that is, if done properly, would ultimately lead to the Cross.

Judah remonstrates to his father that had it not been for this critical issue, the taking of Benjamin, which was demanded by the lord of Egypt, they would have already returned due to the lack of food. The situation has now reached the place to where they have no choice; they must go to Egypt.

THEIR FATHER ISRAEL

"And their father Israel said unto them, If it must be so now, do this; take of the best fruits in the land in your vessels, and carry down the man a present, a little balm, and a little honey, spices, and myrrh, nuts, and almonds:

"And take double money in your hand; and the money that was brought again in the mouth of your

sacks, carry it again in your hand; peradventure it was an oversight:

"Take also your brother, and arise, go again unto the man" (Gen. 43:11-13).

We find here that the Holy Spirit continues to refer to Jacob as *"Israel."*

It was a part of the Divine Plan that Jacob and his family should be settled for a long period in Egypt. So, all of these proceedings are leading toward that conclusion.

So, we see here that the Patriarch is referred to again as *"Israel,"* making it three times in succession (Vss. 6, 8, 11), without the name *"Jacob"* being mentioned once.

We have already addressed ourselves to this particular thought, but due to the great significance of what is happening here, please allow me the prerogative of covering the following point a little more thoroughly:

THE CORRECT OBJECT OF FAITH

It is not so much here Jacob's great Faith which is being applauded, but rather the correct Object of his Faith. The Plan of God for the removal of this family to Egypt is nearing the moment of fulfillment, and everything is now in readiness. Joseph is prime minister of Israel, or one might say, the viceroy, but with Jacob, of course, at this present time unaware of this fact. All he knows is that strange things have been happening. Simeon has been detained in Egypt for no apparent reason except the ridiculous assertion that these men are spies. As well, if the brothers return, they must bring Benjamin with them. Why was such a thing required of them?

Irrespective as to the *"why,"* Jacob acquiesces.

The Patriarch is trying to gather together a little gift for the lord of Egypt, and, as well, taking care that there is enough money to pay not only for this order but for the previous order also. Little does he realize what is actually in store for him.

The little gift which the brothers would present to Joseph, although precious to this family, because of the famine, means nothing to Joseph, with the exception of sentimental value. It is the same with our gifts to Christ. It might look big to us, but its intrinsic worth means nothing to Christ, as should be obvious. But yet, our gifts are precious in His Sight just as this gift was precious in Joseph's sight because he loved his brothers even as Christ loves us.

EL-SHADDAI

"And God Almighty give you Mercy before the man, that he may send away your other brother, and Benjamin. If I be bereaved of my children, I am bereaved" (Gen. 43:14).

Jacob uses here the appellative, *"God Almighty,"* which, in the Hebrew, is *"El-Shaddai,"* and means, *"The All-sufficient One,"* or the *"All-powerful One."* It refers to the Covenant God of Abraham (Gen. 17:1) and of Jacob himself (Gen. 35:11).

Jacob, in essence, is saying, *"I do not understand all that is happening, but I know that God is able to protect both Simeon and Benjamin. I acquiesce to the Divine Will."*

While he is thinking only of the protection of his two sons, little does he realize just how able God actually is. In fact, Simeon and Benjamin are about the least of Jacob's concerns, if he only knew!

In effect, he says, *"If I lose my children, I lose them."* The truth is, he will not only not lose his children, Joseph will be restored, and, as well, the great Patriarch will even see his grandsons, the sons of Joseph.

"When sorrows and storms are besetting my
    track,
"And Satan is whispering 'You'd better turn
    back,'
"How oft I have proved it, tho' dark be the way,
"A little believing drives clouds all away."

"How easy when sailing the sea in a calm,
"To trust in the strength of Jehovah's Great Arm;
"But somehow I find when the waves swamp the
    boat,
"It takes some believing to keep things afloat."

"And others there are full of courage and zeal,
"Who go to the battle like warriors of steel;
"But right in the heat of the conflict with sin,
"Instead of believing they faint and give in."

"Then let us remember in running this race,
"That Faith is not feeling, and trust is not trace;
"And when all around us seem dark as the night,
"We'll keep on believing, and win in the fight."

JACOB

Chapter Thirteen

THE REVELATION

THE REVELATION

JACOB

"And they went up out of Egypt, and came into the land of Canaan unto Jacob their father,

"And told him, saying, Joseph is yet alive, and he is governor over all the land of Egypt. And Jacob's heart fainted, for he believed them not.

"And they told him all the words of Joseph, which he had said unto them: and when he saw the wagons which Joseph had sent to carry him, the spirit of Jacob their father revived:

"And Israel said, It is enough; Joseph my son is yet alive: I will go and see him before I die" (Gen. 45:25-28).

The brothers made their second trip to Egypt, now taking Benjamin with them. The scene that unfolded with Joseph revealing himself to his brothers had to be a moment unequaled. The last time these men had seen their brother was when they sold him to the Ishmaelites as a slave into Egypt. Now they looked upon him as the governor of the land, the second most powerful man in Egypt, and quite possibly the second most powerful man in the world.

Now they came home, and the news they brought was bittersweet. They would be able to relate to their father that Joseph was yet alive, but, as well, they would then have to admit what they had done some 22 years earlier.

If the scene with Joseph revealing himself to his brothers was, in fact, one of, if not the most, poignant in history, then the scene with the brothers before their father, Jacob, had to be a close second.

For 22 years the old man had grieved. A thousand questions loomed large in his mind, but there were no answers. Why would God have him select Joseph for the birthright and then allow him to be killed by wild animals?

Even though the account given here doesn't mention the brothers telling their father what actually happened as it regarded Joseph, and I speak of the situation that took place some 22 years earlier, it is obvious that they had to do so.

All of this we read in the account of Joseph and Jacob was superintended by the Patriarch. So, the following is the way it might have happened:

THE TRUTH

When the brothers arrived back from Egypt, which must have taken them at least three weeks, of course, Jacob was glad to see them and, more than all, glad to see Benjamin. Whether he noticed anything different about them, we aren't told, but their demeanor most definitely must have been somewhat different. As they all gathered together to give an account of their trip, the old man would have been eager to hear all the news. Quite possibly, one of them, maybe Judah, would have requested of his father that he sit down, for they had something to relate to him. If that's the way it happened, Jacob, no doubt, would have been somewhat puzzled as to what it might be. Simeon had been returned to them, and Benjamin was here safe and sound. So, what could it be?

CULPABILITY

More than likely, the brothers would have first related to him their evil intent of those 22 years before. It would have been very difficult to have related such a thing. They had to admit their culpability, their hard hearts, and their efforts to deceive their father, in which they were very successful. As the Patriarch heard this, it must have cut deep, especially considering how much he had suffered all of these years.

They would have related how they put Joseph in a pit and then sold him as a slave into Egypt for 20 pieces of silver. They would have told how they took the coat of many colors and dipped it in the blood of a kid of goats and had someone else to take it to Jacob. They would have confessed how they let him draw his own conclusions that Joseph had been killed by a wild animal.

As they laboriously relived this scene, Jacob, no doubt, felt the pain all over again, wondering why they were revealing this to him now.

It was probably Judah doing the speaking to his father. After making the confessions to Jacob, Judah then said, *"Joseph is yet alive,"* and then he added, *"He is governor over all the land of Egypt."*

JOSEPH IS YET ALIVE

The old man must have sat there for a few moments unable to grasp what he had been told. Then, coming on the heels of the horrible words which had just been revealed to him, he grew faint and could not find it in his heart to believe what he was being told.

Then, very slowly, Judah told his father, Jacob, how that Joseph had revealed himself unto them and had then received permission from Pharaoh to bring the entire family back to Egypt. He had even sent the wagons to help them move.

Jacob slowly arose from where he had been sitting, walked to the front and looked outside, and, sure enough, there were the wagons.

And then the Scripture says: *"And Israel said, It is enough; Joseph my son is yet alive: I will go and see him before I die."*

It is noteworthy that Jacob is referred to in Verse 28 as *"Israel."* Whatever the reasons, to be sure, it is linked to Faith.

It was enough to hear that Joseph was yet alive. That within itself was miraculous, to say the least, but to think that he was now the governor of Egypt made this story even more incredible. How could such a thing be?

No doubt, in the coming years, Joseph would relate all of the happenings to his father, and do so in minute detail.

SACRIFICES

"And Israel took his journey with all that he had, and came to Beer-sheba, and offered sacrifices unto the God of his father Isaac" (Gen. 46:1).

The two names, *"Jacob"* and *"Israel,"* are used here by the Holy Spirit with great emphasis. When the Patriarch does not believe (Gen. 45:26), he faints and is called, *"Jacob"*; when he does believe (Gen. 45:28; 46:1), he takes courage and boldly steps out and is called, *"Israel."*

Several things are said in Verse 1:

We find Jacob starting for Egypt with the Holy Spirit giving him the name *"Israel,"* which reflects a renewed confidence and Faith in God, Who had originally changed his name. In fact, great and mighty things were happening. He knew it was true, but it was still hard to make himself believe what had just happened. *"Joseph is alive?"*

Yes! He is not only alive but the governor over all the land of Egypt. The old man reasoned that only God could do such a thing! With those words, *"Joseph is yet alive,"* every question, in essence, had been answered.

THE WAGONS

As Jacob looked at the wagons with their sides

emblazoned with the seal of Egypt, his mind could hardly contain all that he knew, and, no doubt, again and again, the tears of thankfulness and gratitude came freely.

Now, he came to Beer-sheba where both Abraham, his grandfather, and Isaac, his father, had sojourned for considerable periods and had erected Altars to Jehovah.

He felt moved upon by the Holy Spirit to *"offer sacrifices unto God."* He either used the Altar that had been erected by his father, Isaac, or else, he constructed one himself, for Isaac's Altar could well have been destroyed by vandals.

The Scripture says that he offered *"sacrifices,"* which means that several lambs were offered at this particular time.

THE ALTAR

This Altar represented what all of this was about. It is the reason for all that Abraham, Isaac, and Jacob were led to do. It is the reason for the Miracle birth of Isaac and the Miracle change of Jacob. His sons would form the nucleus of the new Nation, which would be called after the name that the Lord had given to Jacob — Israel. They would one day, some 255 years later, occupy this land of Canaan and would rename it, *"Israel."* From this Nation would come the Prophets, who would give Israel and the world the Word of God as well as the great Law of Moses.

THE SON OF GOD

All of this was being done for but one purpose, and that was for the Entrance of the Son of God into this world, which was prophesied immediately after the Fall in the Garden of Eden (Gen. 3:15). In addition, the very purpose for His Coming would be the Cross, represented by this Altar and untold numbers of other similar Altars, which were all symbolic of Calvary. There Jesus would bleed, suffer, and die, thereby, atoning for all sin that the fallen sons of Adam's lost race might be brought to God.

So, Jacob killed the little animals, with their hot blood pouring out in a basin, which he, no doubt, poured out at the base of the Altar. He then placed the carcasses on the Altar, watching the flames consume each one. A picture is presented here of that coming day when Jesus Christ as the Lamb of God will take away the sin of the world (Jn. 1:29; 3:16).

The manner in which the statement is used, *"The God of his father Isaac,"* proclaims the fact that all that Abraham had handed down to Isaac, likewise, Jacob's father had handed down to him. The Doctrine was unsullied and untainted, which refers to the fact that *"Jesus Christ and Him Crucified"* was the Foundation of this great Plan of God.

ISRAEL — JACOB

"And God spoke unto Israel in the visions of the night, and said, Jacob, Jacob. And he said, Here am I" (Gen. 46:2).

This Verse says that *"God spoke unto Israel,"* and yet, when He spoke to him personally, He said, *"Jacob, Jacob."* Why the seeming contradiction?

Actually, there is no contradiction. When we look at the Second Verse, we are looking at Sanctification in both its positional and conditional forms.

The type of Sanctification that God gives to us, which takes place immediately at Conversion, refers to our position in Christ and never changes. Hence, Jacob would be called *"Israel"* (*"But you are sanctified"*

— I Cor. 6:11). The address by God saying, *"Jacob, Jacob,"* spoke of Jacob's condition, *"Sanctify wholly"* (I Thess. 5:23).

Positional Sanctification is given to us freely by Jesus Christ. We do not earn it or merit it; it is a Work of Grace, hence, Jacob referred to as *"Israel."* As well, there is conditional Sanctification, hence, God saying, *"Jacob, Jacob."* This refers to the fact that the Holy Spirit is making every endeavor to bring our *"condition"* up to our *"position."* In fact, this is a lifelong process and is gained basically in the same manner as our initial Sanctification at Conversion — Faith in Christ and the Cross. Faith maintained in the Finished Work of Christ guarantees the progress that we as Believers must make, that is, if Christlikeness is to be developed within our lives.

EGYPT

"And He said, I am God, the God of your father: fear not to go down into Egypt; for I will there make of you a great nation:

"I will go down with you into Egypt; and I will also surely bring you up again: and Joseph shall put his hand upon your eyes" (Gen. 46:3-4).

The Lord said to Jacob:

• *"I am God"*: In essence, this says, *"I am the El, the Mighty One."* After what Jacob had seen in the last few days, he did not doubt the Power of God.

• *"The God of your father"*: The same Message that God gave to Isaac, He also gave to Jacob. As previously stated, the Message must not be changed in any fashion.

• *"Fear not to go down into Egypt"*: This was evidently said because Jacob obviously had apprehensions about going to Egypt despite the fact that Joseph had sent for him. Isaac had been forbidden to go there (Gen. 36:2). However, the spirit of Jacob was now satisfied because the Lord told him to go.

What a delightful episode in his life that he would take no one's word for this, even his son Joseph's, but must have the personal Leading of the Lord.

• *"For I will there make of you a great Nation"*: Twice it had been predicted by the Lord that Jacob would develop into a multitudinous people (Gen. 28:14; 35:11). The present Promise was an indication that the fulfillment of the Prophecy was at hand.

• *"I will go down with you into Egypt"*: This is not the idea of a local deity following them when they changed their abodes and, thereby, confined to the district in which they happened for the first time to reside, but a metaphorical expression for the efficiency and completeness of the Divine protection.

• *"And I will also surely bring you up again"*: This spoke of the time that Jacob would die, and his body would be brought back to Canaan for burial, which it was.

• *"And Joseph shall put his hand upon your eyes"*: He had never thought to see Joseph again, but the Lord assured him here that he would not only see his son but would live near him for quite some time, and at the last, Joseph would close Jacob's eyes in death.

THE LAND OF THE SOUTH

"And Jacob rose up from Beer-sheba: and the sons of Israel carried Jacob their father, and their little ones, and their wives, in the wagons which Pharaoh had sent to carry him.

"And they took their cattle, and their goods, which they had gotten in the land of Canaan, and came into Egypt, Jacob, and all his seed with him:

"His sons, and his sons' sons with him, his daugh-ters, and his sons' daughters, and all his seed brought he with him into Egypt" (Gen. 46:5-7).

Jacob was 130 years old at this time, and this event was 215 years after the Call of Abraham. The Children of Israel would stay in Egypt, as well, for 215 years. They would spend some 40 years in the wilderness before finally going into the Land of Promise.

Pharaoh had told Jacob not to regard his goods because the good of all the land of Egypt was before him; but the Patriarch did not wish to take advantage of the offer any more than he had to, which was a wise decision on his part.

Out of the great events in God's Dealings with the human race, Jacob coming into Egypt with all of his family, without a doubt, stands high. A threshold was being crossed, and even though it would be some 255 years before Israel would actually possess the Promise as it regarded the land of Canaan, great strides were now being made.

JUDAH

"And these are the names of the Children of Israel, which came into Egypt, Jacob and his sons: Reuben, Jacob's firstborn" (Gen. 46:8).

In the Eighth Verse, the Holy Spirit once again says, *"Israel,"* and this is because of what He would do with and make of this people. Through them, the Messiah would come, hence, *"the Children of Israel."*

The *"Church"* of that day began with Abraham and Sarah. By the time of Jacob, the grandson of Abraham, it was somewhat larger. At this present time, (2013) it numbers into the tens of millions of people, and I speak of those who are truly Saved.

Verse 28 says: *"And he sent Judah before him unto*

Joseph." Judah had natural traits that made him an outstanding leader of men and one to be trusted. In Prophecy, he was destined to have the chief place among the brethren. His was to be the ruling Tribe through which the Messiah would come and rule all nations forever (Gen. 49:10).

In history, Judah had the ruling part in Israel from David to the Babylonian captivity, a period of nearly 500 years. This Tribe, along with Benjamin and multitudes from all the other Tribes, continued as a Nation for over 130 years longer than the apostate northern kingdom of Israel. Judah was the leader in the return from captivity until the Messiah came the first time. Judah, as well, will be the leading Tribe under the Messiah in the Millennium and forever.

THE CHILDREN OF ISRAEL

While we have not printed all the genealogy of Genesis 46:8-28, we will address according to the following: it has to do with the number of individuals under Jacob who went into Egypt.

In tabulating the number of people given in this genealogy which came into Egypt, we are actually given three numbers: 66 and 70, and then in Acts 7:14, Stephen gives the number 75.

The apparent confusion in these different numbers will disappear if it be observed that the first takes no account of Jacob, Joseph, Manasseh, and Ephraim, but these are included in the second computation of 70. And then, Stephen simply added to the 70 of Verse 27 the five grandsons of Joseph, who are mentioned in the Septuagint version from which he quoted, thus making 75 in all. There is no irreconcilable contradiction between the Hebrew historian and the Christian Preacher (Pulpit).

THE LINEAGE OF CHRIST

It was from the Tribe of Judah that the Son of Man would come, the Redeemer of the world. Actually, it was through Jacob that the Prophecy came that the Redeemer would come through this particular Tribe (Gen. 49:10). At first, the Lord merely said that the Redeemer would come through the human race (Gen. 3:15). He then said that the Redeemer would come through a particular people, all from the loins of Abraham (Gen. 12:1-3). He then predicted, as stated, that from this people, the Redeemer would come from a particular Tribe, Judah. The prediction then came forth that of these people and from this certain Tribe, the Redeemer would come from a particular family, David (II Sam., Chpt. 7). And then, in this family, it would be a Virgin who would bring forth this Wondrous Child (Isa. 7:14).

Of the sons of Judah, it would be Pharez who would be in the sacred lineage.

JOB

The *"Job"* mentioned in Genesis 46:13, the son of Issachar, is the same Job of the Book which bears his name. It is believed that this Book was the first one written, probably written by both Moses and Job while Moses was in the wilderness some 40 years before delivering Israel. It is known that Job was contemporary with Moses for a number of years before Job died. In fact, the Book of Job is probably the oldest Book in the world, having been written in collaboration with Job while Moses was in the wilderness, and written before the Book of Genesis was written, etc.

The Book of Job explains the problem of why good men are afflicted. It is for their Sanctification. It is interesting that this difficult question should be the first taken up and answered in the Bible.

At a point in time, it is obvious that Job left his father, Issachar, and the land of Egypt and went into the land of Uz (Gen. 22:20). At what age Job left the land of Egypt, we aren't told; however, he was probably about 70 years of age at the time of his great trial. He lived to be 210.

THE WORTHFULNESS OF CHRIST

In brief, the Book of Job proclaims the worthlessness of self, which is the first step in Christian experience, with the Song of Solomon proclaiming the Worthfulness of Christ, which is the last step in the Christian experience. It takes awhile for the Believer to climb out over the problem of *"self,"* which must be done before one can fully realize the *"Worthfulness of Christ."* However, we must remember that the *"Song of Solomon"* can never be reached until *"Job"* has been passed through.

Job does not symbolize an unconverted, but rather a converted man. It was necessary that one of God's Children should be chosen for this trial; for the subject of the Book is not the Conversion of the sinner, but the consecration of the Saint. It is evident that an unconverted man needs to be brought to an end of himself, but that a man who feared God, who was perfect in his worship, and who hated evil should also need this is somewhat confusing to most. So, here comes the mystery of the Book of Job.

God uses Satan, calamity, and sickness to be His Instruments in creating character and making men partakers of His Holiness, but with the understanding that those things themselves do not and, in fact, cannot create character, etc., but they draw us to Christ

Who can (some of the thoughts regarding Job were derived from George Williams.)

THE MEETING

"And Joseph made ready his chariot, and went up to meet Israel his father, to Goshen, and presented himself unto him; and he fell on his neck, and wept on his neck a good while" (Gen. 46:29).

The Holy Spirit here refers to the Patriarch once again as *"Israel"* as he meets Joseph for the first time in over 20 years. Among other things, the Holy Spirit refers to him as *"Israel"* because of the future meeting that will take place between Israel and the Lord Jesus Christ, of which Joseph was a Type. This meeting will take place at the Second Coming even after such a long estrangement.

Joseph making ready his chariot and going up to meet his father tells us very little in the translation; however, in the Hebrew, such terminology is commonly used of the Appearance of God or His Angels. It is employed here in this manner to indicate the glory in which Joseph came to meet Jacob.

Joseph's chariot was of the royal house and was probably unlike anything Jacob had ever seen. It would have been pulled by the finest and most beautiful horses. As well, there were probably many attendants and guards with Joseph who were also riding in gilded chariots and dressed in the finery of Egypt. We must remember that Joseph was second only to Pharaoh, and with Egypt possibly being the greatest nation in the world, it meant that Joseph was the second most powerful man in the world of that time.

KING OF KINGS AND LORD OF LORDS

As well, Joseph didn't do this solely for his father, but this is actually the manner in which this prime minister traveled, which served to exhibit his authority. However, in all of this, there is a greater spiritual meaning. When Jesus came the first time, He came, in fact, as a Humble Peasant. Israel knew Him as the Carpenter's Son, which means that He definitely was not of the Jewish aristocracy.

When He comes the second time, He will not come as a Peasant, but rather as *"King of kings and Lord of lords."* In fact, as it refers to splendor and Glory, there is absolutely nothing that can even remotely compare with that which will accompany Christ when He comes back to this Earth. So, when Israel sees Him at that time and accepts Him as Lord and Saviour, it will be in a Glory that beggars all description. In fact, the very planetary bodies of the heavens will dance in glee, so to speak, when our Lord shall come back to Earth again (Mat. 24:29-30). The Creator has now come back to His Creation, and we speak of Planet Earth, where He will ultimately make His Eternal Headquarters (Rev., Chpts. 21-22). So, the meeting of Joseph with his father, Jacob, is meant to portray that coming day, hence, the glory which accompanied Joseph.

JOSEPH AND JACOB

The evidence is that Jacob and all of his entourage went first to the area called, *"Goshen."* It would have been in the area very close to modern Cairo, Egypt. How long Jacob had been settled there before Joseph came, we aren't told; however, it could not have been very long, probably only a few days.

When they informed Jacob that Joseph was coming, I wonder what the thoughts were of the great Patriarch. He had never hoped to see Joseph again, and it had been over 20 years since he had laid eyes on him. In fact, Joseph was only 17 years old when he last saw him. He was now about 38 or 39.

When Joseph came into the presence of Jacob, he fell on his neck, which means that he embraced him grandly, with him weeping as, no doubt, Jacob did as well. However, this time, they were tears of joy. Faith had now been honored as heartache of the past 20 and more years had been wiped away. It was now only a dim memory. Joseph was here, and Joseph was yet alive.

Strangely and beautifully enough, this is the story of Israel. The meeting which we are describing here, prophetically speaking, is yet to take place; however, it is closer now than ever. The seven years of dark trouble are yet to come to Israel, which is typified by the seven years of famine, according to the dream that was given to Pharaoh. At the end of those seven years of trouble, *"Jacob's trouble,"* Jesus Christ is coming back and will, in fact, be the Saviour of Israel just as Joseph was the saviour of Israel.

ISRAEL

"And Israel said unto Joseph, Now let me die, since I have seen your face, because you are yet alive" (Gen. 46:30).

Without a doubt, this was the happiest moment of Jacob's life, and no wonder! That which he never dreamed would happen has, Miracle of Miracles, come true.

In the Patriarch's mind, his life's journey had now filled its course. The last earthly longing of his heart had been completely satisfied. He was now ready, whenever God will, to be gathered to his fathers.

However, the Lord would see fit to allow this great man to live another 17 years and to enjoy the fullest of the Blessings of God. The Lord had asked Jacob to go through a great sorrow, so great, in fact, that it defies description. However, He would now make up for that sorrow, and do so manifold. The Lord will never owe any man anything.

The truth is: the Lord has never owed anyone anything. However, even if He asks us to do something that is difficult, He, without fail, will always reimburse us, and will do so exactly as He did with Jacob.

Not counting the five grandsons of Joseph, there would have been 70 people there that day, counting all the children, when Joseph met Jacob. What questions the children must have had! Could they understand that Joseph was the lord of Egypt and yet the son of Jacob and, in essence, their uncle?

The number, *"70,"* became afterwards a symbolic number among the Israelites — as in the 70 Elders of Moses, the 70 of the Sanhedrin, the 70 Disciples of the Lord, etc.

There may be something in the combination of numbers. Seventy is seven times ten. Ten is the Biblical symbol of the complete development of humanity. Seven is of perfection. Therefore, 70 may symbolize the Elect People of God as the hope of humanity — Israel in Egypt. In the Twelve Patriarchs and the 70 souls, we certainly see the foreshadowing of the Saviour's Appointments in the beginning of the Christian Church. The small number of Israel in the midst of the great multitude of Egypt is a great encouragement to Faith. *"Who has despised the day of small things?"*

SHEPHERDS

"And Joseph said unto his brethren, and unto his father's house, I will go up, and show Pharaoh, and say unto him, My brethren, and my father's house, which were in the land of Canaan, are come unto me;

"And the men are shepherds, for their trade has

been to feed cattle; and they have brought their flocks, and their herds, and all that they have.

"And it shall come to pass, when Pharaoh shall call you, and shall say, What is your occupation?

"That you shall say, Your servants' trade has been about cattle from our youth even until now, both we, and also our fathers: that you may dwell in the land of Goshen; for every shepherd is an abomination unto the Egyptians" (Gen. 46:31-34).

Goshen seemed to be the most fertile part of Egypt, at least as it referred to the grazing of cattle and sheep. The Nile River ran through this area, and it finally settled into the marshlands of the Nile Delta, which afforded it much grass, etc.

While flocks of cattle and herds of sheep were held by the Egyptians, and even by Pharaoh, those who attended these flocks and herds were looked down on by the Egyptians. As well, as it regards shepherds, the word, *"Abomination,"* used in Verse 34, means that there was some religious connotation to the attitude of the Egyptians toward the shepherds.

At any rate, Joseph did not attempt to conceal from Pharaoh the low caste of the shepherds, his brothers, but he trusted in God that what was an abomination to the Egyptians would be made acceptable by the Grace of God.

As well, if they kept to themselves in Goshen, the Israelites were not likely to intermingle with the Egyptians and, thereby, to intermarry.

Egypt was an agricultural nation, which meant that her population was made up of farmers, as much as they despised herdsmen. Their monuments picture shepherds as distorted, dirty, and emaciated figures.

"Encamped along the hills of light,
"You Christian soldiers rise,

"And press the battle ere the night,
"Shall veil the glowing skies;"

"His Banner over us is love,
"Our sword the Word of God;
"We tread the road the Saints above,
"With shouts of triumph trod;"

"On every hand the foe we find
"Drawn up in dread array;
"Let tents of ease be left behind,
"And onward to the fray;
"Salvation's helmet on each head,
"With truth all girt about."

JACOB

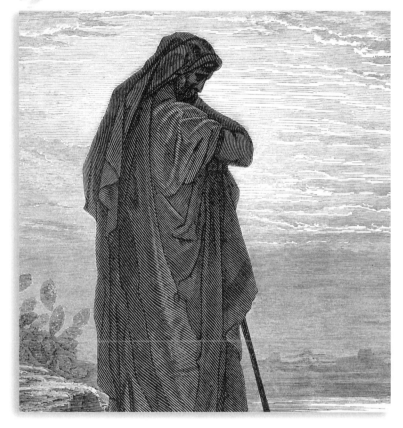

<u>Chapter Fourteen</u>

PHARAOH

PHARAOH

"Then Joseph came and told Pharaoh, and said, My father and my brethren, and their flocks, and their herds, and all that they have, are come out of the land of Canaan; and, behold, they are in the land of Goshen.

"And he took some of his brethren, even five men, and presented them unto Pharaoh" (Gen. 47:1-2).

As far as we know, no one in Egypt ever knew anything about the wickedness of the past deeds of Joseph's brothers; such is true forgiveness. It not only forgives sin, but it forgets as well.

Though Joseph was a great man, and despite the fact that his brothers were shepherds, which means that the Egyptians despised such, yet, he openly owned them. Despite what we were, our Lord Jesus is not ashamed to call us brethren. That the brothers were shepherds, which Joseph had been, as well, served as a Type of the Good Shepherd, Who would someday come and, in fact, did!

In this appearance of Joseph before Pharaoh, it seems that he went in first and told Pharaoh that his father and brethren with all of their flocks were now in the land of Goshen.

He then brought in five of his brothers and presented them to Pharaoh. Last of all, he *"brought in Jacob his father, and set him before Pharaoh."*

THE SAVIOR OF EGYPT

Joseph wanted his family in Goshen, for that was the best place for pasture. In fact, they were there now; but Joseph must observe protocol and ask permission from Pharaoh before everything could be settled, which he did.

Of course, there was no way that Pharaoh would refuse Joseph. In fact, Joseph, as was overly obvious, was the savior of Egypt. Due to the provisions made by Joseph, Egypt, in effect, was now the savior of the world of the Middle East. No nation in that area, the area of the famine, had any sustenance except Egypt, and this was because of Joseph. Pharaoh owed everything to Joseph, so his request was met with instant approval.

Joseph taking five of his brothers in to see Pharaoh after he had the first conference portrays the fact that his request had been granted, which, of course, I'm sure that he knew it would.

It is interesting as to why he took only five of his brothers. Why not all of them? Quite possibly, five was a very special number to the Egyptians even as seven later became to Israel.

GOSHEN

"And Pharaoh said unto his brethren, What is your occupation? And they said unto Pharaoh, Your servants are shepherds, both we, and also our fathers.

"They said moreover unto Pharaoh, For to sojourn in the land are we come; for your servants have no pasture for their flocks; for the famine is sore in the land of Canaan: now therefore, we pray you, let your servants dwell in the land of Goshen.

"And Pharaoh spoke unto Joseph, saying, Your father and your brethren are come unto you:

"The land of Egypt is before you; in the best of the land make your father and brethren to dwell; in the land of Goshen let them dwell: and if you know any men of activity among them, then make them rulers over my cattle" (Gen. 47:3-6).

Occupations were hereditary among the Egyptians, and, thus, the five brothers answered Pharaoh that they were shepherds and that their father and grand-father had been such before them.   Consequently, Pharaoh would conclude that in their case, no change was possible or desired in their mode of life.

They asked for permission to dwell in the land of Goshen even though Joseph had already received such permission. They were, as well, merely following protocol.

Pharaoh answered in a bountiful way, telling them that *"the land of Egypt was before them,"* and that they could have anything they desired; however, if it was Goshen that they desired, then that's what they would have.

He further added that if desired, Joseph could give his brothers employment as being over the vast herds of Pharaoh. In other words, they would be working for the state, which, more than likely, they did, and which these jobs would have been excellent promotions in their case. In other words, they were well taken care of regarding finances.

JACOB

"And Joseph brought in Jacob his father, and set him before Pharaoh: and Jacob blessed Pharaoh" (Gen. 47:7).

Going back for several months, the moment when Joseph revealed himself in his glory to his brethren, was when Judah took the sorrow of the aged Israel to heart and put himself into it. It is a wonderful picture of Christ's Revelation of Himself when Judah in the latter day will voice the sorrow of Israel in connection with the rejection of Jesus, the True Joseph.

Joseph was not ashamed of his brethren. He pre-sented them to the great king. Although he had to confess a short and troubled life and was himself a despised shepherd, yet Jacob blessed the mighty monarch: *"And without contradiction, the less is blessed of the greater."*

All of this means that the least and most faltering of God's Children is superior to the mightiest monarch and is conscious of the superiority.

In the story of Joseph, we have had a series of meetings, which have been astounding in their presentation and far reaching in their consequences.   After bringing in his five brothers to Pharaoh, last of all, he brought in his father, Jacob.

I wonder what Jacob thought when as a lowly shepherd he walked into what must have been one of the grandest buildings, if not the grandest, on the face of the Earth, the palace of Pharaoh, head of the mightiest nation of the world of that day. This was a setting which Jacob in his wildest dreams could never have imagined. But yet, it quickly became obvious that despite the glory and the splendor of this palatial empire, Jacob was the better, and Pharaoh knew that as well.

THE BLESSING

Pharaoh, no doubt, imagined that the tremendous powers possessed by Joseph, which were unequalled anywhere in the world of that day, had to have their seedbed in the life of this aged Patriarch who stood before them, and he was right. As Pharaoh looked at this aged man, little did he realize, but yet, sensed, that a Power greater than anything he knew resided in the heart of this frail Patriarch. As he looked at Jacob, this heathen never dreamed that the man standing before him would be thought of throughout eternal ages as the third one in the great appellative, *"The God of Abraham, Isaac, and Jacob."*

Knowing the protocol of the time, it would have to be that despite the splendor and glory of his surroundings and despite the frailty of this aged man, Pharaoh requested that Jacob would bless him. As stated, *"The less is blessed of the better."*

As Jacob reached out and lay his gnarled, aged hand on the head of Pharaoh and proceeded to bless him, such typifies the coming glad day when Israel, with Jesus standing by her side, will bless the Gentile world. It will happen at the beginning of the great Kingdom Age and will last throughout that definite time.

PHARAOH

"And Pharaoh said unto Jacob, How old are you?

"And Jacob said unto Pharaoh, The days of the years of my pilgrimage are an hundred and thirty years: few and evil have the days of the years of my life been, and have not attained unto the days of the years of the life of my fathers in the days of their pilgrimage.

"And Jacob blessed Pharaoh, and went out from before Pharaoh" (Gen. 47:8-10).

This was a first for Egypt, for never before had such a prayer been heard within an Egyptian palace. Still, we must believe that the conduct of Pharaoh was mostly due to the effect of Joseph's life and ministry. One true man is a great power in any country.

Jacob being 130 years old at that time was evidently much older than most, if not all, of the people in Egypt as it regards longevity. I think the facts are, at least during this particular period of time, that those who served the Lord, as a whole, lived much longer than their contemporaries in the heathen world. I think this was true then in Egypt, and I think it was true in all other countries as well.

From the Text, it seems that Pharaoh knew that Jacob was very aged just by looking at him; consequently, he asked him his age, with Jacob replying that he was 130. I doubt seriously that there was anyone in Egypt at that time who was 100 years old, much less the age of Jacob.

But yet, as Jacob confessed, he was not as old as his fathers. In fact, he would die at 147 years of age, some 17 years after coming into Egypt. His grandfather, Abraham, died at 175 and his father, Isaac, at 180.

THE SUBJECT OF ROMANS, CHAPTERS 9, 10, AND 11

Joseph being raised from the pit to the throne, a Type of Christ, enriched his brethren with all the promises, which they, by their rejection of him, had forfeited, but which were now, upon the ground of Grace, restored to them.

The Egyptians themselves, representative of all the nations of the Earth, were saved from death by Joseph and made by him the willing slaves of the throne and their future assured to them. All of this is a striking picture of what has yet to come to pass but most definitely shall! This is the subject of Romans, Chapters 9, 10, and 11, in which it is pointed out that Israel and the Gentile will inherit the Promises in fellowship solely upon the ground of pure Grace.

Joseph was the greatest benefactor Egypt ever had. In one day by Divine wisdom, he destroyed slavery and landlordism. He set up only one master and one landlord in the nation, and that was the nation itself, as physically embodied in Pharaoh.

THE SEVEN YEARS OF FAMINE

From this account, we learn just how severe the famine actually was. Had it not been for Joseph, no doubt, hundreds of thousands, if not millions, would have died of starvation. However, because of the

Divine wisdom given to him, he was able to forecast the famine, lay in store for that coming time, and then again by Divine wisdom, was able to nourish the people as the famine became more and more severe.

The people seem to have done fairly well in the first year of the famine and possibly even the second year, but by the time of the third year, the situation had become critical and remained that way, even growing steadily worse, to the conclusion of this terrible seven-year period.

When Joseph levied the twenty percent tax, this was one of the fairest arrangements that any people had ever known. In fact, it is seldom equaled in any country presently. For instance, at this particular time (2013), counting state, local, and federal income taxes, it approximates 50 percent in the United States.

DIVINE WISDOM

Some have claimed that Joseph robbed the Egyptians of their liberties and converted a free people into a hoard of abject slaves. Nothing could be further from the truth.

In fact, had it not been for Joseph and the Divine wisdom which he was given during this extremely trying time, as stated, millions of people would literally have starved to death. As it was, the people were looked after, and there is no record that anyone starved.

As well, when the famine ended and once again crops could be grown with the assurance of a bountiful harvest, Joseph allowed all the people to go back to their original land plots and even gave them seed, equipment, and animals to work the land, with Pharaoh only getting twenty percent. To be frank and, as stated, that was and is an excellent arrangement.

ISRAEL

"And Israel dwelt in the land of Egypt, in the country of Goshen; and they had possessions therein, and grew, and multiplied exceedingly" (Gen. 47:27).

In Verse 27, the Nation is called, "Israel," for the first time.

They came in 70 strong and about 215 years later would leave out upwards of three million people.

Horton says: "This is a summary Verse letting us know that though Israel's family came to Egypt intending to stay temporarily, they continued to live in Goshen and settled down to stay. They were prosperous and kept increasing in number."

After the death of Joseph, there would come a day that a Pharaoh, who held no affection for Joseph or the Hebrews, would occupy the throne; consequently, he would make slaves of them.

However, had that not been done, Israel would have had no desire whatsoever to leave Egypt and, in fact, would not have left. The Lord has to allow many things which are negative to come our way in order for us to desire to do His Will.

CANAANLAND

"And Jacob lived in the land of Egypt seventeen years: so the whole age of Jacob was an hundred forty and seven years.

"And the time drew near that Israel must die: and he called his son Joseph, and said unto him, If now I have found grace in your sight, put, I pray you, your hand under my thigh, and deal kindly and truly with me; bury me not, I pray you, in Egypt:

"But I will lie with my fathers, and you shall carry me out of Egypt, and bury me in their buryingplace.

And he said, I will do as you have said.

"And he said, Swear unto me. And he swore unto him. And Israel bowed himself upon the bed's head" (Gen. 47:28-31).

As previously stated, Jacob lived some 17 years in Egypt after arriving in that land, dying at 147 years old. However, he had brought about the sons who would make up the great Tribes of Israel, which would ultimately give the world the Word of God and, as well, serve as the Womb of the Messiah. They were also meant to evangelize the world and, in effect, did so under the leadership of the Apostle Paul who, as is obvious, was Jewish.

Born in Canaan, Jacob had lived 77 years in that land, then 20 years in Padan-aram. He then lived 33 years in Canaan again, and now 17 in Egypt, 147 years in all.

Now the great Patriarch came down to die, but first, he would gloriously predict the future of his sons, or rather the Tribes over which they would serve as the head.

THE AGED PATRIARCH

Mackintosh has a beautiful statement concerning Jacob's last days. He said:

"The close of Jacob's career stands in most pleasing contrast with all the previous scenes of his eventful history. It reminds one of a serene evening after a tempestuous day: The sun, which during the day had been hidden from view by clouds, mists, and fogs, sets in majesty and brightness, gilding with its beams the western sky, and holding out the cheering prospect of a bright tomorrow. Thus it is with our aged Patriarch. The supplanting, the bargain-making, the cunning, the management, the shifting, the shuffling, the unbelieving selfish fears, all those dark clouds of nature and of

Earth seem to have passed away, and he comes forth and all the calm elevation of Faith, to bestow Blessings and impart dignities, in that holy skillfulness which communion with God can alone impact."

Jacob realized, and graphically so, that God had blessed him exceedingly. The son he never hoped to see again now stood by his side. Not only that, his son was the prime minister of the greatest nation on Earth. Along with that, the entirety of his family had been given the choice part of Egypt in which to dwell and to pasture their flocks. In addition, for some 17 years he had lived a life of serenity, peace, and blessing, all coupled with the Presence of the Lord.

THE PROMISED LAND

However, as wonderful as all of this was, Egypt with all its glory was not his home. His heart was in Canaanland, that Promised Land which God promised to his grandfather, Abraham, calling him out of Ur of the Chaldees, and then his father, Isaac. The Promise had been just as clear to him as well.

So, he made Joseph promise, even swear, that he would not bury him in Egypt but that he would put his remains where his heart was — in the land of Canaan, which would one day be called, *"Israel."*

The Twenty-ninth Verse refers to Jacob as *"Israel,"* because his Faith shines brightly. He faced the prospect of death with his Faith in the Promise. It was so real to the Patriarch and so outstanding that he even had Joseph to put his hand under his thigh, the procreative part of man, signifying that a birth would take place in that Land of Promise exactly as the Lord had stated. When Joseph did it as his father demanded, promising that he would carry him out of Egypt and bury him in the buryingplace of his grandfather,

Abraham, and his father, Isaac, the Scripture says that Jacob, i.e., *"Israel,"* bowed down on the head of his bed in praise and worship, which indicated that he was now satisfied.

WORSHIP

Hebrews 11:21 says Jacob *"worshipped, leaning on the top of his staff."* However, there is no contradiction. These are two different incidents.

Jacob's feelings concerning Egypt and the Promised Land should be our feelings, as well, as it regards this world and the portals of Glory. Even though this present world can have some attractions just as Egypt did for Jacob and his family, we must understand that this present world is not our abode. Our future is not here, but rather with the Lord of Glory. No matter its present attractions, there is a *"better country"* awaiting us on the other side. We must live our lives accordingly with our roots in the Promises of God, rather than in this fleeting world.

JOSEPH AND JACOB

"And it came to pass after these things, that one told Joseph, Behold, your father is sick: and he took with him his two sons, Manasseh and Ephraim.

"And one told Jacob, and said, Behold, your son Joseph comes unto you: and Israel strengthened himself, and sat upon the bed" (Gen. 48:1-2).

Hebrews 11:21 throws much light on the beautiful Forty-eighth Chapter of Genesis. In fact, in Chapters 48 and 49, Jacob shines as never before. If it is to be noted, the Holy Spirit refers to him again and again as *"Israel."* This is the great Faith action of his life. Feeble and dying and having nothing except the staff on which he leaned and worshipped, he yet bestowed vast and unseen possessions on his grandsons. To be sure, the Lord honored every word.

When Joseph was informed that his father, Jacob, was ill, he hastened to go to his side, knowing that the old man didn't have long left. However, the Spirit of the Lord impressed Joseph to take his two sons, Manasseh and Ephraim, with him. In fact, great spiritual consequences would be involved. The boys must have been about 18 or 20 years old at the time.

Joseph wanted his two sons to know and realize that even though they had been born in Egypt, and all they had ever known was Egypt, still, they weren't Egyptians, but rather of the house of Jacob, i.e., *"Israelites."*

Such is a portrayal of Believers born in this present world but, nevertheless, not of this world, but rather of the world to come.

Finally, the significance of the change of name from *"Jacob"* to *"Israel"* is not to be overlooked. By Faith (it is always Faith), the great Patriarch, moved upon by the Lord, would claim the Promises and chart the course of Israel. Though the eyes of the Patriarch were very dim in the natural, even as we shall see, his Faith burned brightly, actually, brighter than ever, hence, he is called, *"Israel."*

> *"'Tis the Promise of God,*
> *"Full Salvation to give*
> *"Unto him who on Jesus,*
> *"His Son, will believe."*

> *"Tho' the pathway be lonely,*
> *"And dangerous too,*
> *"Surely Jesus is able*
> *"To carry me through."*

"Many loved ones have I
"In yon heavenly throng.
"They are safe now in Glory,
"And this is their song:"

"There's a part in that chorus
"For you and for me,
"And the theme of our praises
"Forever will be."

JACOB

Chapter Fifteen

GOD ALMIGHTY

GOD ALMIGHTY

"And Jacob said unto Joseph, God Almighty appeared unto me at Luz in the land of Canaan, and blessed me,

"And said unto me, Behold, I will make you fruitful, and multiply you, and I will make of you a multitude of people; and will give this land to your seed after you for an everlasting possession" (Gen. 48:3-4).

In Verses 3 and 4, Jacob reiterated the great Appearance of the Lord as the Lord appeared to Him on a bygone day. He called Him, *"God Almighty,"* which means, *"The Great Provider."* In this, he was telling Joseph that God would continue to provide. Jacob was dying, but God would not die and neither would His Promises.

Jacob referred to God as *"El Shaddai,"* using the same name which God had used of Himself when He appeared to the Patriarch at Beth-el, which was after the sad experience of Shechem (Gen. 35:7-15).

Along with relating this glorious experience, Jacob would also bring the Promise in view. First of all, he proclaimed to Joseph that even though the Promises of God may seem to be so grand and glorious that they are beyond our reach, God, in fact, will provide, and every single Promise will be fulfilled.

As well, the Promise of which he spoke was not material blessings, for Joseph already had that, and so did his sons and Jacob as well. He was looking beyond all of that to something of far greater magnitude. He was looking toward the purpose and reason for which this family had been raised up, brought from the loins of Abraham and the womb of Sarah.

THE GREAT PROVIDER

The *"Great Provider,"* God Almighty, El Shaddai, would provide a Redeemer Who would come into this world to restore the lost sons of Adam's fallen race. This is what all of this is all about! This is the purpose and reason for the struggle! It is to look forward to the Light that will ultimately dispel the darkness, the Salvation which will ultimately dispel the sin, the Life which will ultimately dispel the death, and the freedom which will ultimately dispel the bondage. All of this will be wrapped up in one Man, *"The Man Christ Jesus."*

Jacob again reiterated the Glorious Appearing of the Lord to him at Beth-el when the great Promises were affirmed and reaffirmed.

A great multitude of people will come from Jacob, even as the Patriarch reminded Joseph. In fact, about 200 years later, they would number approximately two and one-half to three million strong.

However, as well, Jacob reminded Joseph that Egypt was not their everlasting possession, but rather only a temporal possession. Canaan was that everlasting possession, and Canaan they would have. Joseph was to understand this, and so were his two sons.

Let the reader understand that as it regards the land of Israel even presently (2013), it belongs to Israel and not the Palestinians, or anyone else, for that matter, and will belong to them forever and forever. When God said, *"Everlasting possession,"* He meant exactly what He said.

OPPOSITION TO THE PROMISE

Though God promises something, not at all does that mean that Satan will not oppose the Promise and actually the fulfillment of the Promise. He will do everything within his power to keep it from being fulfilled. Let the reader understand that the one ingredient he will fight is Faith, and it is because it is Faith that will claim and possess the Promise.

However, as Faith possesses the Promise, Faith also dispels the opposition. Once again, allow me to state the fact that the Faith of which we speak is always Faith in *"Christ and Him Crucified"* (I Cor. 1:23; 2:2). Inasmuch as Jesus and Him Crucified is the Story of the Bible, if one doesn't have such as the Object of his or her Faith, he really doesn't have faith in the Word of God but something else entirely.

Even though Jacob would not have understood the terminology I have just used, still, this, as well, is what his Faith would ultimately produce and, in fact, what it was meant to produce all along.

In essence, one might say that all in the Old Testament had Faith in the Prophetic Jesus, while we now have Faith in the Historic Jesus as well as the Prophetic Jesus. Historically, He has come, lived, died, was resurrected, ascended, and is now exalted at the Right Hand of the Father on high (Heb. 1:2-3). Prophetically, He is coming again and is coming to rule and reign upon this Earth for 1,000 years, during which time, Israel and every Saint of God will reign with Him. To be sure, we speak of every Saint who has ever lived, even from the dawn of time, whoever they may have been (I Thess. 4:13-18).

THE STRUGGLE OF FAITH

Let the Believer always know and understand that the struggle in which he is engaged and, in fact, will be engaged until the Trump sounds or the Lord calls us home is a struggle of Faith. That's the reason the great Apostle told Timothy: *"Fight the good fight of Faith, lay hold on Eternal Life, whereunto you are also Called, and have professed a good profession before many witnesses"* (I Tim. 6:12).

While it is a *"fight,"* it is at the same time a *"good fight"* because it is a fight that we will win. This *"fight"* lays hold on Eternal Life and *"professes a good profession before many witnesses."* This means that we are fighting the same fight of Faith that Jacob fought and, in fact, all others who have gone on before us and have been victorious in this conflict.

This means that in the final, it is not a struggle with finances, with physical well-being, with domestic situations, or social implications, but rather that which is spiritual. It all comes down to the Promises of God that are ensconced in His Word, which proclaims our victorious supremacy. It is all brought about because of Who Jesus is and What Jesus did, and I speak of His Finished Work on the Cross. That is the fight of Faith we are called upon to engage. It transcends all other struggles and if we succeed in that, we succeed in all.

THE MESSAGE OF THE CROSS

The Story of the Bible is the Story of the Cross, even as the Story of the Cross is the Story of the Bible.

About 170 times in his fourteen Epistles, Paul uses the term, *"In Christ,"* or one of its derivatives such as, *"In the Lord Jesus,"* *"In Him,"* etc. Those two words, *"In Christ,"* in effect, say it all.

It refers to Christ and what He did for us at the Cross, which He, in effect, did as our Substitute and Representative Man (I Cor. 15:45-50). Simple Faith in Christ places us in His Death, Burial, and Resurrection (Rom. 6:3-5). The Cross is where the victory was won, and it is where the victory is maintained.

THE RESURRECTION

While the Resurrection is extremely important, even as would be obvious, our Redemption does not rest in the Resurrection, but rather the Cross. Many things prove this.

Some people act as if the Resurrection of Christ was in doubt. It wasn't! On the Cross Jesus atoned for all sin, past, present, and future, thereby, defeating every principality and power of darkness (Col. 2:10-15). Due to the fact that the wages of sin is death, if He had failed to atone for even one sin, He could not have risen from the dead, meaning that Satan legally could have kept Him in the death world. However, Satan could not keep Him there because he had no legal right to keep Him there. With all sin atoned and the bondage of sin broken, meaning all powers of darkness including Satan were defeated, Satan's legal right of death was abrogated.

So, there was no doubt as to the Resurrection of Christ. Satan was not only not going to hold Him in the death world, he was not even going to try because he had no right to do so.

Please understand this: the Cross of Christ was not dependent upon the Resurrection, the Ascension, or the Exaltation of Christ. Rather, the Resurrection, the Ascension, and the Exaltation of Christ were totally dependent upon the Cross. In other words, if Jesus had failed to atone for even one sin, or failed in the slightest to do what He set out to do in the giving of Himself as a Sacrifice, there would have been no Resurrection, no Ascension, and no Exaltation of Christ. All of that was dependent upon the Cross. Allow me to say it again, *"The Cross was not at all dependent on those things we have mentioned."*

At the moment Jesus died on the Cross, there is every evidence that the Holy Spirit actually told Him when to die, which He did by simply breathing out His Life (Heb. 9:14). This means that His Death was neither an execution nor an assassination, but was rather a Sacrifice. No man took His Life from Him; He offered it up freely (Jn. 10:17-18).

THE VEIL

The moment He died, the Scripture says: *"And, behold, the Veil of the Temple was rent in twain from the top to the bottom"* (Mat. 27:51).

The *"Veil"* in the Temple separated the Holy Place from the Holy of Holies, the latter being where God was to reside. No one was allowed to go into the Holy of Holies with the exception of the High Priest. He could only go in once a year, the Great Day of Atonement, and not without blood from the sacrifice. However, the Veil being ripped from top to bottom, and done so by God, proclaimed to the entirety of mankind for all time that the price was now paid. Jesus had died on the Cross, atoning for all sin, that *"whosoever will may come and take of the Water of Life freely"* (Rev. 22:17). In other words, due to what Christ did at the Cross and our Faith in that Finished Work, anyone, even the vilest sinner, can come directly to the Throne of God where he will always find pardon and peace.

Now, if Redemption awaited the Resurrection to be complete, the Veil in the Temple would have rent or torn when Jesus was resurrected. However, God did not wait for the Resurrection because, even though the Resurrection is of supreme significance, it was the Cross which afforded Redemption and which afforded Redemption in totality (Rom. 6:3-10; 8:1-11; I Cor. 1:17, 18, 23; 2:2; Col. 2:10-15).

RESURRECTION PEOPLE?

We sometimes use the term that we are *"people of the Resurrection."* That is correct but only as we properly understand what we are saying. Paul said:

"For if we have been planted together in the likeness of His Death, we shall be also in the likeness of His Resurrection" (Rom. 6:5).

This means that all that His Resurrection affords cannot be had or held unless we first understand that we have this not because of His Resurrection, but rather because we know and understand that *"we have been planted together in the likeness of His Death."*

Let not the reader think that we are minimizing in any fashion the significance of the Resurrection. We aren't! We are merely putting it in its proper place. In fact, the Death, Burial, Resurrection, Ascension, and Exaltation of Christ are all looked at as *"the Finished Work"* (Heb. 1:2-3). Correspondingly, we should think of His Finished Work in that capacity. However, at the same time, we should know that it is the Cross that is the primary objective, and the Cross which made everything possible. That's the reason that Paul also said:

"But God forbid that I should glory, save in the Cross of our Lord Jesus Christ, by Whom the world is crucified unto me, and I unto the world" (Gal. 6:14).

He didn't say: *"But God forbid that I should glory, save in the Resurrection. . . ."*

As well, he said: *"For Christ sent me not to baptize, but to preach the Gospel: not with wisdom of words, lest the Cross of Christ should be made of none effect"* (I Cor. 1:17).

He didn't say: *"Lest the Resurrection of Christ should be made of none effect."*

He also said, *"But we preach Christ Crucified"* (I Cor. 1:23). He didn't say, *"But we preach Christ Resurrected,"* although he most definitely did preach the Resurrection of Christ (I Cor., Chpt. 15), but Paul's emphasis was always on the Cross.

THE RATIFICATION

Again I emphasize that the Resurrection was of supreme significance. One might say that it was the ratification of all that had been done on the Cross. Still, it is the Cross to which we must look because it was at the Cross that Christ as a Sacrifice atoned for all sin, past, present, and future, at least for all who will believe, thereby, satisfying the demands of the broken Law. This then abrogated Satan's legal right to hold man in captivity. His legal right is *"sin,"* but with all sin atoned, he has lost that legal right. Therefore, the bondage in which he now holds mankind is a pseudo-bondage, and he does so by a pseudo-authority, meaning that it's authority that we give him, whether in an unsaved state or even as a Believer.

SATAN'S PSEUDO-AUTHORITY

What do we mean by the term, *"Pseudo-authority"*?

We are meaning that Satan really doesn't have the authority to hold a single soul in bondage, Jesus having finished the Work of Atonement at the Cross. So, if he doesn't have the authority to do so, how is it that most of the world is still under satanic domination with even most Christians falling into this category?

The unsaved are held in bondage by Satan simply because they have not availed themselves of the great Redemption afforded by Christ at the Cross. They refuse to believe and with Faith being the means by which Redemption is afforded (Jn. 3:16), Satan can continue to hold them in bondage by and through a pseudo-authority.

When it comes to Christians, in fact, it is the same principle. Whenever you as a Believer came to Christ, you did so by simply evidencing Faith in Christ. This means that you then received Salvation because you were *"Born-Again"* (Jn. 3:3). Satan's authority over you was then broken.

However, regrettably, after Conversion, because of erroneous teaching, many, if not most, Christians then try to maintain their Salvation by a system of works and performance. This means that they are not continuing to evidence Faith in Christ and the Cross. In effect, they are giving Satan a pseudo-authority over them because their Faith is misplaced. Now, remember this:

It is never the quantity of Faith but always the quality of Faith. The quality of Faith is brought about by the correct Object of Faith, which is always the Cross. When we evidence Faith in the Cross and keep our Faith in the Cross, we rob Satan of any authority he might have. Jesus has atoned for all sin and by keeping our Faith in the Finished Work of Christ, Satan has no more authority over us (Col. 2:14-15; Rom. 6:14).

MY PERSONAL EXPERIENCE

Personal experiences are not to be taken as examples, that is, within themselves. If, however, personal experiences line up totally with the Word of God, then they most definitely can serve as examples.

For some six years, even on a daily basis and with tears, I sought the Lord, asking Him to reveal to me the way of victorious living. When I speak of *"victorious living,"* I'm not speaking of victory some of the time but victory all of the time. No, that doesn't mean sinless perfection because no Believer can honestly claim such. However, it does mean that the sin nature is not to have dominion over you (Rom. 6:14).

In respect to this petition, I began to cry out to the Lord in October, 1991. In 1997, the Lord began to answer that prayer. I use the word, *"Began,"* simply because the Revelation which He began to give to me has continued unto this hour. I speak of its expansion, which I believe it will ever continue and ever expand. The reason is simple: this great Covenant of Grace is *"an Everlasting Covenant."* In fact, the term is used, *"Through the Blood of the Everlasting Covenant,"* proclaiming the fact that it is the Cross which made possible this great Covenant and made possible its everlasting duration. The price was fully paid, therefore, it can be everlasting (Heb. 13:20). For the New Covenant to fail, Christ would have to fail, which is not possible.

THE SIN NATURE

The first thing the Lord showed me was an explanation of the *"sin nature,"* as Paul explained in Romans, Chapter 6. He then showed me that total and complete victory over the sin nature is maintained by Faith in the Cross of Christ and, in fact, Faith continuing in the Cross of Christ. This is the way, and the only way, to the victorious, overcoming, Christian walk. This is the manner in which we *"walk the walk,"* so to speak! What the Lord gave me is exactly what He gave to the Apostle Paul, even as Paul explained it in Romans, Chapter 6. In fact, Romans, Chapter 6, is what the Lord used to open up to me this great Truth. In Chapter 7 of Romans, the great Apostle went on to give his own personal experience of trying to live for God with misplaced faith. Instead of Faith in the Cross, it was rather faith in *"self,"* which God, the Holy Spirit, can never condone or honor. Paul bluntly said in Romans 8:8, *"So then they who are in the flesh cannot please God."* In fact, the great Apostle referred to Believers as *"spiritual adulterers,"* who try to live for God by placing their faith in something other than Christ and what He did for us at the Cross (Rom. 7:1-4). In other words, such a Christian is being unfaithful to his Lord. As should be obvious, that's quite an indictment!

As the Lord continued to open up this Revelation to me, I found that the manner in which the Lord explained the meaning of the New Covenant to me is the same way in which He gave it to Paul and, no doubt, many others as well. It is obvious to all in Romans, Chapter 6. The Lord explained to Paul the meaning of the sin nature and how to have victory through the Cross. As by now should be obvious, that was not only for Paul but, as well, for all other Believers.

THEOLOGICAL AND MORAL

Even though I have already addressed these things after a fashion, because of their great significance, please permit me to look again at the following:

The way of the Cross demands a change, and that change is total in its complexion and total in its movement.

Satan has been very successful at pulling the faith of the church away from the Cross to other things. He really doesn't care what the other things are or how holy they might be in their own right, just so that it's not the Cross. That's why Paul said, *"Christ sent me not to baptize"* (I Cor. 1:17). Paul wasn't denigrating Water Baptism, but rather telling Believers that their emphasis must always be on the Cross and never on the side issues, as important as those side issues might be in their own right.

THE WORD OF FAITH?

I suppose that the greatest weapon that Satan has used in these last several decades to destroy the *"Message of the Cross"* has been the *"Word of Faith message."* Now, that particular name or title may definitely include people who do not have erroneous doctrines, but for the most part, it refers to an erroneous direction, which is always nurtured by false doctrine.

As Judaism was the great hindrance to the Message of Grace during the time of Paul, the so-called *"Faith Message"* is the great hindrance presently. In fact, in my opinion, it is worse even than Judaism.

The faith that is proposed is really no faith at all, at least that which God will recognize. Let us say it again:

If it's not Faith in *"Jesus Christ and Him Crucified,"* then it's not faith that God will condone (I Cor. 1:17-18, 21, 23; 2:2; Col. 2:10-15; Eph. 2:13-18). The *"Word of Faith"* teaching totally denigrates the Cross. The Cross in those circles is referred to as, *"Past miseries,"* or even as, *"The greatest defeat in human history."* Some of its teachers even claim that if one preaches the Cross, one is preaching death and will hurt and hinder the Believer. It also teaches, at least after a fashion, that the Blood of Jesus Christ didn't atone. While it will say out of one side of its mouth that the Blood does atone, it will then turn around and denigrate the Cross. Well, if one denigrates the Cross, one has denigrated the Blood. The two are indivisible.

THE JESUS DIED SPIRITUALLY DOCTRINE

They teach that Jesus became a sinner while on the Cross, died as a sinner, which means that He died spiritually, thereby, went to Hell, and we speak of the burning side of Hell, and there suffered for three days and nights the agony of the damned. At the end of the three days and nights, they continue to teach, God then said, *"It is enough,"* meaning that Jesus had suffered enough. He was then *"Born-Again,"* even as any sinner is Born-Again when he or she comes to Christ, and then Christ was resurrected. So, when they talk about a person's Faith in Christ in order to be Saved, they are speaking of trusting Christ and what He did in the pit of Hell as a lost sinner. Incidentally, all of this is pure fiction with not a shred of it being in the Bible. However, sadly, millions believe it!

BLASPHEMY!

The teaching of the *"Word of Faith"* message, which I have given in brief, is none other than blasphemy. It cannot be construed as anything else. To believe such a doctrine, which is the worst perversion of the Atonement that Satan has ever concocted, is none other than believing a lie. That's why Paul also said:

"Examine yourselves, whether you be in the Faith (Jesus Christ and Him Crucified is the Faith)*; prove your own selves. Know you not your own selves, how that Jesus Christ is in you, except you be reprobates?"* (II Cor. 13:5).

As should be obvious, these are strong terms given by the Holy Spirit through the Apostle. In effect, he is saying that any doctrine or any teaching that eliminates the Cross, because this is what the term, *"the faith,"* actually means, can only be termed as a reprobate doctrine that produces *"reprobates." "Reprobates"* in the Greek is, *"Adokimos,"* and means, *"Rejected, worthless, castaway."* So, in effect, he is saying that any other type of faith is a *"worthless faith."* This means that if it's faith other than *"Jesus Christ and Him Crucified,"* then it is a worthless faith, irrespective as to what it might be or what it might claim.

The truth is, anyone who takes unto himself the false message of the *"Word of Faith"* doctrine has taken a path that will ultimately lead to spiritual hurt and possibly even spiritual ruin.

THE SPIRIT OF GOD

A lady wrote me the other day and asked this question: *"If the Word of Faith doctrine is wrong, why does the Spirit of God move in these meetings where it is preached and proclaimed?"* My answer to her was after the following:

The Spirit of God is not moving in those particular services. The Spirit of God cannot condone erroneous doctrine. While there are many things which might be labeled as the Spirit of God, the truth is, it isn't.

What is being projected is that which looks like God, sounds like God, and at times may even feel like God. However, what is at work is that which Paul referred to as an *"Angel of light."* He said:

"For such are false apostles, deceitful workers, transforming themselves into the Apostles of Christ.

"And no marvel; for Satan himself is transformed into an Angel of light.

"Therefore it is no great thing if his ministers (Satan's ministers) *also be transformed as the ministers of righteousness; whose end shall be according to their works"* (II Cor. 11:13-15).

That's why he also said, *"Now the Spirit* (Holy Spirit) *speaks expressly, that in the latter times* (the times in which we now live) *some shall depart from the Faith* (Jesus Christ and Him Crucified)*, giving heed to seducing spirits, and doctrines of devils* (demons)*"* (I Tim. 4:1).

THE SACRIFICE

Does all of this mean that no one is Saved who believes the Jesus died spiritually doctrine? No, not at all! In fact, there are many people who believe this doctrine who are truly Saved; however, the truth is, if they continue in that doctrine, more and more their spiritual experience will be weakened. In fact, many will lose their souls because of this doctrine, as it is with any false doctrine. This is what Satan intends!

It all goes back to Cain and Abel as outlined in Genesis, Chapter 4. Cain didn't refuse to offer up a sacrifice. He only refused the sacrifice that God demanded, which was a slain lamb, an innocent victim that was a portrayal of Christ. He wanted to offer up the labor of his own hands, which meant his own concoction. God would not accept it and, in fact, could not accept it. It hasn't changed from then until now.

There is one Sacrifice that God will honor and that is the Sacrifice of His Only Son, the Lord Jesus Christ, which was carried out at the Cross. He will accept nothing else. However, Satan has pushed and promoted, and done so through the church, every other type of sacrifice that one could begin to imagine. These sacrifices, whatever they might be, look good. To the unspiritual eye, it would seem that surely the Lord would want this. However, no matter how pretty the altar, if it's not the slain Lamb on that altar, so to speak, God will never accept it. Let the following also be understood:

If the sacrifice is rejected, then the sacrificer is rejected as well. If the Sacrifice is accepted, then the sacrificer is accepted. The latter places Faith in the Sacrifice and not self, while everything else places Faith in self or other things. So is the *"Word of Faith"* doctrine. It is faith in faith, which, in effect, means faith in self, which God cannot accept. As we've said over and over again and will continue to say, if it's not faith in the Cross, which refers to what Jesus did there, then it's not faith that God will recognize.

IS IT WHO HE IS OR WHAT HE DID?

The question of my heading is far more important than meets the eye at first glance. Many, if not most, Christians think that everything we have from the Lord comes to us simply because of Who Jesus is. I refer to Him being the Son of God, etc. In other words, to these people, the Cross is meaningless; however, that's not the case at all.

If the mere fact of Jesus being God, which He definitely is and, in fact, always has been and always will be, could bring us Salvation from our sins, then He would never have had to be born of the Virgin Mary and then die on a Cross. However, the truth is, that fact cannot save us.

While the Lord definitely could have regenerated man without the Cross, His Righteousness, Justice and, in fact, His Very Nature would not allow such. In other words, the terrible debt of sin owed by man to God must be paid. Inasmuch as man cannot pay this debt, if it is to be paid, God Alone must pay it, for He is the only One Who can.

God could have allowed man to be eternally lost, but at the same time, love would not allow such. It was love that created man, and it was love that must redeem man (Jn. 3:16).

So, for the Nature and Righteousness of God to be satisfied, as it must be satisfied, the debt had to be paid.

THE CROSS

There was only one way it could be paid, at least as far as we know, and that was by Jesus going to the Cross. There He would shed His Life's Blood, which would effect payment and, in fact, atone for all sin, past, present, and future, at least for those who will believe (Eph. 2:13-18; Rom. 10:9-10; Jn. 3:16).

While Jesus was the Only One Who could do this, in fact, before Salvation could come to Adam's fallen race, He would have to go to the Cross, which refers to *"what"* He did. That's the reason I keep saying, even as Paul said, that it's always *"Jesus Christ and Him Crucified"*

(I Cor. 1:17, 18, 23; 2:2; Gal. 6:14). If we try to separate Jesus from the Cross, irrespective as to whether we do it through ignorance or not, the results are always the same. We conclude by preaching *"another Jesus."*

ANOTHER JESUS

In writing to the Corinthians, Paul said: *"For if he who comes preaches another Jesus, whom we have not preached, or if you receive another spirit, which you have not received, or another gospel, which you have not accepted, you might well bear with him"* (II Cor. 11:4). The Apostle, in effect, was saying that preachers were coming into the Church at Corinth and elsewhere, as well, and were not preaching the Cross but rather something else. He likened that something else to *"another Jesus,"* which produced *"another spirit,"* and which played out to *"another gospel."*

That being the case, what was being proclaimed was not truly Christ and was not truly the Gospel but something else altogether.

To make it easier to understand, if any preacher separates Christ from the Cross, in other words, placing emphasis on something else other than the Cross, he is, in effect, preaching *"another Jesus."* Regrettably, that's where the far greater majority of the modern church presently is. The Cross has been ignored, laid aside, or disbelieved altogether, as it is by the Word of Faith people. This means that what is presently being produced is none other than *"another Jesus."*

As a result, no lives are changed, no one is baptized with the Holy Spirit, no one is delivered, and no one is healed by the Power of God.

ANOTHER GOSPEL

Very few attempts in modern church circles are

even made presently for the Salvation of souls. Very little effort is made, as well, regarding Believers being baptized with the Holy Spirit. Also, Deliverance from sin and shame is nonexistent. While grandiose claims are made regarding Healings and Miracles, the truth is, it's mostly sham and scam.

Yes, some few people definitely are being saved and some few definitely are being baptized with the Holy Spirit, etc., but the truth is, that number is abysmally small. Why? It's because it's *"another Jesus"* that is being promoted, which produces another spirit, and which plays out to another gospel.

When one turns on Christian television, with some few exceptions, what is seen is about the same as modern professional wrestling. In other words, what professional wrestling is to the sports world, the modern church is, for the most part, to the spirit world. It's a joke! The tragedy is, the church has drifted so far away from the Truth because it has drifted so far away from the Cross that it little knows the difference any more. That's the tragedy of it all! Far too often it claims things to be of the Holy Spirit which, in fact, are of *"another spirit,"* producing *"another gospel"* (II Cor. 11:4).

SALVATION AND SANCTIFICATION

Many, if not most, Believers understand the Cross as it refers to the initial Salvation experience; however, even that knowledge is very sparse, which I will come back to in a moment. As it regards the Cross and Sanctification, the modern church is almost totally illiterate respecting this single most important aspect of the Christian experience.

The modern church little knows the part the Cross plays in our everyday living before God, which plays out to our overcoming, victorious, Christian experience. If this life is lived as it ought to be lived, it is the most wonderful, joyous, and fulfilling life that man has ever known (Jn. 10:10). However, not knowing and understanding how Sanctification works, most Believers, whether they realize it or not, set out to sanctify themselves, which is an impossible task. The truth is this:

THE POWER OF THE CROSS

What Jesus did at the Cross not only provides Salvation for the sinner but, as well, Sanctification for the Saint. This means that not one single Christian ought to be bound by any power of darkness in any capacity. In other words, if we follow the Word of the Lord and do so as we should, at a point in time, *"Sin shall not have dominion over you"* (Rom. 6:14).

However, the facts are, sin, or rather the sin nature, in some way dominates most Christians. It does so simply because they do not know and understand God's Prescribed Order of Victory. What is that Prescribed Order?

GOD'S PRESCRIBED ORDER OF VICTORY

Even though the Bible is extremely short on formulas, still, I'm going to use one that hopefully will help us to understand a little better.

If the Believer can totally adhere to the following, the victory that Jesus procured at the Cross, which He did all for us, can be ours in totality. To be sure, such a victory gained is as Simon Peter said, *"Joy unspeakable and full of glory."* What we will give you is very simple, but if it's properly understood, you now know God's Prescribed Order of Victory.

• JESUS CHRIST IS THE SOURCE OF ALL THINGS WE RECEIVE FROM GOD: our Lord paid the price at Calvary's Cross for all that we have in the Lord. That's the reason the Holy Spirit always defers to Christ (Rom. 6:1-10; Col. 2:10-15).

• THE CROSS OF CHRIST IS THE MEANS BY WHICH ALL THINGS ARE GIVEN TO US: the Cross of Christ is the Means, and the only Means, by which all of these wonderful things are given to us (I Cor. 1:17, 18, 23; 2:2).

• THE CROSS OF CHRIST MUST EVER BE THE OBJECT OF OUR FAITH: when I say the Cross of Christ, I'm not speaking of the wooden beam on which Jesus died, but rather what He accomplished at the Cross. Without fail, this must be the Object of our Faith. The Story of the Bible is the Story of *"Jesus Christ and Him Crucified"* (Gal., Chpt. 5; 6:14; Col. 2:14-15).

• With Jesus as the Source, the Cross of Christ as the Means, and the Cross as the Object of our Faith, THEN THE HOLY SPIRIT WILL GRANDLY HELP US, WITHOUT WHICH, WE CANNOT DO WHAT WE SHOULD DO (Rom. 8:1-11).

In effect, all the things that Abraham, his son, Isaac, his grandson, Jacob, and all the great Prophets of the Old Testament experienced all labored toward one grand conclusion, and that is *"Jesus Christ and Him Crucified."* This was the direction, and it is still the direction.

EPHRAIM AND MANASSEH

"And now your two sons, Ephraim and Manasseh, which were born unto you in the land of Egypt before I came unto you into Egypt are mine; as Reuben and Simeon, they shall be mine.

"And your issue, which you beget after them, shall be yours, and shall be called after the name of

their brethren in their inheritance.

"And as for me, when I came from Padan, Rachel died by me in the land of Canaan in the way, when yet there was but a little way to come unto Ephrath: and I buried her there in the way of Ephrath; the same is Beth-lehem" (Gen. 48:5-7).

The Holy Spirit through Jacob would now claim the two sons of Joseph, in effect, as his own sons even though they were actually his grandsons. He claimed them on the same level as his first two sons, Reuben and Simeon. Concerning this, Horton said: *"By this Jacob indicated he was bypassing the older sons and was making sure that Joseph would get the double portion of the birthright. This would apply only to Ephraim and Manasseh. Any other children Joseph might have would get their inheritance through Ephraim and Manasseh. Jacob named Ephraim first in anticipation of the leadership Ephraim would have."*

Jacob first recited the gift of the land of Canaan to him by God, then making Joseph his firstborn, he adopted Joseph's two sons as his own, actually setting the younger above the elder.

In effect, Joseph had a double claim; he merited the birthright, and, also, he was the firstborn of Rachel, who was Jacob's true wife.

By Jacob doing this, and I speak of taking Ephraim and Manasseh, Joseph's sons, as his own, this filled out the complement of 13 sons. He had 11, and these two would make 13, as is obvious, which were needed to fill out the entirety of the Twelve Tribes of Israel plus the Priestly Tribe, totaling 13.

WHO ARE THESE?

"And Israel beheld Joseph's sons, and said, Who are these?

"And Joseph said unto his father, They are my sons, whom God has given me in this place. And he said, Bring them, I pray you, unto me, and I will bless them" (Gen. 48:8-9).

Pulpit says: *"That Jacob did not at first discern the presence of these two boys shows that his adoption of them into the number of the theocratic family was prompted not by accidental impulse of a natural affection excited through beholding these young men, but by the inward promptings of the Spirit of God."*

Even though Jacob was blind, or nearly so, the Tenth Verse portrays the Holy Spirit referring to him as *"Israel"* because he could *"see"* by Faith.

THE HOLY SPIRIT

None of this that Jacob was doing was contrived out of his own mind. He was led by the Holy Spirit in every action. In fact, making these two sons of Joseph his own finished out the complement which God intended, as stated, of the Thirteen Tribes of Israel. They would stay in Egypt some 215 years, at least that's how long it was from the time that Jacob came into Egypt and when they would go out under Moses, delivered by the Mighty Power of God. They would go out approximately three million strong.

As Joseph stood that day before his father, his two sons, Ephraim and Manasseh, were with him. The implication seems to be that Jacob could dimly see them but not well enough to make out who they were. If, in fact, my statements are correct, this shows that Jacob was not entirely blind but nearly so. At any rate, he did not recognize the two boys even though he had been speaking of them to Joseph.

In the Eighth Verse, the Holy Spirit refers to Jacob as *"Israel"* because what he was doing was a Work and Word of Faith.

The two sons of Joseph stood before the aged Patriarch, and he blessed them. A further Work of the Spirit took place.

THE EYES OF FAITH

"Now the eyes of Israel were dim for age, so that he could not see. And he brought them near unto him; and he kissed them, and embraced them.

"And Israel said unto Joseph, I had not thought to see your face: and, lo, God has shown me also your seed.

"And Joseph brought them out from between his knees, and he bowed himself with his face to the earth" (Gen. 48:10-12).

A number of things are said in these Verses:

Jacob is referred to as *"Israel,"* once again signaling his great Faith. In fact, the entirety of this Chapter throbs with Faith. Jacob is referred to as *"Israel"* nine times in this one Chapter. It speaks of Faith. It's not so much that Jacob's Faith was perfect, for possibly, that cannot be said of anyone, but that he had carried out and was carrying out all that God had called him to do, and without reservation.

Naturally speaking, his eyes may have been dim because of age, but even though he could little see in the physical sense, concerning his Faith, he had never had greater illumination. In effect, he could now *"see"* as he had never seen before.

He now recalled to Joseph that he had never thought to see Joseph again, but not only had he seen Joseph, he had also seen Joseph's sons, his grandsons. He gave God all the praise and glory for this, even as he should have done.

As Jacob said these things, Joseph bowed low before his father, realizing the tremendous import of what was being said.

THE BLESSING

"And Joseph took them both, Ephraim in his right hand toward Israel's left hand, and Manasseh in his left hand toward Israel's right hand, and brought them near unto him.

"And Israel stretched out his right hand, and laid it upon Ephraim's head, who was the younger, and his left hand upon Manasseh's head, guiding his hands wittingly; for Manasseh was the firstborn.

"And he blessed Joseph, and said, God, before whom my fathers Abraham and Isaac did walk, the God which fed me all my life long unto this day,

"The Angel which redeemed me from all evil, bless the lads; and let my name be named on them, and the name of my fathers Abraham and Isaac; and let them grow into a multitude in the midst of the Earth" (Gen. 48:13-16).

The Blessing that Jacob bestowed upon these two boys was no empty blessing, but rather rich with eternal wealth, even as Faith very well knew.

Jacob feared the influence of Egypt upon his sons. His nature led him all his life to grasp at wealth and position, but now, Faith shone brightly and he earnestly pointed Joseph and his sons to the true riches promised by God. In fact, they were in great danger. Joseph was viceroy of Egypt and brilliant prospects were within his reach for his children. The aged Patriarch urged him not to make his home in Egypt but to set his heart on Canaan.

Just before Jacob blessed these young men, the aged Patriarch retook his staff and leaning upon it so as not to fall bowed in grateful worship before God. This is the time of which Paul spoke when he wrote: *"By Faith Jacob, when he was dying, blessed both the sons of Joseph; and worshipped, leaning upon the top of his staff"* (Heb. 11:21). Strengthening himself once more upon the bed, he bade his grandsons yet again to come near him and crossing his hands, he blessed them. As stated, it was no empty blessing but rich with eternal wealth, even as Faith very well knew.

THE PROMISE

All of this shows that Jacob was not set upon the wealth of his luxurious bedchamber, which Joseph, no doubt, had provided for him, but was far away in God's Chosen Land. If he for a moment did lie upon such a costly couch, yet was he a worshipper of God thereon.

Manasseh was the firstborn, and Joseph expected Jacob to give him the greater part of the blessing. However, the Holy Spirit, Who Alone knows all the future, told Jacob to put his right hand, which pronounced the greater blessing, upon the head of Ephraim, who was the younger.

He specified that the blessing about to be pronounced came from God, Who had guided both Abraham and Isaac, and Who had also guided him all the days of his life.

He gave the Lord the praise for redeeming him from all evil and then said *"Let my name be named on them, and the name of my fathers Abraham and Isaac."* And finally, *"Let them grow into a multitude in the midst of the Earth."*

The first pertained to the Promise, and I speak of the God of Abraham, Isaac, and Jacob, while the second spoke of blessing. The Promise had to do with the coming Redeemer, Who definitely did come. The Blessing concerning the multitude is yet to be fulfilled but definitely will be fulfilled in the coming Millennium when Israel will be the leading Nation on the Earth.

EPHRAIM

"And when Joseph saw that his father laid his right hand upon the head of Ephraim, it displeased him: and he held up his father's hand, to remove it from Ephraim's head unto Manasseh's head.

"And Joseph said unto his father, Not so, my father: for this is the firstborn; put your right hand upon his head.

"And his father refused, and said, I know it, my son, I know it: he also shall become a people, and he also shall be great: but truly his younger brother shall be greater than he, and his seed shall become a multitude of nations.

"And he blessed them that day, saying, In you shall Israel bless, saying, God make you as Ephraim and as Manasseh: and he set Ephraim before Manasseh.

"And Israel said unto Joseph, Behold, I die: but God shall be with you, and bring you again unto the land of your fathers.

"Moreover I have given to you one portion above your brethren, which I took out of the hand of the Amorite with my sword and with my bow" (Gen. 48:17-22).

Thinking his father's dim eyesight had caused him to confuse the two boys, Joseph proceeded to take the right hand of the Patriarch from the head of Ephraim and place it on the head of Manasseh who was the firstborn. However, Jacob refused to do this and, in effect, said that he knew what he was doing.

CANAAN

Jacob had done this, putting the younger before the elder, simply because the Holy Spirit had guided him accordingly. Ephraim, although the younger, would be the greater of the two Tribes and, in fact, would be greater than any of the Twelve Tribes of Israel, with the exception of Judah.

Jacob wanted Joseph and his two grandsons, as well as all of his sons, to know that even though they were greatly blessed in Egypt, Canaan was, in fact, their home. He bade them to always look to yonder land.

Jacob told Joseph that the land was a doubly precious land; first, because God gave it to him; and second, because there he buried Rachel. In effect, he said to Joseph, *"That land should be doubly precious to you because of these two facts."*

All of this presents a scene of touching tenderness! The aged eyes of the dying Patriarch glowed once more with the love of early manhood. He looked eagerly into Joseph's eyes as much to say: *"Joseph, I loved her, and she was your mother."* Thus, he laid these two great pleas upon the heart of Joseph so that they should save him from making Egypt his country.

We aren't told exactly what Jacob meant by his statement, *"Which I took out of the hand of the Amorite with my sword and with my bow."* It could mean one of two things, or even both:

1. This very well could have been a conflict with the Amorites of which we are given no information.

2. As well, it could speak of the coming day when Israel would vanquish this foe, which is probably the meaning.

Jacob giving the blessing to the sons of Joseph, and especially the double blessing to Ephraim, in essence, was giving it to Joseph. Esau sold his birthright, and Reuben forfeited his. Jacob, therefore, could bestow it on whom he would.

> *"Is there a mountain in your way?*
> *"Do doubts and fears abound?*
> *"Press on, O hear the Spirit say,*
> *"'This mountain shall come down.'"*

"Is there a river in your path,
"A river deep and wide?
"Step in, the waters will roll back,
"You'll reach the other side."

"Is there a fiery furnace trial
"Far more than you can bear?
"Behold the Blessed Son of God,
"Is walking with you there."

"Then trust Alone the Mighty God,
"He speaks the winds obey.
"Take courage then, O fainting heart,
"For you He'll make a way."

JACOB

Chapter Sixteen
THE PROPHECY

THE PROPHECY

THE LAST WORDS OF JACOB

"And Jacob called unto his sons, and said, Gather yourselves together, that I may tell you that which shall befall you in the last days.

"Gather yourselves together, and hear, you sons of Jacob; and hearken unto Israel your father" (Gen. 49:1-2).

In Verses 1 and 2, the Holy Spirit impresses the use of both names, *"Jacob"* and *"Israel."* As the twelve sons gathered in his presence, he was referred to as *"Jacob."* However, when it refers to the Prophecies that would be given, *"Hearken unto Israel your father,"* he was referred to by his princely name, *"Israel."*

The *"last days"* of Verse 1 are mentioned some 33 times in Scripture. It refers here to days before both the First and Second Advents of the Messiah. The Holy Spirit through Jacob will now give the prophetic direction of the Tribes from the day that Jacob gave them to the eternal future.

At a point in time, probably very soon after the Patriarch had blessed the two sons of Joseph, he called all his sons together, sensing that he didn't have long left. As well, he had a Prophetic Word from the Lord that he must give unto them.

Concerning this particular time, Henry says: *"His calling upon them once and again to gather together, intimated both a precept to them to unite in love, to keep together, not to mingle with the Egyptians, not to forsake the assembling of themselves together, but that they ever should be one people."*

Henry went on to say: *"We are not to consider this address as the expression of private feelings of affection, resentment, or partiality, but as the language of the Holy Spirit, declaring the purpose of God respecting the character, circumstances, and situation of the Tribes which should descend from them."*

Even though the information given would be very abbreviated, as is normally the Practice of the Holy Spirit, still, in what few words that were used, tremendous information can be derived.

THE PLAN OF GOD

The great Plan of God, as it involves Redemption for the fallen sons of Adam's lost race, began with the sacrifice as portrayed in Genesis, Chapter 4.

The sacrifice is paramount throughout the entirety of the Bible, which actually constitutes the Plan. Until Christ came, it consisted of a clean animal, such as a lamb, etc. All of this pointed to Christ Who was to come and, in fact, did come and became the ultimate Sacrifice. So, everything revolves around Jesus Christ and the Cross.

To get this great Work accomplished, the Nation of Israel was formed in order that Faith may be generated in the Earth. Fallen man has no faith in God. God would reveal Himself in some way to Abraham just as He did to Isaac and to Jacob. However, the Revelation to Isaac and Jacob and all others following was predicated on instruction being given first of all by Abraham.

The Nation of Israel was to give the world the Word of God, which they did, and, as well, was to serve as the Womb of the Messiah, which they also did. However, Israel lost her way, crucified her Messiah, and was consequently destroyed. The Church was raised up to take her place, even as Paul describes in Romans, Chapters 9, 10, and 11. But, Miracle of Miracles, this great Chapter, plus many others in the Old Testament, proclaims the fact that Israel will be brought back. This will take place at the Second Coming.

THE SON OF MAN

At that time (the Second Coming), the Son of Man shall take the reigns of government into His Own Hand by Divine appointment and rule over the whole redeemed Creation; His Church — the Bride of the Lamb — occupying the nearest and most intimate place according to the eternal councils.

The fully restored House of Israel shall be nourished and sustained by His Gracious Hand, and all the Earth shall know the deep blessedness of being under His Sceptre. Finally having brought everything into subjection, He shall hand back the reigns of government into the Hands of God that *"He may be all in all"* (I Cor. 15:24, 28).

From all of this we may form some idea of the richness and copiousness of Joseph's history. In short, it sets before us distinctly in Type the Mission of the Son to the House of Israel, His Humiliation and Rejection, the deep exercises and final Repentance and Restoration of Israel, the union of the Church with Christ, His Exaltation and Universal Government, and finally, it points us forward to the time when *"God shall be all in all."*

While we do not build all of this entirely upon Joseph's history, still, it is edifying to find such early foreshadowings of these great Truths in his own life and experience.

It proves to us the Divine unity which pervades Holy Scripture. Whether we turn to Genesis or to Ephesians — to the Prophets of the Old or those of the New Testament — we learn the same Truths, *"All Scripture is given by inspiration of God"* (Mackintosh).

REUBEN

"Reuben, you are my firstborn, my might, and the beginning of my strength, the excellency of dignity, and the excellency of power:

"Unstable as water, you shall not excel; because you went up to your father's bed; then you defiled it: he went up to my couch" (Gen. 49:3-4).

Reuben had some admirable qualities in his character; unfortunately, they were offset by his incestuous act with Bilhah, his father's concubine (Gen. 35:22). It was Reuben who advised his brothers not to kill Joseph and returned to the pit to release him (Gen. 37:21, 29). Later he accused them of bringing calamity upon themselves when they were held in the Egyptian court as suspected spies (Gen. 42:22). Again, it was Reuben who offered his own two sons as sufficient guarantee for the safety of Benjamin (Gen. 42:37).

In the blessing of the sons of Jacob, Reuben is recognized legally as the firstborn, although in actual fact the double portion, which went with the birthright (Deut. 21:17), was symbolically bequeathed to Joseph through his two sons, Ephraim and Manasseh.

However, after a eulogy of Reuben, no doubt, sincerely meant, there is added a significant and Prophetic Utterance by this Patriarch: *"Unstable as water, you shall not have preeminence."*

The Tribe of Reuben was involved in the rebellion in the wilderness (Num. 16:1). Its pursuits would be mainly pastoral, but those to the west of Jordan were mainly agricultural. This may have lead to a separation of interests, for Reuben took no part in repelling the attack of Sisera (Judg. 5:15).

However, a place is reserved for the Tribe of Reuben in Ezekiel's reconstructed Israel (Ezek. 48:7, 31), which will take place in the coming Kingdom Age. As well, they are numbered among the 144,000 sealed out of every Tribe of the Children of Israel in the Revelation of John the Beloved (Rev. 7:5).

SIMEON AND LEVI

"Simeon and Levi are brothers; instruments of cruelty are in their habitations.

"O my soul, do not come into their secret; unto their assembly, my honor, with them do not be united: for in their anger they killed a man, and in their selfwill they dug down a wall.

"Cursed be their anger, for it was fierce; and their wrath, for it was cruel; I will divide them in Jacob, and scatter them in Israel" (Gen. 49:5-7).

Simeon and Levi are perfect examples of those who take matters into their own hands instead of putting it into the Hands of the Lord.

Because of the slaughter at Shechem, Simeon and Levi were truly divided and scattered in Israel. Actually, when the land would be parceled out at the command of Joshua upon the arrival across the Jordan, Simeon would receive no inheritance but, in fact, would have their part in the inheritance of Judah.

As well, Levi would have no inheritance at all but would have their curse turned into a blessing as they became the Priestly Tribe of Israel.

In fact, it might even be said of Simeon that their curse was turned into a blessing because of having the privilege of being in the inheritance of Judah, the Messianic Tribe.

Simeon and Levi are perfect examples of the human race in general. The wickedness and iniquity mark humanity. As such, it is cursed, cursed by the broken Law. However, when the land was parceled out when Israel came into Canaan, Simeon was given an inheritance in the possession of Judah, which was a Type of Christ (Josh. 19:1-9).

Likewise, when the believing sinner comes to Christ, the curse is removed because Jesus has paid the price at the Cross, and then we are given a possession, an inheritance in Christ, our Heavenly Judah.

DIVIDED AND SCATTERED

Verse 6 speaks of *"their secret"* and refers to the plans to murder the inhabitants of Shechem, which they carried out.

They assembled the other brothers in order to carry out this gruesome task. As would be obvious, this greatly impacted the *"honor"* of Jacob. The Holy Spirit says that one must not be *"united"* with such people and such actions.

The phrase, *"In their anger they killed a man,"* in the Hebrew tenses refers to many men.

Their *"digging down a wall"* actually referred to them hamstringing the oxen of Shechem, which is the way it should have been translated.

The word, *"Divided,"* pertains to Simeon in that they were divided from their inheritance, meaning they had none. As stated, their inheritance was in the Tribe of Judah.

"Scatter" pertains to the Tribe of Levi, which became the Priestly Tribe and saw the curse turned into a blessing exactly as did Simeon. While their inheritance was scattered here and there, still, this Tribe was involved in the greatest blessing of all, that of caring for the Tabernacle and the Temple and all their administration.

JUDAH

"Judah, you are he whom your brethren shall praise: Your hand shall be in the neck of Your enemies;

your father's children shall bow down before You"
(Gen. 49:8).

Of all the Tribes of Israel, the premier Tribe was
Judah because through this Tribe the Messiah, the
Redeemer, the Son of God, would come, Who would lift
the fallen sons of Adam's lost race. As the very name,
"Judah," means, *"Praise,"* the One Whom Judah would
produce would be the object of continual praise. He
is the Son of God, the Fairest of Ten Thousands, Who
is worthy of all praise because *"He has redeemed us to
God by His Blood out of every kindred, and tongue, and
people, and nation;*

*"And have made us unto our God kings and priests:
and we shall reign on the earth"* (Rev. 5:9-10).

VICTORY

The phrase, *"Your hand shall be in the neck of Your
enemies,"* speaks of the great Victory that Christ would
win over Satan and all the powers of darkness, which
He would do through the Cross, typified by Verses 11
and 12.

The phrase means that He will put His Foes to
flight, literally grasping them by the neck, signifying
that He would *"bruise the head"* of Satan.

Let the reader understand that God doesn't give
victories to fallen man, but only to His Son, the Lord
Jesus Christ. Now, if you will think a moment, this
statement speaks volumes:

JESUS CHRIST

• It tells us that irrespective of our own efforts,
and I speak of efforts outside of Faith in the Cross, we
will win no victories by that method. It makes no difference how religious our efforts are, even how right

they may be in their own way; victory can never be secured in this manner.

• We obtain victory by placing our Faith exclusively in Christ because God has given all Victory to Him. We secure that victory by simple Faith and never by works.

• This Victory has already been won by Christ. In other words, as they say on the street, *"It's a done deal!"* So, that means that it doesn't matter how pitiful one's situation might be. Every single unbeliever in this world can totally and instantly have all that Christ has purchased on the Cross if they will only turn to Christ and trust Him. In fact, that's the manner in which all people have been saved.

• As well, it speaks to every Christian who at this moment is bound by the sin nature in some way. You can be totally and completely free. It's already done. All you have to do is trust Christ. You must be very careful that you are trusting that which He did at the Cross, all on your behalf. If you will rest your Faith in the Cross of Christ and refuse to allow it to be moved, the Holy Spirit through Paul plainly said, *"Sin* (the Sin Nature) *shall not have dominion over you"* (Rom. 6:14).

JESUS CHRIST IS GOD

The phrase, *"Your father's children shall bow down before You,"* refers to the fact that the glorious One Whom Judah will produce, and we speak of the Incarnation, will, in fact, be the Son of the Living God. As such, and because He is God, untold millions bow down before Him, and rightly so!

"Bowing down before Him," is not merely a matter of paying homage, but rather an admission that the One before Whom we are bowing is, in fact, the Son of God, the Saviour of the world, the Baptizer with the Holy Spirit, the Giver of Eternal Life, and *"The Man, Jesus Christ."*

THE LION OF THE TRIBE OF JUDAH

"Judah is a lion's whelp: from the prey, My Son, You are gone up: He stooped down, He couched as a lion, and as an old lion; who shall rouse Him up?" (Gen. 49:9).

Even though Judah is addressed here, as is obvious, all of this actually refers to Christ. He Alone is the *"Lion of the Tribe of Judah"* (Rev. 5:5). In the Hebrew language four things are implied here:

1. Christ is likened to a young lion.

2. He is described, as well, as *"an old lion,"* referring to one ripening into its full strength and ferocity;

3. It roams through the forest in search of prey;

4. It is heightened by the alternate image of a lioness, which is particularly fierce in defending its cubs.

The phrase, *"Judah is a lion's whelp,"* refers to a young lion in the power of its youth absolutely invincible. This represented Christ in the flower of His Manhood, full of the Holy Spirit, healing the sick, casting out demons, raising the dead, and doing great and mighty things, with every demon spirit trembling at His Feet.

A lion seeks out *"prey,"* meaning that Christ is always on the offensive. He never fights a defensive mode, so to speak, but only that which is offensive. It is true that the weapons of our warfare, as described in Ephesians, Chapter 6, are mostly defensive in nature. However, the idea is, as we wield the sword of the Spirit, which is the Word of God and which is offensive, it is meant to protect us while in the offensive mode, which we should be at all times.

ON THE OFFENSIVE AND NEVER DEFENSIVE

In fact, the Child of God should never be defensive. The lion was always seeking the prey and never the prey seeking the lion. The words, *"Defeat"* and

"Defensive," go hand in hand, while the words, *"Offend"* and *"Offensive,"* go hand in hand. It is my business as a Child of God to offend the Devil at all times.

THE SCEPTRE

"The sceptre shall not depart from Judah, nor a Law-Giver from between His Feet, until Shiloh come; and unto Him shall the gathering of the people be" (Gen. 49:10).

The word, *"Sceptre,"* in the Hebrew is, *"Shebet,"* and means, *"A stick or baton for punishing, righting, fighting, ruling, walking, etc."* It is also defined as, *"A staff of office and authority,"* which is the meaning in this Tenth Verse.

Due to the fact that the Tribe of Judah would bring forth the Messiah, it would hold the sceptre of power until He came, which this Tribe did. However, when He came, the sceptre was taken from Judah and placed in the Hands of the Son of God, where it was intended all the time.

The Sceptre held by Christ, which He still holds this Power and, in fact, will ever hold this Power, has reference to more than the fact that He is God, which He definitely is. To cut straight through to the bottom line, it refers to what He did at the Cross, which satisfied the demands of the broken Law, and which, thereby, took away Satan's legal right to hold mankind captive (Col. 2:14-15). Let the reader understand that the Sceptre of Power is now in the Hands of Christ, and it will remain in the Hands of Christ forever and forever. Due to the fact that every Believer is *"in Christ,"* that means, as well, that the sceptre of power is in our hands also. However, it is there only as long as our Faith is anchored in Christ and what Christ did at the Cross. It is the Cross which made it possible for us to have such power (Acts 1:8).

LAW-GIVER

The phrase, *"Nor a Law-Giver from between His Feet, until Shiloh come,"* refers to the fact that the Tribe of Judah was meant to be a guardian of the Law, which they were. The Temple was in Jerusalem, which was a part of the Tribe of Judah, and which had to do with the Law.

When Jesus came, typified by the name, *"Shiloh,"* Who, in fact, was and is the True Law-Giver, He fulfilled the Law in totality by His Life and His Death, thereby, satisfying all of its just demands. Now the Law is totally and completely in Christ, and every Believer becomes a Law-keeper, and does so automatically when Faith is expressed in Christ Who has perfectly kept the Law all on our behalf. In other words, we don't try to keep the Law, but, in fact, it is kept because Christ has kept it perfectly, and our Faith in Him gives us His Victory in totality. So, in effect, we keep the Law by placing our Faith and trust in Him Who has kept the Law perfectly. As stated, we then actually become Law-keepers instead of Lawbreakers. Naturally, we're speaking of the moral Law.

UNTO HIM

The phrase, *"And unto Him shall the gathering of the people be,"* proclaims the fact that Christ is All in All. Israel was raised up for the express purpose of pointing the world to Christ. Unfortunately, they tried to make themselves bigger than Christ and, thereby, fell by the wayside. Nevertheless, the Objective of the Holy Spirit was Christ and unto Him, not Israel, etc., *"shall the gathering of the people be."*

It didn't say that people would gather to Muhammad, the Pope, Buddha, or any other fake luminary, but unto Christ.

There are about two billion people in the world presently who make some type of claim on Christ in one way or the other, whether Catholic or Protestant. The number truly Born-Again would be far, far smaller. Nevertheless, Biblical Christianity with Christ as its head is the most powerful driving force in the world and, in fact, always has been, even from the beginning of the Church. I speak of the true Church!

THE BLOOD OF GRAPES

"Binding his foal unto the vine, and his animal's colt unto the choice vine; He washed His Garments in wine, and His Clothes in the blood of grapes" (Gen. 49:11).

The *"vine"* speaks of fruit and, in fact, *"the blood of grapes"* speaks of what He did on the Cross in the shedding of His Life's Blood in order to bring forth this fruit. In John 15:1, He said: *"I am the True Vine, and My Father is the Husbandman."*

The *"fruit"* He would bring forth would be those who are *"in Him."* In fact, He said: *"For without Me you can do nothing"* (Jn. 15:5). The fruit is made possible as it grows on the Vine, with us being *"in Him"* because of the fact that He paid the price on the Cross. *"He washed His Garments in wine,"* i.e., *"in Blood."*

RIGHTEOUSNESS

"His Eyes shall be red with wine, and His Teeth white with milk" (Gen. 49:12).

This speaks of the Righteousness of Christ. It is Righteousness which He has always had but now is made possible to us due to what He did in His Sufferings, i.e., *"the blood of grapes."*

These Passages have been applied to the coming Millennium with others applying them to the Judgments of the Tribulation, etc.

While all of those things definitely will happen, that, however, is not the thrust of these Passages. This speaks of the Redemption which He affords because of Who He is and What He has done, and I speak of the Cross.

Genesis, Chapter 49, forms one of the great Dispensational Prophecies of the Word of God. It concerns the *"latter days"* and the *"last days"* (Vs. 1). It is believed that these predictions give Prophetic Direction from the day that Jacob gave them to the eternal future.

• It is said that Reuben, Simeon, and Levi contain the moral history of Israel up to the Birth of Christ.

• Judah portrays the time of the Messiah and His Rejection.

• Zebulun and Issachar portray the dispersion and subjugation of the Jews among the Gentiles.

• Dan portrays the appearing and kingdom of the Antichrist. It is even believed that the Antichrist may possibly come from the Tribe of Dan.

• Verse 18 portrays the cry of anguish of the elect sons of Israel for the Second Coming of Christ; Gad, Asher, and Naphtali, those who will cry.

• Joseph and Benjamin together predict the Second Coming and Glory of Israel's Messiah.

ZEBULUN

"Zebulun shall dwell at the haven of the sea; and he shall be for an haven of ships; and his border shall be unto Zidon" (Gen. 49:13).

This portrayal of Zebulun is not so much geographical as it is occupational.

The closest that Zebulun came to the Mediterranean was about 10 miles; however, the great trade routes from north to south, etc., went through Zebulun with them being very active in commerce.

As well, the phrase, *"And his border shall be unto*

Zidon," should have been translated, *"And his borders shall be toward Zidon."*

ISSACHAR

"Issachar is a strong animal couching down between two burdens:

"And he saw that rest was good, and the land that it was pleasant; and bowed his shoulder to bear, and became a servant unto tribute" (Gen. 49:14-15).

The Tribe of Issachar bordered the Jordan River and as a result favored some of the best agricultural areas in all of Israel.

As well, the phrase, *"And became a servant unto tribute,"* has to do with its agricultural pursuits and not subjugation by another nation.

DAN

"Dan shall judge his people, as one of the Tribes of Israel.

"Dan shall be a serpent by the way, an adder in the path, that bites the horse heels, so that his rider shall fall backward" (Gen. 49:16-17).

Dan had the ability to bear rule and yet became a treacherous serpent. It is certainly observable that the first introduction of idolatry in Israel is ascribed to the Tribe of Dan (Judg., Chpt. 18), and that in the numbering of the Tribes of Revelation, Chapter 7, the name of Dan is omitted.

As well, it is believed that the Antichrist, who will be Jewish, could spring from the Tribe of Dan, once again likened to *"an adder in the path,"* a most venomous serpent.

GAD, ASHER, AND NAPHTALI

"I have waited for Your Salvation, O LORD.

"Gad, a troop shall overcome him: but he shall over-come at the last.

"Out of Asher his bread shall be fat, and he shall yield royal dainties.

"Naphtali is a hind let loose: he gives goodly words" (Gen. 49:18-21).

As we mentioned in the overview, if it is correct that these Tribes portray Israel all the way from Jacob's day to the eternal future, then the cry, *"I have waited for Your Salvation, O LORD,"* speaks of the Second Coming when the Messiah will miraculously rout the Antichrist, thereby, saving Israel from sure destruction.

This is the first time that the word, *"Salvation,"* is used in the Bible. As Jacob and, in fact, all of Israel would see such, it pertains to the ancient people's most trying time even yet to come. Jesus Himself said: *"For then shall be great tribulation, such as was not since the be-ginning of the world to this time, no, nor ever shall be.*

"And except those days should be shortened, there should no flesh be saved: but for the elect's sake (Israel's sake) *those days shall be shortened"* (Mat. 24:21-22).

THE SECOND COMING

Jacob's ancient prayer will then be answered, and answered in such a graphic way as to defy all descrip-tion. The Coming of the Lord will be the most cataclysmic happening the world has ever known in all of its his-tory or will ever know.

"Gad" will be overcome by the Antichrist during the Great Tribulation but *"shall overcome at the last,"* which speaks of the Second Coming.

"Asher" could well be the first of the Tribes to wel-come Christ upon His Second Coming. The phrase, *"Yield royal dainties,"* pertains to an excellent presenta-tion for the king. That King is the Lord Jesus Christ.

"Naphtali" will have wonderful words for Christ upon His Return. They will be words of Repentance (Zech. 13:1).

While these predictions definitely had to do with the Tribes of Israel in their coming formation as a Nation, which is borne out in the Old Testament, I have by and large ignored that and dealt with the Prophetic predictions, even as I believe the Holy Spirit gave to Jacob.

JOSEPH

"Joseph is a fruitful bough, even a fruitful bough by a well; whose branches run over the wall:

"The archers have sorely grieved Him, and shot at Him, and hated Him:

"But His Bow abode in strength, and the Arms of His Hands were made strong by the Hands of the mighty God of Jacob; (from thence is the Shepherd, the Stone of Israel:)

"Even by the God of Your Father, Who shall help You; and by the Almighty, Who shall bless you with blessings of heaven above, blessings of the deep that lie under, blessings of the breasts, and of the womb:

"The Blessings of Your Father have prevailed above the blessings of my progenitors unto the utmost bound of the everlasting hills: they shall be on the head of Joseph, and on the crown of the head of Him Who was separate from His Brethren" (Gen. 49:22-26).

A TYPE OF CHRIST

Joseph, as Judah, is a Type of Christ, hence, the flowing and glowing superlatives.

Judah is portrayed as Christ in His Sufferings, while Joseph is portrayed as Christ in His Millennial Blessings. It is the same as David portraying Christ in His

Conquering Mode, while Solomon portrays Christ in His Rulership of peace and prosperity. Consequently, this of Joseph portrays Christ in the coming Kingdom Age.

He is described as a *"fruitful bough,"* and greater still, *"a fruitful bough by a well."* In fact, the branches are so outspreading and so full of fruit that they *"run over the wall,"* which means that in that coming age there will be an abundance of everything.

As Joseph's brethren hated him, likewise, Israel hated Christ and, in fact, crucified Him. However, what they didn't seem to know was the One they hated was actually *"the Shepherd, the Stone of Israel."* As such, God would raise Him from the dead with His *"Arms being made strong by the Hands of the mighty God of Jacob."*

BLESSINGS

As Joseph is a Type of Christ, the Holy Spirit through the Patriarch is here actually referring to Christ. It is Christ Alone Who enjoys the Blessings of the Father, and those Blessings come upon Him in every manner. For instance, He has all Blessings from Heaven, and, as well, the Earth will literally spew out Blessings upon Him. The *"blessings of the breasts and of the womb"* proclaim the fact that untold numbers will be born into the Kingdom of God, all because of what Christ did at the Cross and, in effect, will be His Brothers and Sisters.

As well, He has blessed more than the Patriarchs, Prophets, and Apostles of old, and as long as the hills endure, His Blessings will endure.

These Blessings shall rest on the Head of Christ and shall settle on His Crown, for He is *"King of kings and Lord of lords."*

BLESSINGS ON BELIEVERS

The Believer must understand that our Blessings are received only through Christ. Apart from Christ, God blesses no one, for apart from Christ, God cannot bless anyone.

Jesus is our Substitute and, in effect, our Representative Man (I Cor. 15:45-47). As the Federal Head of all Believers, He stands in our place. In other words, God does not really look to us or at us, but rather to Him and at Him. Whatever He is, we are.

The way we obtain this is solely by Faith. When we use that statement, we are referring to Faith in Christ and what He did for us in His Finished Work. Faith in Him exclusively, which, if it is proper Faith, always refers to what He did on the Cross, guarantees to such a Believer all that Christ is.

Every Christian wants Blessings, and rightly so! However, we must understand that God does not bless us because of our works, labors, enthusiasm, zeal, or efforts on His Behalf, as dedicated as all of these things might be. Our Blessings come exclusively through Christ and are obtained strictly by Faith.

Whenever our Faith is properly placed, all that is said here regarding Joseph, i.e., *"Christ,"* applies to us as well. It is Blessings of every description and from every direction.

Now, what I've said in these previous few paragraphs constitutes a great truth. As we've already stated, every Believer wants Blessings, but there is only one way those Blessings can be obtained. Because it's so important, let us say it again:

God does not really bless individuals per se, whomever they might be; at least He doesn't bless us apart from Christ. The Blessings rest upon Christ and rest upon Christ exclusively. When we have Faith in Him, which refers to what He did at the Cross, then His Blessings become our Blessings.

BENJAMIN

"Benjamin shall ravin as a wolf: in the morning he shall devour the prey, and at night he shall divide the spoil" (Gen. 49:27).

Benjamin is addressed last possibly because he was the youngest.

It concerns the conclusion of the Millennial Reign when Satan will be loosed for a season; however, at that time, the Lord will make short shift of Satan. The Tribe of Benjamin may very well be the leading Tribe to oppose the Evil One, even as the Scripture says: *"In the morning he shall devour the prey, and at night he shall divide the spoil."*

Concerning Benjamin, Jacob said, *"He shall ravin as a wolf."* It is plain from this that Jacob said what he said by the Spirit of Prophecy and not by natural affections, else he would have spoken with more tenderness of his beloved son, Benjamin, concerning whom he addressed and foretold this.

The warlike spirit of Benjamin carried over to Paul the Apostle who was of this Tribe (Rom. 11:1; Phil. 3:5). Paul shared the Blessings of Judah's lion and was the recipient of His Victories. So are we!

THE TWELVE TRIBES OF ISRAEL

"All these are the Twelve Tribes of Israel: and this is it that their father spoke unto them, and blessed them; every one according to his blessing he blessed them" (Gen. 49:28).

Even though Reuben, Simeon, and Levi were under the marks of their father's displeasure, yet he is said to bless them every one according to his blessing, for none of them were rejected as was Esau.

Whatever rebukes of God's Word or Providence we are under at any time, yet as long as we have an interest in God's Covenant, a place and a name among His People, and good hopes of a share in the Heavenly Canaan, we must account ourselves blessed.

CANAAN

"And he charged them, and said unto them, I am to be gathered unto my people: bury me with my fathers in the cave that is in the field of Ephron the Hittite,

"In the cave that is in the field of Machpelah, which is before Mamre, in the land of Canaan, which Abraham bought with the field of Ephron the Hittite for a possession of a buryingplace.

"There they buried Abraham and Sarah his wife; there they buried Isaac and Rebekah his wife; and there I buried Leah.

"The purchase of the field and of the cave that is therein was from the children of Heth" (Gen. 49:29-32).

While Jacob died in Egypt, his heart was in Canaan, for this was God's Land. We are in this world, but our hearts must ever be in the Heavenly Canaan.

His demand to be buried in Canaan presented itself as an act of Faith that one day the entirety of the land would be his. Presently, as Paul said, we only *"have the Firstfruits of the Spirit,"* but the Firstfruits guarantee the remainder (Rom. 8:23).

The Spirit of God concludes the Prophecies given by Jacob concerning his sons and actually the Twelve Tribes of Israel, and now he charges his sons to surely bury him in the land of Canaan. He didn't even want his bones to remain in Egypt.

He had lived in this land for some 17 years and had, no doubt, enjoyed ease and splendor. He was blessed to see Joseph as the second most powerful man in Egypt and, thereby, the world of that day. However, the great Patriarch never allowed all of this splendor and ease to turn his Faith from its correct Object. It burned brightly to the end, and he says to his sons, *"Bury me with my fathers in the land of Canaan."* Him being buried in Canaan, just as it had been with his grandfather, Abraham, and his father, Isaac, proclaimed itself and made a statement that all of these were staking claim to the entirety of the land. God had promised it to them, and ultimately, that promise would be realized.

"Wounded for me, wounded for me,
"There on the Cross He was wounded for me;
"Gone my transgressions, and now I am free,
"All because Jesus was wounded for me."

"Dying for me, dying for me,
"There on the Cross He was dying for me;
"Now in His Death my Redemption I see,
"All because Jesus was dying for me."

"Risen for me, risen for me,
"Up from the grave He has risen for me;
"Now evermore from death's sting I am free,
"All because Jesus has risen for me."

"Living for me, living for me,
"Up in the skies He is living for me;
"Daily He's pleading and praying for me,
"All because Jesus is living for me."

"Coming for me, coming for me,
"One day to Earth He is coming for me;
"Then with what joy His Dear Face I shall see,
"Oh how I praise Him! He's coming for me."

JACOB

Chapter Seventeen

THE DEATH OF JACOB

THE DEATH OF JACOB

"And when Jacob had made an end of commanding his sons, he gathered up his feet into the bed, and yielded up the ghost, and was gathered unto his people" (Gen. 49:33).

The last hours of the great Patriarch were filled with Prophecies and predictions concerning the Twelve Tribes of Israel, which would ultimately bring the Redeemer into the world. He died when that Prophecy was completed, but he did not die until it was completed. What a way to go!

The great Patriarch had ultimately realized that which God had called him to do. The main thing is he had kept the Faith that was once delivered unto Abraham and his father, Isaac. He had not allowed that torch to fall to the ground or even be dimmed. At his death, it burned brightly and, in fact, brighter than ever.

So concludes the Ministry of the blessed trio, *"Abraham, Isaac, and Jacob,"* but the *"God of Abraham, Isaac, and Jacob"* will never conclude. Because He lives, they and we shall live also!

It was Faith that made these men great! It was Faith that burned their lives, Testimonies, and experiences into our hearts. Despite their failures and their foibles, and they had those because they were human, it was Faith that shone so brightly at the last because Faith is ever greater than its counterparts.

What was said of Abraham, *"He believed God, and it was counted unto him for Righteousness,"* can be said of all three. Nothing could be greater than that!

DEATH

"And Joseph fell upon his father's face, and wept upon him, and kissed him" (Gen. 50:1).

Joseph closed his father's eyes as predicted by the Lord to Jacob in Chapter 46, Verse 4.

Verse 1 is a picture of Christ weeping over Israel. Jacob was dead physically and alive spiritually. Israel was alive physically and dead spiritually.

Of all the sons, Joseph knew and understood the Faith of his father as no other. He was standing there when the great Prophecies were given those last hours and, as well, understood them to a degree that his brothers didn't. But yet, I'm not sure if Joseph or anyone at that time could have even remotely grasped the totality of what was happening or the eternity of such.

When a man comes down to die, the only thing he can really take with him is his Faith. Faith characterized Jacob as it characterizes every Saint of God. When it all comes down to the bottom line, it is Faith and Faith alone.

MOURNING

"And Joseph commanded his servants the physicians to embalm his father: and the physicians embalmed Israel.

"And forty days were fulfilled for him; for so are fulfilled the days of those which are embalmed: and the Egyptians mourned for him seventy days" (Gen. 50:2-3).

Jacob's body was embalmed, but his soul and spirit went into Paradise to be there with his grandfather, Abraham, his father, Isaac, and every other Believer who had lived up unto that time, which included Enoch, Noah, and Abel, plus many others.

They mourned for Jacob 70 days, for death is an enemy. It is the last enemy that will be defeated (I Cor. 15:26). Jesus took the sting out of death at the Cross, but at the end of the Kingdom Age when Satan and all his minions shall be locked away in the Lake of Fire forever and forever, death will then be totally defeated (Rev., Chpt. 20).

The embalmers were not normally physicians. So, it is more than likely that Joseph commanded the physicians to superintend the process, which they, no doubt, did.

According to Pliny, the study of medicine originated in Egypt. The physicians employed by Joseph were those attached to his own household or the court practitioners, the latter of which was probably the case.

Due to the fact that they were going to have to take Jacob's body the long distance back to Canaan, which would take several weeks, Jacob would have to have the most extensive process.

PHARAOH

"And when the days of his mourning were past, Joseph spoke unto the house of Pharaoh, saying, If now I have found grace in your eyes, speak, I pray you, in the ears of Pharaoh, saying,

"My father made me swear, saying, Lo, I die: in my grave which I have dug for me in the land of Canaan, there shall you bury me. Now therefore let me go up, I pray you, and bury my father, and I will come again.

"And Pharaoh said, Go up, and bury your father, according as he made you swear" (Gen. 50:4-6).

Joseph did not go in directly to Pharaoh, but rather spoke to the monarch through the members of the royal household.

According to Egyptian custom, Joseph would have let his beard and hair grow during the time of mourning, the appearance of which forbade him approaching the throne. Pharaoh's answer would, of course, be conveyed through the courtiers.

A VERY GREAT COMPANY

"And Joseph went up to bury his father: and with him went up all the servants of Pharaoh, the elders of his house, and all the elders of the land of Egypt,

"And all the house of Joseph, and his brethren, and his father's house: only their little ones, and their flocks, and their herds, they left in the land of Goshen.

"And there went up with him both chariots and horsemen: and it was a very great company.

"And they came to the threshingfloor of Atad, which is beyond Jordan, and there they mourned with a great and very sore lamentation: and he made a mourning for his father seven days.

"And when the inhabitants of the land, the Canaanites, saw the mourning in the floor of Atad, they said, This is a grievous mourning to the Egyptians: wherefore the name of it was called Abel-mizraim, which is beyond Jordan.

"And his sons did unto him according as he commanded them:

"For his sons carried him into the land of Canaan, and buried him in the cave of the field of Machpelah, which Abraham bought with the field for a possession of a buryingplace of Ephron the Hittite, before Mamre" (Gen. 50:7-13).

FUNERAL PROCESSION

This funeral procession must have been one of the largest ever conducted in Egypt up to that time. Of course, all of the family of Jacob was present with the exception of the babies and little children. As well, the household of Pharaoh attended, and also the members of his cabinet, all accompanied by chariots and horsemen.

Funeral processions in Egypt were generally headed up by servants who led the way carrying tables laden with fruit, cakes, flowers, vases of ointment, wine, and other liquids, with three young geese and a calf for sacrifice, chairs and wooden tablets, napkins, and other things.

Then others followed bearing daggers, bows, fans, and the mummy cases in which the deceased and his ancestors had been kept previous to burial.

Next came a table of offerings, couches, boxes, and a chariot. After these things, men appeared with gold vases and more offerings. To these succeeded the bearers of a sacred boat and the mysterious eyes of Osiris as the god of stability.

THE CAVE OF THE FIELD OF MACHPELAH

Placed on the consecrated boat, the hearse containing the mummy of the deceased was drawn by four oxen and by seven men under the direction of a superintendent who regulated the march of the funeral. Behind the hearse followed the male relations and friends of the deceased who either beat their breasts or gave token of their sorrow by their silence and solemn steps as they walked, leaning on their long stick, and with these, the procession closed.

Of course, the procession described was only for a short distance. Consequently, the funeral procession of Jacob, while certainly having some of these trappings, of necessity would have been scaled down due to the long trip to Canaan.

Joseph had the entire procession to stop when they came to the *"threshingfloor of Atad,"* where they underwent a second mourning of seven days. Then Jacob was taken to the *"cave of the field of Machpelah,"* where Abraham and Isaac were also buried. Sarah was also buried there along with Rebekah and Leah.

THE PATRIARCHS

While the inhabitants of the land of Canaan did not know or understand the significance of these burials, the Patriarchs readily understood what they were doing. God had promised them this land, and their burial in the land by Faith staked a claim not merely to the buryingplace, but to the entirety of this country, which would one day be called, *"Israel."*

As well, there was something else in mind which did transcend all other principles, and I speak of Resurrection. Even though the subject was then dim, still, their Faith was sure as it regarded this Miracle of Miracles which they believed that one day would happen. It has not yet happened, but we are four thousand years closer than Abraham was when he was buried.

In fact, the Resurrection could take place at any moment. Concerning that coming event, the great Apostle Paul said:

"But I would not have you to be ignorant, Brethren, concerning them which are asleep, that you sorrow not, even as others which have no hope.

"For if we believe that Jesus died and rose again, even so them also which sleep in Jesus will God bring with Him.

"For this we say unto you by the Word of the Lord, that we which are alive and remain unto the coming of the Lord shall not prevent them which are asleep.

"For the Lord Himself shall descend from Heaven with a shout, with the voice of the Archangel, and with the Trump of God: and the dead in Christ shall rise first:

"Then we which are alive and remain shall be caught up together with them in the clouds, to meet the Lord in the air: and so shall we ever be with the Lord.

"Wherefore comfort one another with these words" (I Thess. 4:13-18).

RESURRECTION

We do know that the Doctrine of the Resurrection was known as early as Job, who was the son of Issachar. As well, as it regards the Bible, the Book of Job is probably the first Book written and was probably written by Moses in collaboration with Job who was contemporary with Moses for some years. Job said:

"If a man die, shall he live again? all the days of my appointed time will I wait, till my change come" (Job 14:14).

Job would have learned of the Resurrection from his grandfather, Jacob, who learned it from Isaac, who learned it from Abraham. No doubt, the Doctrine was known from the very beginning.

Enoch, who lived about 1,200 years before Jacob, said, *"Behold, the Lord comes with ten thousands of His Saints"* (Jude, Vs. 14).

This speaks of Resurrection!

"Death has no terrors for the Blood-bought one,
"O glory hallelujah to the Lamb!
"The boasted victory of the grave is gone,
"O glory hallelujah to the Lamb!"

"Our souls die daily to the world and sin,
"O glory hallelujah to the Lamb!
"By the Spirit's Power as He dwells within,
"O glory hallelujah to the Lamb!"

"We seek a city far beyond this vale,
"O glory hallelujah to the Lamb!
"Where joys celestial never, never fail,
"O glory hallelujah to the Lamb!"

"We'll then press forward to the Heavenly Land,
"O glory hallelujah to the Lamb!
"Nor mind the troubles met on every hand,
"O glory hallelujah to the Lamb!"

"We'll rise someday just as our Saviour rose,
"O glory hallelujah to the Lamb!
"Till then shall death be but a calm repose,
"O glory hallelujah to the Lamb!"

BIBLIOGRAPHY

CHAPTER 3

George Williams, *Williams' Complete Bible Commentary*, Grand Rapids, Kregel Publications, 1994, pg. 31.

Gene E. Veith, *Postmodern Times: A Christian Guide to Contemporary Thought and Culture*, Good News Publishers, Wheaton, 1994, pg. 215.

Ibid., pg. 230.

Matthew Henry & Thomas Scott, *A Commentary upon the Holy Bible: Genesis to Deuteronomy*,The Religious Tract Society.

Ellicott's Commentary on the Whole Bible, Zondervan Publishing House, Grand Rapids, pg. 106.

CHAPTER 5

C.H. Mackintosh, *Notes on the Book of Genesis,* Loizeaux Brothers, New York, 1880, pg. 282.

George Williams, *Williams' Complete Bible Commentary*, Grand Rapids, Kregel Publications, 1994, pg. 32.

CHAPTER 6

C.H. Mackintosh, *Notes on the Book of Genesis*, Loizeaux Brothers, New York, 1880, pg. 291.

H.D.M. Spence, *The Pulpit Commentary: Genesis*, Grand Rapids, Eerdmans Publishing Company, 1978.

Ellicott's Commentary on the Whole Bible, Zondervan Publishing House, Grand Rapids, pg. 113.

Ibid.

CHAPTER 7

Stanley M. Horton, *Genesis: The Promise of Blessing*, World Library Press, Missouri, 1996, pg. 136.

C.H. Mackintosh, *Notes on the Book of Genesis*, Loizeaux Brothers, New York, 1880, pg. 297.

CHAPTER 9
H.D.M. Spence, *The Pulpit Commentary: Genesis*, Grand
  Rapids, Eerdmans Publishing Company, 1978.
Ibid.

CHAPTER 10
George Williams, *Williams' Complete Bible Commentary*,
  Grand Rapids, Kregel Publications, 1994, pg. 36.

CHAPTER 11
H.D.M. Spence, *The Pulpit Commentary:* Genesis, Grand
  Rapids, Eerdmans Publishing Company, 1978.
Ibid.
C.H. Mackintosh, *Notes on the Book of Genesis*, Loizeaux
  Brothers, New York, 1880, pg. 316.

CHAPTER 14
Stanley M. Horton, *Genesis: The Promise of Blessing*,
  World Library Press, Missouri, 1996, pg. 187.
C.H. Mackintosh, *Notes on the Book of Genesis*, Loizeaux
  Brothers, New York, 1880, pg. 332.

CHAPTER 15
Stanley M. Horton, *Genesis: The Promise of Blessing*,
  World Library Press, Missouri, 1996, pg. 188.
H.D.M. Spence, *The Pulpit Commentary: Genesis*, Grand
  Rapids, Eerdmans Publishing Company, 1978.

CHAPTER 16
Matthew Henry & Thomas Scott, *A Commentary upon
  the Holy Bible: Genesis to Deuteronomy*, The Religious
  Tract Society, pg. 111.
Ibid., pg. 112.

NOTES

NOTES

NOTES

NOTES

NOTES

NOTES

NOTES

NOTES

NOTES

NOTES

NOTES

NOTES